The Deals of
Warren Buffett
Volume 2

Despite holding positions of Professor of Investment and Professor of Corporate Finance, Glen Arnold concluded that academic life was not nearly as much fun, nor as intellectually stimulating, as making money in the markets. As an investor in his fifties, he now spends most of his time running his equity portfolio from an office in the heart of rural Leicestershire, far from the noise of the City of London.

For decades, his research focus explored the question *what works in investment?* – drawing on the ideas of the great investors, academic discoveries and his own experience, good and bad (see www.glen-arnold-investments.co.uk). While he used to teach on this subject in the City, and supervise PhD students researching stock market inefficiency, he would now rather concentrate on actual investment analysis, but does explain the reasons behind his share purchases and sales as he goes along. He also discusses investment philosophy and ideas at newsletters.advfn.com/deepvalueshares.

He is the author of the UK's bestselling investment book and bestselling corporate finance textbook.

Also by Glen Arnold

The Deals of Warren Buffett

Volume 2
The Making of a Billionaire

Glen Arnold

Hh

HARRIMAN HOUSE LTD
18 College Street
Petersfield
Hampshire
GU31 4AD
GREAT BRITAIN
Tel: +44 (0)1730 233870
Email: enquiries@harriman-house.com
Website: www.harriman-house.com

First published in Great Britain in 2019

The right of Glen Arnold to be identified as the Author has been asserted in accordance with the Copyright, Design and Patents Act 1988.

Hardback ISBN: 978-0-85719-647-7
eBook ISBN: 978-0-85719-648-4

British Library Cataloguing in Publication Data
A CIP catalogue record for this book can be obtained from the British Library.

Whilst every effort has been made to ensure that information in this book is accurate, no liability can be accepted for any loss incurred in any way whatsoever by any person relying solely on the information contained herein.

No responsibility for loss occasioned to any person or corporate body acting or refraining to act as a result of reading material in this book can be accepted by the Publisher, by the Author, or by the employers of the Author.

To great children:
Oliver, Sophie, Millie Sunshine, Lyla,
Thom, Lola and Alys

Acknowledgements

I would like to thank the very supportive and professional team at Harriman House. Craig Pearce, senior commissioning editor, helped me tremendously in developing the concept for this series of books and in shaping the work. Charlotte Staley, Lucy Scott, Sally Tickner, Emma Tinker and Suzanne Tull have all put in a great deal of effort to make this book a success – thank you all.

Contents

Every owner of a physical copy of this edition of

The Deals of Warren Buffett – Volume 2

can download the eBook for free direct from us at Harriman House,
in a format that can be read on any eReader, tablet or smartphone.

Simply head to:

ebooks.harriman-house.com/dealsofwb2

to get your free eBook now.

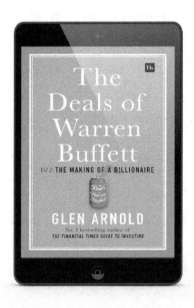

The Origins of This Book Series

It all began in 2013, when I took the big decision to stop other activities to allow full concentration on stock market investing. This meant giving up a tenured professorship, ceasing lucrative teaching in the City of London and, ironically, pulling back sharply on writing books.

To create a record of the logical process in reaching a decision to select a share, I wrote blogs laying out my analysis on a simple website and made it free to all. It was galvanising to be forced to express clearly and publicly the reasoning behind allocating capital in a particular way. And besides, I needed a way to review, a few months down the line, the rationale for the investments made.

The blog became popular, and then the investment website ADVFN asked if I would transfer it to their newsletter page. I accepted, and one strand of my writing there became a series of articles about the investment deals of Warren Buffett (I didn't always have a potential investee company to analyse and I thought readers might be interested in Buffett's rationales and lessons). It is from those articles that this book has been created.

The 'Why?' question

You might think that Warren Buffett has been covered in dozens of published volumes and there is nothing new to say. But having read much of this literature myself, I was left unsatisfied. Other writers address what he invested in and how much he made from it. But I wanted to know why. What were the special characteristics of the companies Buffett chose that made them stand out? Was it in the balance sheet numbers, the profit history, the strategic positioning and/

or the qualities of management? I wanted to know the detail. How did Buffett go from step to step in rational investing, from having virtually no money to being very rich?

For each of his major moves, I tried to get to greater depth on the *why* angle. For each investment, this required fresh investigation, tapping many sources. The priority was to focus on the analysis of Buffett's selected companies, which meant very little time spent on his personal life, which has been thoroughly covered elsewhere.

There were scores of key investment deals to cover and each needed a full analysis. Justice would not be done if they were squeezed into one book and so it made sense to stop the first volume at the point where Buffett reached the milestone of $100m net worth, and when he had consolidated his investments in one holding company, Berkshire Hathaway. This second volume describes the ten key investments that took Buffett from $100m to a billionaire; remarkably, he achieved this by the end of the 1980s.

The Buffett connection

My eyes were opened to the wisdom of Buffett decades ago. Naturally, I became a shareholder in Berkshire Hathaway, and regularly visited Omaha for the Berkshire Hathaway AGM. My favourite anecdote from my visits to Omaha is the one where I, and I alone, definitely forced Buffett to give away $40bn. You may think Buffett is strong-minded and couldn't possibly be swayed by a visiting Brit. But I know differently – and I know I'm right!

It happened in 2006, when Bill Gates (this is serious name dropping now!) was with Buffett. Gates is a close friend of Buffett and a director of Berkshire Hathaway. I thanked Gates for the great work he and his wife Melinda were doing with their Foundation – I was most effusive, perhaps a little over the top.

Then I turned to a listening Buffett, standing next to Gates, and said, "Thank you for all you are doing for Berkshire Hathaway shareholders." I don't know what it was, but my voice did not convey quite as much excitement about Buffett's achievements as it had about Gates'.

Would you believe it? In a matter of weeks Buffett announced that he was going to hand over the vast majority of his fortune to the Bill & Melinda Gates Foundation, to be used for charitable purposes around the world. Clearly, Buffett had deeply pondered why this Brit was less impressed by Berkshire Hathaway, his creation, than by the Gates Foundation, his friends' creation. He took action to do something about that.

That's my story and I'm sticking to it until the day I die!

I hope you enjoy reading how Buffett turned $100m into $1bn.

Glen Arnold,
summer 2019

Preface

What this book covers

This book describes the deals that turned a 40-something Buffett with $100m into a 59-year-old billionaire and, more importantly, it illustrates the lessons on the best approach to investing that he picked up along the way – lessons for all of us.

This is the most exhilarating period of his career. He found gem after gem in both the stock market and in tightly-run family firms with excellent economic franchises, such as Nebraska Furniture Mart and Scott Fetzer.

In adding to the collection of wholly-owned subsidiaries, he was helped by the reputation he was building as the kind of owner who gives space for talented families or professional managers to just get on with the job. He induced an amazing level of loyalty from the company founders which, in turn, helped to produce terrific returns on capital. Thus, cash was being thrown off; cash for Buffett to invest in yet more great businesses. He created a wonderful virtuous circle.

The controlled businesses were not the only sources of cash to invest; the fast-growing insurance companies, such as National Indemnity and GEICO, held large floats which needed to be invested somewhere. Buffett was the man to make good use of this money. Much of it went to buy significant shareholdings in some market-dominating US giants – like Coca-Cola, Gillette and Capital Cities/ABC.

While this book explains Buffett's reasoning for making his key investments, it does not shy away from the errors he made along the way; he learned from them and so can we. The net effect of his triumphs and mistakes was a personal holding of well over $1bn by 1989, and a foundation from which to grow Berkshire Hathaway yet further to become one of the world's ten largest companies.

The stories of his stunning investment deals are told in the following sequence (in order of first investment made):

1. GEICO (1976)

2. The Buffalo Evening News (1977)

3. Nebraska Furniture Mart (1983)

4. Capital Cities–ABC–Disney (1986)

5. Scott Fetzer (1986)

6. Fechheimer Brothers (1986)

7. Salomon Brothers (1987)

8. Coca-Cola (1988)

9. Borsheims (1989)

10. Gillette–Procter & Gamble–Duracell (1989)

Over the first ten years of this period, the S&P 500 index doubled. Not a bad return for a decade, you might think. But look at Berkshire Hathaway shares – they jumped 29-fold, from under $89 to over $2,600. See Figure A.

In the following four years, the S&P again performed quite well by conventional standards, rising 39%. But Buffett does not operate according to conventional standards – Berkshire's shares multiplied over three-fold. This is shown in Figure B.

To put these numbers in context, remember that when Buffett first bought into Berkshire Hathaway, in 1962, he paid $7.50 per share.

Figure A: Berkshire Hathaway share price compared with the
S&P 500 index (1976–1985)

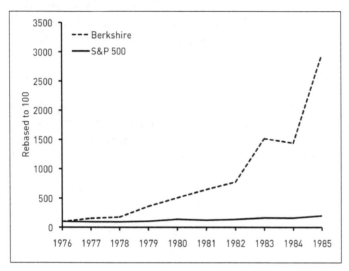

Sources: Yahoo Finance; R. J. Connors, *Warren Buffett on Business*
(Penguin, 2013). S&P index values do not include dividends reinvested.

Figure B: Berkshire Hathaway share price compared with the
S&P 500 index (1986–1989)

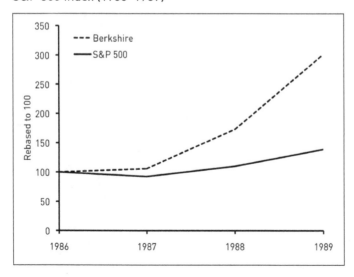

Source: Yahoo Finance. S&P index does not include dividends reinvested.

Who this book is for

This book is for investors who want to learn, or be prompted to bring again to the front of the mind, the vital rules for successful investment, through a series of fascinating investment case studies.

How the book is structured

It is arranged as ten cases studies. You can dip in and read about particular deals that take your interest if you wish, but I would encourage you to read chronologically to achieve an understanding of how Warren Buffett developed as an investor.

A Recap: How Warren Buffett Got to His First $100m

B efore we look at the path from $100m to $1bn, let's briefly recap the story from Volume 1 – the journey to $100m.

In 1941, the 11-year-old Buffett managed to scrape together $114.75 to buy his first shares in Capital Cities. They did not perform very well, but the experience stimulated reflection and the desire to search for an understanding of what are good and bad approaches to share selection.

In his teenage years, he did all sorts of things to make a dollar, from buying and renting pinball machines to retrieving lost golf balls, but the largest contributor to his growing pot was the five daily newspaper rounds delivering *The Washington Post*.

Graham and GEICO

By the time he was 20, he had about $15,000 and discovered the investing principles developed by Benjamin Graham, by reading his book *The Intelligent Investor*.

So keen was he to learn more that Buffett enrolled on a course Graham presented at Columbia University. During the second term, he found that Graham's investment fund had held a significant stake in a small insurance company called Government Employees Insurance Company (GEICO), and Graham was a director.

After some research – which included knocking on the front door of GEICO's Washington DC offices on a Saturday, and bombarding Lorimer Davidson, the assistant to the president, with questions for four hours – Buffett invested two-thirds of his savings into GEICO shares.

Within a year he had sold them for a 50% profit. Not bad, but he later kicked himself for not holding onto shares in a company with such a high-quality economic franchise. If they had been retained, and he had gone fishing for the next 19 years, they would have been worth $1.3m.

GEICO will always be remembered with affection. It was a memorable investment for Buffett because it kick-started the first phase of his investing career. He had gone out from the classroom and engaged in practical employment of the key principles taught by his mentor:

1. Conduct a thorough analysis of a company.

2. Make sure there is a margin of safety in the difference between your estimated intrinsic value and the price at which the share is selling.

3. Do not aim at more than a satisfactory return.

4. Remember that Mr Market comes up with some strange valuations from time to time, so you need independence of mind to decide whether Mr Market is being sensible or undervaluing a company.

During his absence from the share register, GEICO became very successful, but Buffett left it alone for 24 years. During that time, the market could see that it was a good business and, consequently, priced its shares too high for a value-focused investor. In sum, it was a good company, but not a good investment to buy.

No matter, he found other brilliant investments such as Sanborn Maps, American Express and Disney. His net worth shot past the $1m mark, and then past the $10m milestone. He was having great fun managing his investment partners' money, and charging them one-quarter of what he made above a 6% threshold.

Every now and then, his eye would glance GEICO's way, but it wasn't until disaster struck the firm in the mid-1970s, and the share fell from $62 to $2, that he really got excited. Almost everyone on Wall Street concluded it wouldn't be long before the demise of the company. It was at this point of maximum market apprehension that Buffett stepped in, and Berkshire Hathaway (BH) bought a substantial proportion of GEICO's shares. Over the next few years, he kept adding to the holding.

As well as being the foundation stone for the first phase of his career, GEICO was crucially important for the start of the second phase.

Between 1976 and 1980, BH spent $45.7m buying one-half of GEICO's shares. There followed a period of brilliant performance by its new team of managers. The company was doing so well that, in 1996, Buffett and Charlie Munger judged a fair price for the other half of the shares to be $2.3bn, and so they paid it – an amazing 50-fold increase on the $45.7m paid for the first half.

But even that seems cheap when you look at the benefits GEICO brought to Berkshire Hathaway. In most years, it made insurance underwriting profits – the difference between revenue from selling policies and the costs of claims and expenses. (Making a surplus on underwriting is not all that common with insurance companies; they are content with breaking even on the operating business while hoping to make money on investments.)

In fact, GEICO's business model was so good that in many years it made $1bn from underwriting, providing more money for Buffett to invest elsewhere. On top of that, it had an enormous float – money held in the company in preparation to pay out on claims. Much of this could be used to invest in shares and gain a return. In some years, the float generated another $1bn of capital gains and dividends. So, Buffett's available cash for investment grew larger and larger.

But we are getting ahead of the story… First, we ought to get back to understanding the circumstances Buffett found himself in the mid-1970s.

Warren Buffett's collection of businesses in the mid-1970s

Before moving on to understand the investments Buffett made in the second half of the 1970s and beyond, we need to remember the cards he had to play at that time. We'll start by looking at the extent of the empire the 40-something Buffett controlled.

After closing the Buffett Partnership in 1970, he and his wife Susan put the largest proportion of their money into Berkshire Hathaway shares, which was then principally a New England textile manufacturer, struggling to make profits. He had taken control of this $20m enterprise in May 1965, attracted by the net assets and, for sure, not by the quality of its operating business, although there were brief flickers of hope that it could be turned around.

Immediately, Buffett ordered investment in textiles to be strictly limited – every dollar put in must generate at least a dollar of true value, a good return on capital employed. Rarely did Buffett think this was likely and so he generally said no to expansion or fancy new machinery. Instead, BH accumulated dollars from asset sales and the occasional profit. The search was on for good places for that cash, places where it would create much more than a dollar of value.

National Indemnity

In 1967, Buffett found in his home town of Omaha just such an investment: National Indemnity, a motor and casualty insurer, which Berkshire Hathaway bought for $8.6m. It had, like GEICO, an excellent business model run by competent and honest managers. It was, therefore, capable of producing an underwriting profit in a competitive market – by being an efficient, low-cost operator with reliable high-quality service.

Just as important to Buffett was the float, standing at $17.3m in 1967. It wasn't long before Buffett had built this up to over $70m. This large amount of money could go on making capital gains and receiving dividends/interest for Berkshire from its holdings of securities, even if the insurance underwriting business suffered from low premium rates for a while.

Buffett became hooked on insurance businesses, especially those with some prospect of profits (or only small loses) and a large float. BH bought more property and casualty insurers, workmen's compensation insurers, and embarked on reinsurance.

The Rockford Bank

Berkshire had also invested over $15m (in 1969) in a small bank situated in Rockford, called Illinois National Bank and Trust. This produced bumper profits after tax of between $2m and $4m for BH year after year. The cash flowing from this could be used by Buffett to buy other wonderful businesses and stock market shares selling at value prices.

The Washington Post

In 1974, Berkshire Hathaway spent $10.6m buying 9.7% of The Washington Post's shares. Once the threats to the paper from the Nixon administration were over, the value started to rise.

Retailing, with some extras

The second key company – after Berkshire – in the Buffett family portfolio to emerge from the closing of the Buffett Partnership was Diversified Retailing. When the Buffett Partnership, in 1966, had bought its 80% stake in the company, it was a simple department store retailer – a struggling one, but with impressive net assets.

It later bought a chain of about 75 dress shops (Associated Cotton Shops) and, to Buffett's great relief and embarrassment, managed to off-load the department stores at only a *small* loss. That sale brought in about $11m of cash which he used for other investments in the early 1970s. Also, the dress shop chain was making about $1m post-tax each year, giving Buffett even more investment firepower.

That is how Diversified Retailing started but, by the mid-1970s, Buffett had directed that it also enter the insurance market. It underwrote fire, casualty and workers' compensation policies. Thus, Buffett had yet another source of money for investments via the insurance float.

A goodly proportion of the cash resources of Diversified Retailing were used to buy stakes in other Buffett-controlled enterprises. It owned about one-seventh of Berkshire's shares and 16% of the third pillar of the Buffett Empire, Blue Chip Stamps.

Blue Chip Stamps

Blue Chip Stamps was attractive because it too had a float. But its float was not created because of the delay between selling insurance policies for up-front premiums and the paying out on claims. It had a pile of cash from selling stamps to retailers, such as gasoline stations, who then gave away the stamps to customers. Customers would collect the stamps in books, and later redeem them for items such as kettles and toasters.

There was often a long gap between Blue Chip receiving payments from retailers and it having to part with a toaster – and many times people simply forgot they had the stamps. Thus Blue Chip built up a float of $60m–$100m as a reserve to buy toasters, etc. Buffett could see where that cash could be deployed. He made one of his greatest ever investments with Blue Chip Stamp's money, by buying See's Candies for $25m in 1972. This produced an ever-growing stream of income for him to invest in shares (by 2019, over $2bn has been handed over).

Another great Blue Chip Stamp holding was, and is, Wesco, which was originally focused on the savings and loan market (S&L). Once Buffett and Munger had taken control, its focus was switched to holding cash and securities, with the S&L business becoming a tag end within what was to become a large diversified holding company and insurance business.

The state of play in the mid-1970s

Buffett, in his pursuit of value investments, had created, as a by-product, a tangle of cross holdings. Within this collection were at least three pools of money for Buffett to invest:

1. Berkshire Hathaway's insurance float of over $70m (and growing fast). As well as dividends, interest and capital gains made from these investments, there was a flow of annual profits from insurance, textiles and banking (varying between $6.7m and $16m).

2. Diversified Retailing's embryonic insurance float, plus income from clothing stores (around $1m pa), and from holdings in Berkshire and Blue Chip.

3. Blue Chip's float of $60m–$100m. Dividends, interest and capital gains flowed from this investment pool, plus the company held commanding positions in See's Candies (annual profits about $3m) and Wesco (profits around $3m–$4m).

Figure C: Shareholdings – approximate fractions in mid-1970s

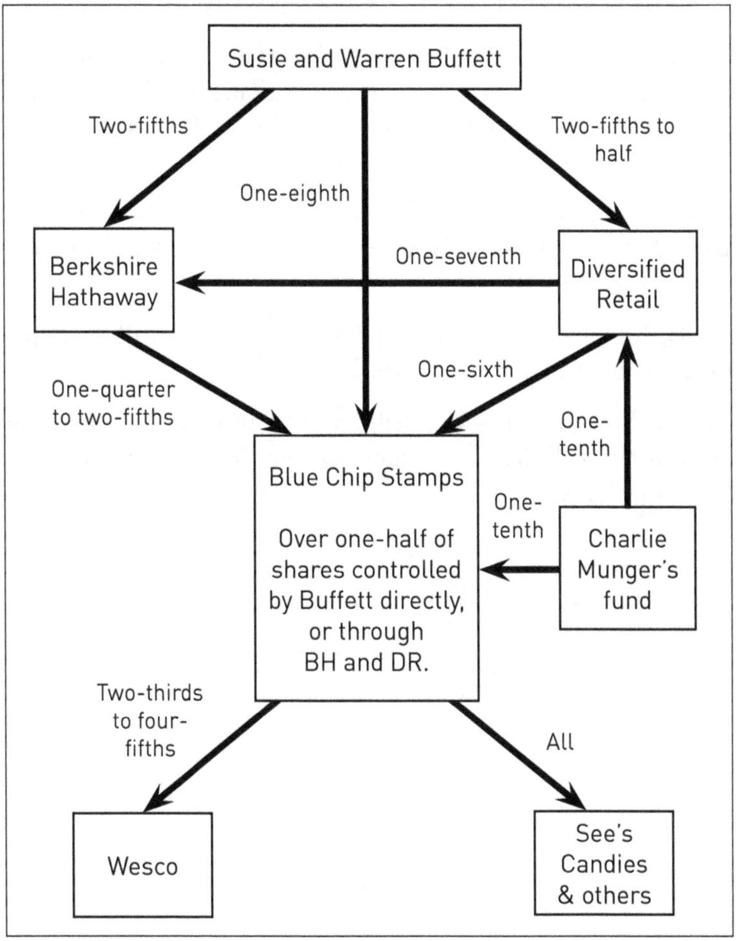

There was a drawback in having this convoluted web of holdings: the Securities and Exchange Commission (SEC) noticed the potential for Buffett to take actions prejudicial to the interests of minority shareholders in some of the companies.

Buffett had not set out to create a tangle or to discriminate against fellow shareholders who had placed their faith in him; he regarded these people as partners to be treated with integrity and fairness. But the mere existence of a perception, that conflicts of interest were possible, led him and Charlie Munger to simplify the whole structure in 1978.

Diversified Retailing merged with Berkshire Hathaway at year-end 1978 (Berkshire bought all Diversified shares in exchange for shares in itself). In return for Charlie Munger's Diversified shares, he was given 2% of Berkshire Hathaway and made vice-chairman.

Berkshire then controlled Blue Chip Stamps, holding about 58% of its shares. Buffett held 43% of Berkshire and 13% of Blue Chip. His wife, Susie, owned 3% of BH.

In 1983, Berkshire bought all the remaining shares in Blue Chip to neaten up the structure even more.

With the background established, let's now move on to look at the deals which took Buffett from $100m to $1bn. We begin, as mentioned above, with GEICO.

Investment 1

GEICO

Summary of the deal

Deal	GEICO
Time	1976–present
Price paid	$45.7m for 51% (1976–1980). $2.3bn for the remainder in 1996
Quantity	Initially 1.99m convertible preferred shares ($19.42m) and 1.29m common stock ($4.12m)
Sale price	Still part of Berkshire Hathaway
Profit	Tens of billions of dollars, and counting
Berkshire Hathaway in 1976	Share price: $40–$80 Book value: $92.9m Per share book value: $95

Warren Buffett has described the 1970s purchase of GEICO shares as "probably the single best investment" he made.[1] It certainly made a lot of money – the original stake of around $45.7m has been multiplied by at least 100-fold.

Three virtuous circles

The operating cost virtuous circle

The GEICO story is a tale of three virtuous circles. The first is what could be called the *operating cost virtuous circle*, put in place by the founders Leo Goodwin and his wife Lillian in the 1930s, and built upon by successive brilliant managers. The Goodwins recognised that auto insurance is a very competitive business. Indeed, it is a commoditised industry in which it's very difficult to charge a higher price by offering a differentiated product. Most purchasers just want the lowest price and will switch providers at the drop of a hat.

Figure 1.1: The operating cost virtuous circle

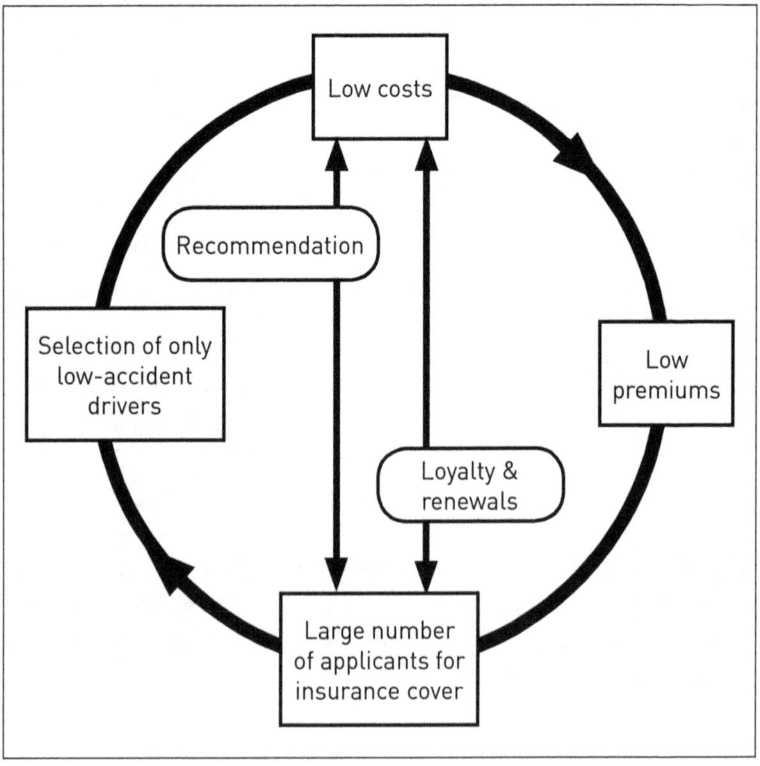

As a result, many insurance companies struggle to make satisfactory returns on capital employed because they are pinned to pared-down prices to maintain volume. The key to raising returns in this sort of business, therefore, is to continuously hammer down costs. The question then is how you do that?

The vast majority of insurance companies in the middle decades of the 20th century adopted distribution methods which involved paying large sums to insurance agents and sales staff to sell policies to the ultimate customer. This middle-man method means that, when commission costs are added to general overheads, something like 40% of what is taken in premiums is spent on administration and sales. GEICO found a way to knock off over one-third of that. This was done through the operating cost virtuous circle.

The starting point – low cost – has two aspects. First, sell insurance direct to the customer without the need to pay agents. This can be achieved through selling by mail or telephone (and today via smartphones).

As the 21-year-old Buffett wrote in an article published in the *Commercial & Financial Chronicle* titled 'The Security I like Best', this direct-selling method has another advantage: "There is no pressure from agents to accept questionable applicants or renew poor risks."

Which leads us onto the second aspect: to sell only to a select group which is known to include a high proportion of safe drivers, each with a steady monthly income, who can be easily target-marketed.

GEICO, conscious of competition and very keen to hold on to existing clients, has a self-imposed rule that all or most of any cost savings are to be passed on to consumers. Buffett today looks to obtain a maximum 4% underwriting profit on GEICO's sales; if the figure creeps above this, policy prices are reduced. In this way, the customer gains the majority of any savings made by cutting operating expenses.

For the first two decades of the company's life, it self-prohibited marketing to anyone outside of a prescribed group. You've guessed the group from the name of the firm: government employees (including military personnel). This targeting both lowered marketing costs and reduced the number of claims, because this group contained an above-average proportion of responsible and sober people (low-risk drivers).

It wasn't until 1958 that non-government workers were permitted to buy GEICO insurance. But even then, the offer was extended only to civilian professional, technical, and managerial occupation groups.

GEICO, by developing a quality service both in administration and in assisting clients following an accident was, and is, very good at retaining existing customers. This helps feed the low-cost model. High quality of service also helps with another aspect of the business model: having such a great volume of applications allows great selectivity in selling policies only to those offering the greatest likelihood of financial reward relative to the risk of a claim.

Many new customers were, and are, won over because existing customers are so impressed that they recommend GEICO to their friends – another way of lowering customer acquisition costs.

The confidence virtuous circle

This second virtuous circle occurred during the crisis facing the company in 1976. I need to explain it in much more detail later, so I'll not say much more now other than to note that the company was headed for bankruptcy because of a lack of confidence among equity and bond investors, and reinsurers, that it could survive. Faith in the managers and in the balance sheet had evaporated.

It was desperate for equity capital to be pumped-in to survive. If someone came up with the money then others in the financial markets would start to figure that it had a reasonable prospect of long-term viability. This, in turn, generated sufficient trust for it to regain policyholders, and to attract lenders and reinsurers.

But no one would take the first step, leading to a catch-22 situation, as each potential finance provider waited for someone else to make the very risky move of picking the company up off the floor with an injection of tens of millions of dollars. The thinking went, that the first capital injection might work… or, on the other hand, it might not. More skeletons might tumble out of the cupboard, or they might not. So why take such an extreme risk? Best to stay clear.

That was the attitude of all, except one. Buffett could see that the economic franchise – low-cost method and reputation with loyal clients – was intact, even if hidden behind some appalling recent insurance practice.

Buffett's capital intervention switched the cycle from a downward vicious one to a virtuous one, as Berkshire Hathaway's money brought strength to the balance sheet and confidence in the marketplace. Reinsurers returned to take some of the policy risks; regulators and lenders became more amenable.

The liabilities-make-money virtuous circle

Figure 1.2: Liabilities-make-money virtuous circle

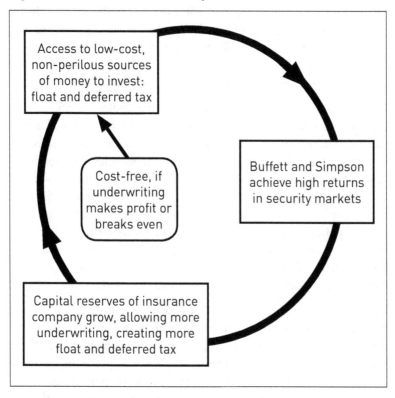

In the story of Warren Buffett, we've already seen – with National Indemnity – how he can turn what accountants classify as a liability into an asset that creates millions in profit for Berkshire. He does this by employing the insurance float to gain good returns on securities, producing interest on fixed-rate instruments, and earning dividends and capital gains on shares.

He could see that GEICO's business model resulted in a large and predictable float of money, waiting to be invested elsewhere. There was also a government source of cash within GEICO – the delay between a tax payment being provided for in the accounts, under 'deferred tax' provision, and the actual outflow of the money.

What brought GEICO to its knees?

GEICO lost its way terribly in the early 1970s. It was dreadfully unprofitable because its managers had pushed revenue without paying sufficient attention to likely future claims. As was the case in so many insurance firms, the executive directors' minds were set on volume of deals, neglecting to think much about long-term profits.

Looking from the outside, it was very sad for Buffett to witness this loss of self-control, with his fond memories of his first significant value investment in 1951. It was also sad for Lorimer Davidson, who, in 1958, had taken over as president from the founder Leo Goodwin. Over Davidson's 12-year period of leadership, premiums grew from $40m (with 485,443 policies) to $250m and GEICO became the fifth largest auto insurance company in the United States, with nearly two million policies sold in a year. Importantly, this steady growth was under conditions of strict underwriting discipline – i.e. turning away business rather than accepting premium income that was inadequate relative to the likely eventual claims and administrative costs.

By the end of 1970, the 71-year-old Davidson had stepped down as president and chairman, and then the business rot set in. Despite his counsel still being sought, in his new position as merely one of the board directors he was outnumbered by those who pushed for growth, enthusiastic about the prescience of new-fangled computer programmes able, supposedly, to assess insurance risk so much better than the old boys and girls.

The dash for growth

In 1973, GEICO removed all occupational restrictions on eligibility for insurance – anyone could apply. It took on blue-collar workers and under 21s, both groups with poorer accident statistics than GEICO's traditional customer. But never mind, the brilliant new software would work out with great accuracy the appropriate risk premiums for these groups, wouldn't it?

The opening up to all adult Americans drove demand so much that GEICO became the fourth-placed publicly-listed auto insurer, with more than $479m annual premium income. GEICO's shares soared to $61 as investors gazed on the growth.

In their haste to expand, direct mail advertisements were sent out to 25m people, and the managers created 123 field offices employing salaried agents to sell insurance policies. These offices were quite costly to set up, with property expenses, large numbers of new employees and computer equipment costs. This office-establishment drive was all part of the general mood of nonchalance about cost control – the very thing on which the firm's wealth was founded.

The executives were confident about the future and let the markets know about their confidence. But as Buffett is fond of saying, "it's only when the tide goes out that you discover who's been swimming naked."

The tide turned

At the height of its hubris, the company was hit by a change in the laws governing insurance. Previously, the insurer of the driver at fault in an accident was responsible for paying all parties. This worked well for GEICO because, traditionally, it had purposely collected only the most careful drivers, rarely at fault. Thus it paid little in claims.

But under the new 'no-fault insurance' laws, passed in 26 states, payouts after an accident were determined by the extent of damage, not by who was at fault. The laws were motivated by a desire to reduce the amount of drawn-out court litigation following accidents. Under no-fault insurance, each driver could draw payment from their own policy for injuries they suffered.

Another burden was placed on GEICO by state regulators responding to public criticism of rising insurance rates; they decided to restrict what insurers could charge. Coming after GEICO had grown its policy numbers aggressively in a short period, these two government burdens caused much more suffering to GEICO than they did to its main competitors. To make matters even worse, this was a period of rapidly rising costs for hospital stays, surgery and auto repair.

Managerial inadequacy

Over the period of expansion, the senior team had been making estimates of likely losses on claims, which flowed through to estimates of balance sheet strength. They had been doing this year in, year out. But when they looked back from 1975, the officers found that they had been woefully over-optimistic – losses had been underestimated by $100m. In all, there were 2.3m loss-generating policies on GEICO's books.

When the consequences of the errors were totted up, the directors were forced to make a bombshell announcement in 1975 – they had made a loss of $126.5m. Dividends were suspended and the shares fell to $5.

In a 1976 interview, a now retired Benjamin Graham – a GEICO director for 17 years until 1965 – said, "I ask myself whether the company did expand much too fast… It makes me shudder to think of the amounts of money they were able to lose in one year. Incredible! … You have to be a genius to lose that much money."[2]

Lorimer Davidson was shaken. He knew he had to interrupt his semi-retirement to try to save the company. One action taken was to form a select company committee to seek new leadership for the stricken firm.

Warren Buffett takes an interest in GEICO

At its April 1976 annual general meeting, hundreds of irate GEICO shareholders made their displeasure felt. They really didn't want the current executive directors to carry on. Piling on the pressure, insurance commissioners from many states came knocking, wanting to know if GEICO was sufficiently strong to avoid bankruptcy and thus meet obligations to policyholders.

The regulators saw that the company desperately needed both reinsurance to lay off some of its exposure, and a large injection of long-term share capital. Despite the company's protestations, the Washington DC insurance superintendent was not convinced that it could survive and was minded to declare it insolvent very soon.

The company needed a very strong-minded CEO with a plan, and a rugged determination to see the scheme through to the end. Someone who had the strength to battle against the odds.

But within days of the AGM, the CEO was sacked, so leadership was even more degraded. Sam Butler, the lead director, took over as temporary chief with a brief to find someone capable of rescuing the firm. Time was very tight.

Jack Byrne: company saviour

Jack Byrne was to become Buffett's key man at GEICO. I think it is fair to say that without Byrne, Buffett would not have invested. Buffett needed to ensure that he had someone in place who: (a) could see the real strategic strengths of the company – the strengths that the previous CEO had lost sight of in the enthusiasm for growth; and (b) had the sheer guts and drive to pull the company from the edge of a crumbling cliff. Buffett later called Jack, "the Babe Ruth of insurance."

Byrne was a no-nonsense New Jersey man with insurance in his blood. He grew up listening to his father talk insurance at the dinner table, and cut his business teeth, as a teenager, in the family insurance agency. In his 20s, as a trained actuary, Byrne gained reinsurance sales and managerial experience working for a couple of companies.

But the place where he really flourished was Travelers Insurance Company. Joining it in 1966 aged 34, he rose rapidly through the ranks becoming an executive vice president. He gained a reputation as a tough-love kind of manager – you wouldn't want to be on the wrong side of him, but if you performed well you were rewarded. In 1975, after he was passed over for president, he decided it was time to move on.

Butler called Byrne shortly after GEICO's explosive AGM. He persuaded him that saving the firm was important not just for shareholders, but for the insurance sector and for wider American society. Byrne worked out a plan of action to get GEICO out of its mess, which he presented to the formal appointment committee. They were impressed and he started as CEO in May 1976.

On the to-do list

There was no time to lose. The first task was to persuade the insurance commissioners not to close the business. He visited the District of Columbia's insurance superintendent almost daily to explain his plan and how much progress was being made. The superintendent remained sceptical, but he did grant a few weeks grace for Byrne to put something together. He was given until late June, or it was curtains.

The second task was to relieve the pressure created by the large book of insurance policies. Byrne's intention was to put together a consortium of other insurers to take 40% of the risks the firm covered – over $25m of policies.

It might seem strange that he thought competitors would stump up to save his company – after all, wouldn't they benefit from poaching customers upon its death?

But Byrne put forward the argument that the regulators would insist fellow industry players make sure that policyholders were not disadvantaged if GEICO did fail – i.e. they would eventually have to fork out for any unpaid claims. Also, the reputation of the insurance industry would take a hit if one of the major players failed, thus reducing consumer demand for insurance generally.

Despite Byrne's doggedness, he didn't make much progress. Wily competitors calculated they would prefer to take the hit from claims arising from a dead GEICO, than have GEICO revived and fighting for market share.

Byrne was only a few days into the job and it was already clear that time was running out fast. Had he made a serious error boarding this sinking ship?

Many longstanding shareholders bailed out and the share price fell to $2, a decline of 97% from its 1972 price. Both Benjamin Graham and Lorimer Davidson, however, kept their shares.

To stem cash outflows, Byrne started the process of closing scores of GEICO offices around the country, cutting the workforce in half. He also implemented rate increases.

There was one sliver of good news: the Washington insurance regulator did not close the company down in June, but allowed it to limp through into July.

Buffett meets Byrne

Buffett had been watching the struggle from the sidelines. Before he made a move, he needed to find out if Byrne really had the qualities required to not only save the company but grow it.

He asked his friend, Kay Graham, publisher of *The Washington Post* and consummate networker (see the movie *The Post*), to arrange a meeting. Byrne, busy in his battle for survival and never having heard of Buffett, turned down a meeting flat.

Lorimer Davidson got to hear about this snub of Buffett and proceeded to give Byrne a roasting, telling him in no uncertain terms to arrange a meeting. When Buffett and Byrne did get together on a July evening, they talked well into the night.

In particular, Buffett needed to know: the chances of survival; the plan for raising capital; whether there was a meeting of minds on the nature of GEICO's low-cost economic franchise and whether the franchise was still there under the debris; and finally, if Byrne was the kind of guy to lead the company through the difficult days ahead.

Buffett was satisfied on all counts. He knew there was a chance of losing everything he might put into GEICO. But, on the other hand, if it could be turned around, it would return many times the initial investment.

With Byrne in charge, the odds were good that the company would survive and take its rightful place again as the leader in low-cost auto insurance.

Warren Buffett's purchase of shares in GEICO

The day after Warren Buffett met Jack Byrne, Berkshire Hathaway bought over $1m shares in GEICO and Buffett left instructions for the purchase of many more. In total, $4.116m was spent on 1,294,308 shares, an average of $3.18. This purchase must have been a real boost for Byrne; someone besides himself believed in the possibility of reviving the company.

Another glimmer of hope came in mid-July, when the Washington insurance superintendent eased up on his hurdles to permit GEICO to continue. Now all that was required was for GEICO to persuade a group of other insurance companies that it should be able to pass on 25% of its risk exposure to them. Oh, and it needed to raise at least $50m of new capital!

This was being asked of a company that had a combined ratio of 124 – one of the worst ever for an insurance company. This meant that for every dollar it took in on policies, it paid out $1.24 in claims liabilities and expenses.

In the long history of the company, this was the first time it had reported an annual loss on underwriting. Byrne, clutching at straws, highlighted that, in the second quarter of 1976, the combined ratio had improved to 113. But everyone could see that was still a loss on its core business. It was, therefore, a very hard sell to other insurers being asked to take on GEICO's policy risks, and to potential shareholders.

Buffett and Byrne roll up their sleeves

Confidence in the GEICO name was very low, but Byrne had a new card to play. He had the backing of Warren Buffett, a man who was increasingly recognised on Wall Street as a shrewd investor and the leader of a well-run insurance company, National Indemnity.

Not only was Buffett prepared to give an opinion on Byrne's plan, on the quality of GEICO's economic franchise and on Byrne's character, but he had backed his judgement with a $4.116m buy. His involvement had the power to change the dynamic in negotiations with others.

Now that he and Byrne were working for a common cause, Buffett went to see the Washington superintendent. Buffett explained that he had committed millions of dollars and agreed that BH would take on some of GEICO's insurance risk. Surely, even the strictest of regulators would allow enough time (a few months) to bring in other insurers and to sell newly minted shares?

The problem was that the other insurance companies would not take 25% of the risks off GEICO, unless it had raised the additional $50m. On the other side, the financial institutions were not willing to put in $50m unless a quarter of the insurance risks had been removed.

The solution lay in getting the two actions to take place at the same time. Byrne had his work cut out. By early August, he managed to persuade 27 insurers to reinsure one-quarter of its exposure. But this was on the strict condition that GEICO succeeded in selling at least $50m of new shares.

There was the rub – Byrne had to get bankers involved to underwrite a share issue. He traipsed around the big investment banks of Wall Street to gain their support for an issue, but one after another they rejected him.

He was getting desperate when he went to see a relatively small firm called Salomon which specialised more in bond-trading than in equity raising. It so happened that they wanted to build up the equity side of the business and so they listened to Byrne's pitch. They had heard of Buffett's commitment to GEICO and could see how it could be saved and thereafter generate a good return for shareholders.

A share offer

On 18 August 1976, *The New York Times* ran a story that "a major investment bank had offered to purchase and reoffer to the public any of the new preferred shares" GEICO was selling. Salomon would take any of the 10m shares ($76m) not subscribed for either by existing shareholders, through the rights offering, or subscribed for by "members of the casualty insurance industry that have agreed to participate in a reinsurance arrangement with GEICO."

The preferred shares offered 8% per year, and were convertible to common stock. Thus the reinsurers could rescue GEICO, avoid a lowered reputation for the insurance sector, and receive reinsurance premiums. They would also gain from any upside in the fortunes of GEICO by converting their preferred shares into common shares in the future.

Jack Byrne later said: "The interlocking puzzle of constituents we had to bring together was staggering. The greatest challenge was the human element. We had to sell, persuade, negotiate, pressure and flatter – all in a period when we had negative press coverage. It was an intricate, sensitive series of small victories which finally made it all work. But, bit by bit, we succeeded."[3]

It took until November to complete the share offering. Buffett was so confident in GEICO's future that he had already told Salomon that BH would take all the preferred shares that others did not buy. That was a bold move for Berkshire, which then had a market capitalisation of not much more than the cost of all those GEICO shares.

In the end, the share offering (and thus the reinsurance deal) was a success and Berkshire bought only 1,986,953 of GEICO convertible preferred for $19.42m. This was a considerable proportion of BH's portfolio of share investments, which totalled $75.4m in December 1976.

They had done it! Byrne and Buffett had turned a vicious downward spiral of falling confidence and leaking capital into a virtuous circle of optimism and the pulling-in of capital and insurance policies. By year end, GEICO had $137m in capital, enough to allow growth.

The participants in the reinsurance treaty made good profits out of the deal and those insurers brave enough to buy shares saw them soar in value.

One note of sadness: former GEICO chairman, Benjamin Graham, whose investment fund first bought into the firm in 1948, did not get to see the completion of the fundraising and the turnaround of the company under the leadership of Byrne, and Graham's one-time apprentice, Warren Buffett, because he passed away in September 1976 aged 82.

Figure 1.3: The confidence virtuous circle of 1976

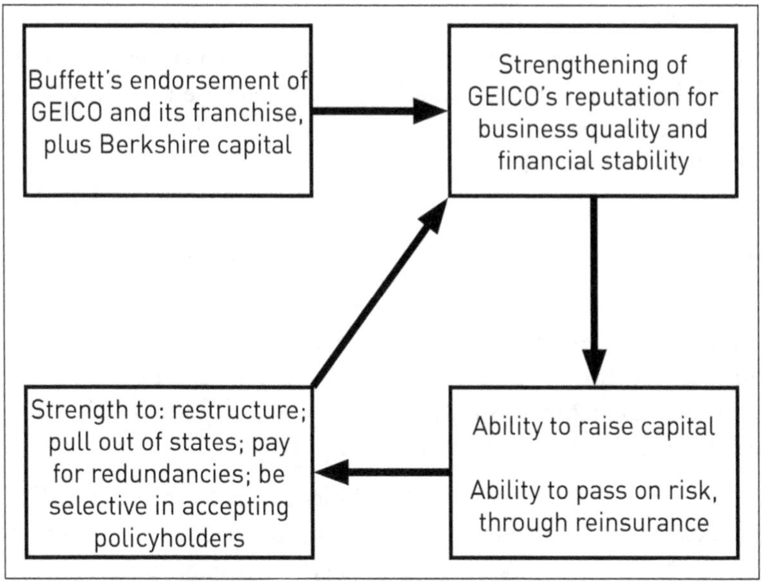

Buffett reflects on why he bought

In 1980, Buffett wrote to Berkshire Hathaway shareholders in his annual chairman's letter to explain his logic for investing such a large proportion of their money in GEICO.

He said that they had witnessed hundreds of attempted turnaround situations over the years and concluded that "with few exceptions, when a management with a reputation for brilliance tackles a business with a reputation for poor fundamental economics, it is the reputation of the business that remains intact."

He went on to say that GEICO might be an exception, having been turned around from the very edge of bankruptcy in 1976. Managerial brilliance had been needed for its resuscitation, and Jack Byrne had supplied it in abundance.

"But it also is true that the fundamental business advantage that GEICO had enjoyed – an advantage that previously had produced staggering success – was still intact within the company, although submerged in a sea of financial and operating troubles."

Buffett compared GEICO's problems to that of American Express in 1964 following the salad oil scandal. Both, he said, were one-of-a-kind companies, temporarily reeling from the effects of a managerial blow that did not destroy their exceptional underlying economics.

Warren Buffett's investment in GEICO takes off

GEICO's Tony Nicely started there in 1961, as an 18-year old in the underwriting department. He became CEO in 1993 and retired in 2018. At the time of the 1975–1976 crisis, Nicely was an assistant vice president, and recalls a stormy time, but was grateful that Jack Byrne was at the helm to steer the ship to safety.

He said in an interview with Robert Miles that Byrne saved "GEICO from complete destruction. There are few people, if any, who could have done it at the time. Jack was charismatic, convincing, and everything he had to be."[4]

Tony Nicely learned a lot about insurance from Byrne. "He understood the business well… he installed a whole new management process at GEICO, much of which still exists today… those of us who were survivors learned a tremendous amount from Jack – about the insurance business, about management and about a lot of other things."

Byrne found the employees and business systems he inherited in isolated silos: the pricing guys did their thing, the claims people did theirs, and the reserves were looked after by someone else. He was appalled by the number of times he heard, "I don't know and it's not my job." Plainly there needed to be a greater sense throughout the whole organisation of the overall objective – generating an acceptable profit on premiums received – so that everyone pulled in the same direction.

Byrne, with some force, pushed and pulled it into shape. He was very demanding and the turnaround was hard on the workforce. "I started out as a young man, and in two to three years I became an old man," said Tony Nicely. "Because of all the hours I had to put in, for a couple of years I was neither a father nor a husband. But it wasn't the long hours or the lack of time off that changed me. It wasn't even the stress of not knowing... whether or not it would still be there at the end of the day. What made me an old man was all the times that I had to look people in the eye... and say... I am sorry... but, through no fault of your own, as of Monday you no longer have a job."[5]

Smaller, but still standing

As expected, losses were reported for 1976. By 1977, however, GEICO was producing an operating profit and trumpeting its return to financial solvency. The volume of business was much reduced – market share fell from 4% to under 2% – but now it consisted of policies with a good likelihood of generating a positive underwriting result.

Byrne was determined to return the company to its roots of being a low-cost provider. So keen was he on cost-cutting that he shared a secretary for many years. In terms of motivating extraordinary performance, Buffett said of him that he was like the chicken farmer who rolls an ostrich egg into the chicken coup and says "Ladies this is what the competition is doing."

In the same way that he interacted with the key person at other investee companies – such as Kay Graham at The Washington Post or Chuck Higgins at See's Candies – Buffett did not second-guess the person on the ground. He let them get on with the job without interference, only giving advice if expressly asked for. Buffett displayed complete trust and these independently-minded executives greatly appreciated that.

One thing Buffett did impress on Byrne was the need to manage GEICO for the long run, definitely not for a short-term boost to volume or earnings. He would encourage him to manage it as though the business was the only one in which his family had a stake, and couldn't sell it for 100 years.

Despite his reluctance to intervene, Buffett did get a buzz out of reading the key metrics weekly. GEICO sent figures every Tuesday on such matters as the percentage of telephone inquiries resulting in a policy purchase.

Too much of a good thing can be wonderful

Buffett liked the developments he saw at GEICO so much that, in 1979, he added another $4.76m to BH's original stake of $23.53m, by which time the preferred shares had been converted to common stock. In the following year, BH bought another $18.85m, taking the total invested to $47.14m (for 7.2m shares). The average price paid over the four years was $6.55. Berkshire then held 33% of GEICO's equity.

He wrote of his excitement concerning GEICO's future in his 1980 letter to Berkshire Hathaway shareholders: "GEICO represents the best of all investment worlds – the coupling of a very important and very-hard-to-duplicate business advantage with an extraordinary management, whose skills in operations are matched by skills in capital allocation."

The sharp-eyed will have picked up that I've stated previously that BH spent only $45.7m for its one-half stake, but now I'm saying that BH laid out over $47m. The reason for the difference is that GEICO, like many companies where Buffett had influence, introduced a policy of share repurchases.

On one occasion, BH sold some of its GEICO shares back to the company. But on many others it did nothing and watched as the shares in issue declined when others sold. Eventually, in the mid-1990s, what had been a holding of one-third of GEICO's equity became one-half because other investors sold their shares to the firm.

A fantastic 19-year run

Between the end of 1976 and the beginning of 1996, GEICO grew at a phenomenal rate. It only took a year for the common stock to rise from the $3.13 BH paid to $8.13. But that was just the start of its impact on Berkshire Hathaway and Buffett's reputation. In 1980, GEICO generated so much in earnings that BH's one-third share amounted to $20m – in one year producing almost one-half of what BH had paid for its holding.

The next year was even better. In 1981, GEICO's shares doubled in price, accounting for over half of the gain in Berkshire's net worth that year (totalling $124m or about 31%). By then the shares were priced at

$27.75 – a nine-bagger in five years – and the value of BH's holding had risen to $200m.

Table 1.1: The meteoric rise in value of Berkshire's holding in GEICO

Year	Share price ($)	Total market value of BH's GEICO holding ($m)
1976	3.13	24
1977	8.13	44
1978	7.00	37
1979	11.88	68
1980	14.63	105
1981	27.75	200
1982	43.00	310
1983	58.13	398
1984	58.00	397
1985	87.00	596
1986	98.50	675
1987	110.50	757
1988	124.00	849
1989	152.50	1,045
1990	162.12	1,111
1991	198.98	1,363
1992	325.00	2,226
1993	256.87	1,760
1994	245.00	1,678
1995	349.34	2,393
1996	BH bought the remaining 49% for $2.3bn	

Source: W. Buffett, letters to shareholders of BH (1976–1996). Ignoring GEICO's 1992 scrip issue (four additional shares for each share already held).

By 1982, BH's one-third interest in GEICO represented $250m of premium volume, which was considerably greater than the total direct volume of all the other BH insurance companies put together, including National Indemnity. And only two years later, GEICO's premium income jumped to $885m, meaning that BH's interest was $320m, well over double BH's own insurance premium volume. At that point (beginning of 1984), with the shareholding worth around $400m, the GEICO investment represented 27% of Berkshire's net worth.

By the early 1990s, GEICO shares had rocketed to over $320, giving Buffett a 100-bagger on BH's common stock investment of 1976 (by then the shares had been split five for one, so the actual price was around $64).

In the engine room

Byrne was very conscious of the need to generate good rates of return on capital. Linked to that, he was aware of a crucial indicator of good management, discernible when a company is producing lots of cash from operations: do they hang on to that cash by investing it in business expansion and a growing cash pile, or do they return that money to shareholders through dividends and/or share repurchases?

Good managers know that the answer depends on whether the marginal dollar can be invested within the business at a satisfactory rate of return. If it can't, it should go to shareholders to invest elsewhere.

Byrne did invest within the business, but only where a dollar invested produced significantly more than a dollar of return. No empire-building for the sake of managerial pride or remuneration. Any dollars beyond that were used to greatly increase the dividend, raising it over six-fold between 1980 and 1992. He also started to repurchase the company's shares – eventually 30% of the shares would be bought back.

The management team also exercised impressive restraint by accepting only truly remunerative insurance business. Buffett wrote that they "have maintained extraordinary discipline in the underwriting area (including, crucially, provision for full and proper loss reserves), and their efforts are now being further rewarded by significant gains in new business."[6]

They were also disciplined on the cost side:

"The total of GEICO's underwriting expense and loss adjustment expense in 1986 was only 23.5% of premiums. Many major companies show percentages 15 points higher than that. Even such huge direct writers as Allstate and State Farm incur appreciably higher costs than does GEICO. The difference between GEICO's costs and those of its competitors is a kind of moat that protects a valuable and much-sought-after business castle. No one understands this moat-around-the-castle concept better than Bill Snyder, Chairman of GEICO [successor to Byrne]."[7]

The effectiveness of their focus on low-cost business is shown in the chart. Whereas most insurance companies had a combined claims and business expenses outflow greater than premium income (a combined ratio greater than 100), in the 16 years to 1992 GEICO showed underwriting profit in 14 years, with a combined ratio more than 100 in only two years – a remarkable achievement.

Figure 1.4: Combined ratios of GEICO and the wider insurance industry (1977–1992)

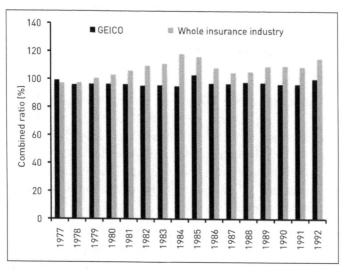

Sources: W. Buffett, letters to shareholders of BH; R. G. Hagstrom, *The Buffett Way* (John Wiley & Sons, 1995).

A permanent one

Buffett admired GEICO so much that even when he sold virtually all other shares in 1986, he held on to GEICO along with those in only two other stock market listed holdings, Capital Cities/ABC and The Washington Post. He regarded these three as permanent holdings, not for sale even if the market should appear to significantly overprice them.

He made a similar commitment to GEICO that he did to See's Candies: he would not sell even "if someone were to offer us a price far above what we believe those businesses are worth. This attitude may seem old-fashioned in a corporate world in which activity has become the order of the day… we will stick with our 'til-death-do-us-part' policy. It's the only one with which Charlie and I are comfortable, it produces decent results, and it lets our managers and those of our investees run their businesses free of distractions."[8]

Shortly after this statement was made, GEICO reported after-tax operating earnings per share of $9.01. So, a decade after buying, in one year BH was earning more from GEICO than the average price it had paid for a share in 1976, 1979 and 1980 (i.e. $6.55). And plenty more value was still to come from this investment goldmine.

Warren Buffett's rival in the investment hall of fame

GEICO is probably the best investment Buffett ever made. Much of this success is linked to what we've already looked at: the terrific performances coming from the underwriting side of GEICO's business. But what turbocharged the return for Berkshire Hathaway was the amazing amount of wealth generated by the person in charge of the equity investments of GEICO's insurance float. Lou Simpson's record rivals that of Buffett at Berkshire.

In the period when Berkshire owned about one-half of GEICO (1976–1996) it was important for the other shareholders to have someone without a potential conflict of interest in charge of the investment side of the business. So that excluded Buffett because he could, if so inclined, invest or divest money from his other pots, such as Blue Chip Stamps, into company shares that GEICO also held and thereby manipulate the market (at least as a theoretical possibility to suspiciously-minded regulators). Lou Simpson was appointed GEICO's investment chief in 1979 and proved to be an inspired choice.

The great hire

After working for a number of investment fund companies, Lou Simpson, 42, responded to an advertisement placed by Jack Byrne in 1979 for a new chief investment officer. He and three others were shortlisted for interview.

Interviewing investors was something that Buffett could help with, given his keen interest in investment approaches and the temperament required of a good investor. Thus it was that the controller of 33% of GEICO was asked to interview the four candidates.

Immediately after spending four hours with Simpson, Buffett called Byrne and told him to stop the search – they had found the guy they needed. Perhaps what Buffett said to *Institutional Investor* magazine seven years later gives us a clue as to what Buffett discovered at that meeting. He said Simpson "has the ideal temperament for investing... He derives no particular pleasure from operating with or against the crowd. He is comfortable following his own reason."

Buffett so admired Simpson that he regularly praised his handling of the GEICO portfolio in letters to BH shareholders.

He wrote, "Lou has the rare combination of temperamental and intellectual characteristics that produce outstanding long-term investment performance. Operating with below-average risk, he has generated returns that have been by far the best in the insurance industry."[9] And also, "Lou takes the same conservative, concentrated approach to investments that we do at Berkshire, and it is an enormous plus for us to have him on board."[10]

Buffett really did hand over the baton to Simpson, being satisfied not to hear about transactions Simpson had made until ten days after the end of the month.

What prompted Buffett to think so highly of Lou Simpson?

In this section, I set out what Simpson achieved at GEICO in his first 25 years. When he started, the firm's annual income from selling insurance policies was about $0.7bn. By 2004, successful expansion of the client base had grown annual revenue to $8.9bn.

Directly related to those premium volumes was the amount in the float. In the 1980s this was merely a few hundred million dollars, but it grew to $2.5bn by the mid-1990s, and to $6bn in 2004. Much of the float would have been invested in government bonds and other securities rather than equities, so Simpson generally had less than half the float for his share portfolio.

Table 1.2: The growth of GEICO's insurance float and Lou Simpson's equity portfolio

Year	Berkshire Hathaway float including GEICO's ($bn)	GEICO float ($bn)	Lou Simpson's portfolio ($bn)
Start 1996	6.4	2.6	
1997	7.1	2.9	
1998	22.8	3.1	
1999	25.3	3.4	
2000	27.9	3.9	
2001	35.5	4.3	2.0
2002	41.2	4.7	
2003	44.2	5.3	
2004	46.1	6.0	2.5

Source: W. Buffett, letters to shareholders of BH.

Table 1.3 shows the returns that Simpson earned on that money. Note two things:

1. **Outperformance**: Most fund managers would consider themselves well ahead of the pack if they managed an annual average

outperformance of a mere 1% per year. Simpson achieved 6.8%. To give you some idea of the long-term significance of this, a $10,000 investment compounding at 13.5%, the rate on the S&P, gives $237,081 after 25 years. If compounded at Simpson's 20.3%, it produces $1,015,408.

2. **Underperformance**: All investors have years where they underperform the market – Simpson underperformed for three years in a row (1997–1999). When this happens, don't worry, stick to sound investment principles and you'll be OK over the long run. Simpson the value investor seemed out of step with the irrational exuberance of the late 1990s dot-com boom. He stuck to his principles and produced great results in the years following the 2000 crash.

Buffett regularly joked about his "embarrassment" with how well Simpson was doing relative to himself. In 1986 he wrote, "Only my ownership of a controlling block of Berkshire stock makes me secure enough to give you the following figures, comparing the overall return of the equity portfolio at GEICO to that of the Standard & Poor's 500."[11]

In 2001: "Lou's thinking, of course, is quite similar to mine, but we usually end up in different securities. That's largely because he's working with less money and can therefore invest in smaller companies than I. Oh, yes, there's also another minor difference between us: In recent years, Lou's performance has been far better than mine."[12]

And in 2004: "Sometimes, it should be added, I silently disagree with his decisions. But he's usually right."[13]

Praise does not come any higher than this: "One point that goes beyond Lou's GEICO work: his presence on the scene assures us that Berkshire would have an extraordinary professional immediately available to handle its investments if something were to happen to Charlie and me."[14]

Simpson said that he had an advantage over Buffett. While they were both running concentrated portfolios of less than 15–20 shares (often seven companies or less), Buffett had to manage up to $40bn whereas Simpson only had single digit billions.

This meant that Simpson had a much wider range of companies to choose from. He could put $400m into one company without taking an inconvenient controlling stake or a stake so great that it became illiquid.

Table 1.3: Portrait of a disciplined investor – Lou Simpson

Year	Return from GEICO equities	S&P return	Relative results	BH change in market value
1980	23.7%	32.3%	–8.6%	32.8%
1981	5.4%	–5.0%	10.4%	31.8%
1982	45.8%	21.3%	24.4%	38.4%
1983	36.0%	22.4%	13.6%	69.0%
1984	21.8%	6.1%	15.7%	–2.7%
1985	45.8%	31.6%	14.2%	93.7%
1986	38.7%	18.6%	20.1%	14.2%
1987	–10.0%	5.1%	–15.1%	4.6%
1988	30.0%	16.6%	13.4%	59.3%
1989	36.1%	31.7%	4.4%	84.6%
1990	–9.9%	–3.1%	–6.8%	–23.1%
1991	56.5%	30.5%	26.0%	35.6%
1992	10.8%	7.6%	3.2%	29.8%
1993	4.6%	10.1%	–5.5%	38.9%
1994	13.4%	1.3%	12.1%	25.0%
1995	39.8%	37.6%	2.2%	57.4%
1996	29.2%	23.0%	6.2%	6.2%
1997	24.6%	33.4%	–8.8%	34.9%
1998	18.6%	28.6%	–10.0%	52.2%
1999	7.2%	21.0%	–13.8%	–19.9%
2000	20.9%	–9.1%	30.0%	26.6%
2001	5.2%	–11.9%	17.1%	6.5%
2002	–8.1%	–22.1%	14.0%	–3.8%
2003	38.3%	28.7%	9.6%	15.8%
2004	16.9%	10.9%	6.0%	4.3%
Avg. annual 1980–2004	20.3%	13.5%	6.8%	n/a

Source: W. Buffett, letters to shareholders of BH (2004, 2015).

If Buffett, in contrast, invested say 5% of his portfolio in one company that might be $2bn. There are few share registers around that can take that amount of money. The alternative of splitting the money up into, say, $400m lumps does not appeal, because that would mean holding stakes in scores of companies, most of which Buffett could not possibly know enough about. This would mean moving a long way down the attractiveness curve, or the best-ideas curve.

Lou Simpson decided to retire in 2010. Clearly, Buffett did not want him to go; in his letter of that year, Buffett named Simpson "one of the investment greats."[15]

Simpson's investment approach

Lou Simpson's investment approach, like his friend Buffett's, developed through trial and error, evolving over decades. It's worth spending a few minutes looking at how the highly successful strategies of both men bore more than a few similarities.

Examine facts rather than valuing hope

Earlier in his career, long before being hired by GEICO, Simpson was a growth investor. He often failed to properly consider whether that growth was being offered at a reasonable price; he was aiming for a spectacular return from a few star performers, hoping that he had guessed the future correctly.

But, through bitter experience, he learned that good long-run results come from buying companies with established and proven high performance, low risk and a low price. Businesses that promised future riches without solid evidence in the past were rarely good investments.

Read all day if you can

Simpson had a voracious appetite for financial newspapers, other intelligent press, annual reports, industry reports, and generally read for five to eight hours a day. He, like Buffett, was not trading-intensive but reading-intensive and thought-intensive.

Think independently

Be sceptical of conventional wisdom. Obtain your own information and do your own analysis. Do not get caught up in waves of irrational behaviour and emotion. Be willing to consider unpopular and unloved companies, as they often offer the greatest opportunities.

Invest in high-return businesses run for shareholders

Look at the rate of return on shareholders' money used within the business. If it is high and, in your judgement, sustainable given the strategic position of the company and the quality of management, then there is a good chance of long-run appreciation in the share price. Cash flow return, rather than profit return, can be a useful additional metric, given that it is more difficult to manipulate than profit.

Make few investments

At a Kellogg School of Management Q&A session in November 2017, Simpson said, "The more you trade, the harder it is to add value because you're absorbing a lot of transaction costs, not to mention taxes." (After retiring from GEICO, he maintained an interest in investing through his chairmanship of SQ Advisors, and as an adjunct professor of finance at Kellogg.)

Making only a few investments means you can devote the requisite amount of time to understand the companies very well, which leads on to: "What we do is run a long-time-horizon portfolio comprised of ten to fifteen stocks... Basically, they're good businesses. They have a high return on capital, consistently good returns, and they're run by leaders who want to create long-term value for shareholders while also treating their stakeholders right."[16]

Good investment ideas – companies meeting his investment criteria – were hard to find. Thus when Simpson found one, he made a large commitment. "You can only know so many companies. If you're managing 50 or 100 positions, the chances that you can add value are much, much lower. So far, this year we bought one new position, and we're looking pretty seriously at one more. I don't know what we'll decide to do. Our turnover [proportion of the portfolio changed in a year] is 15–20%. Usually, we add one or two things and get rid of one or two things."[17]

Sometimes the best plan is to do nothing. Simpson admitted that masterly inactivity is difficult to do because it "is very boring", but is often the right thing.

Scuttlebutt

Get to know the management teams in the investee companies. Also, seek out the views of customers, suppliers and competitors on the company, its strategy and its managers, before making an investment. Simpson has said that he likes to visit senior people at a company in their own office, which is "like kicking the tires."[18] It is important to know how senior management at a company think.

Key questions to explore include whether managers have a substantial shareholding in the business and whether they are straightforward in their dealings with the owners. Also, are they willing to divest unprofitable operations and do they use excess cash to buy back the company's shares, rather than empire-build by investing in low-profit areas?

Simpson told Robert Miles that the thrill comes from "really understanding businesses. I get excited when we get some insights on a business that's not really well understood."[19]

Make long-term investments

Guessing the direction of the stock market or individual shares over periods of a few months is a pointless game because short-term movements are too unpredictable.

What is much more predictable is share returns over the long term (many years) of quality companies: "Over time the market is ultimately rational, or at least somewhat rational."[20]

Simpson liked Buffett's fare card punching analogy: "You should think of investing as somebody giving you a fare card with 20 punches. Each time you make a change, punch a hole in the card. Once you have made your twentieth change, you have to stick with what you own. The point is just to be very careful with each decision you make. The more decisions you make, the higher the chances are that you will make a poor decision."[21]

Simpson would often have more than 10% of the fund in one company, and over 50% in five companies.

Buy at a reasonable price

Once a superior business has been identified, then its shares should only be bought if the price is not excessive relative to its prospects. "Even the world's greatest business is not a good investment if the price is too high."[22] Simpson used indicators such as earnings yield (or its inverse, the price to earnings ratio) and price to free cash flow.

Sell your mistakes, but hold the successes

There is a body of literature examining the psychological tendency to hold on to losing shares (because they might come back and I don't want to face the realisation of my mistake by crystallising losses) while selling early the shares that are performing well (nobody ever went broke by selling for a profit).

Simpson expresses his opposition to these notions with a reference to weeds and flowers: "One thing a lot of investors do is they cut their flowers and water their weeds. They sell their winners and keep their losers, hoping the losers will come back."[23] He says that we should resist our instincts and sell those investments not working out, while holding onto those performing as well as expected or better. He claims his biggest mistakes were when he sold really good companies too soon. The right investment will generally go on producing good returns for a long time.

You need a combination of quantitative and qualitative skills

Simpson tells us that most share buyers quickly develop the requisite quantitive skills, but the vital qualitative skills take longer. The importance of the qualitative in analysing companies is captured in Buffett's aphorism, "You're better off being approximately right than exactly wrong." Here are some of the qualitative factors Simpson thought crucial, despite the impossibility of precision: Are the managers of high integrity? Do they treat the people in the organisation well? Are they suitably long-term focused for shareholders' benefit, rather than obsessed with short-term window dressing?

Jack Byrne comments on Simpson

Jack Byrne was interviewed by *The Washington Post* and said the following about Lou Simpson: "I pondered for eight years what makes Lou knock the cover off the ball. Lou is very bright, with an economics background from Princeton. But the woods are filled with bright guys. It has more to do with his personality. He is very, very sure of his own judgements. He ignores everybody else. He gets one or two really strong ideas a year and then likes to swing very hard."[24]

The Tony Nicely years

Even great businesses take the wrong path from time to time, and in the early 1990s the senior managers at GEICO stumbled. Yet again, they saw visions of things being better on the other side. They expanded away from their core competitive advantage in auto insurance with a low-cost distribution model, into aviation insurance, home insurance and finance. This resulted in a loss of focus and poor returns.

Without Jack Byrne there to constantly keep the senior executives focused, they drifted. Byrne resigned in 1986, attracted by the prospect of running an insurance company, Fireman's Fund, spun out of American Express.

Another hit was received from Hurricane Andrew in 1992. The resultant and significant payouts led to an underwriting loss that year.

GEICO's shares had reached a peak at over $300, with a market capitalisation of around $4.5m, but fell to not much over $200. (This is measured using the share price before the 1992 split. After the five-for-one split, the shares were actually trading at slightly over $40.)

Buffett became concerned with the firm's direction away from its circle of competence, and even considered selling Berkshire's stake.

Tony Nicely took over as co-CEO in charge of the operational side of the business in 1993, with Lou Simpson co-CEO responsible for investments.

Under Nicely, the business distractions were dropped and additional investment was put into the low-cost direct selling of auto insurance. We know how Buffett likes companies with moats and he later said that "thanks to Tony and his management team, GEICO's moat widened."[25]

Buying the other half

Now that GEICO was refocused on its no-agent model of selling auto insurance, Buffett wanted Berkshire to own the whole company. He and Charlie Munger started negotiating a price with Chairman Sam Butler, Lou Simpson and Tony Nicely in 1994. The tough but friendly talks dragged on into 1995. Butler, Simpson and Nicely took their fiduciary responsibilities to GEICO's minority shareholders very seriously and, commendably, negotiated robustly – demanding a high but fair price for the remaining 49% of the company.

Buffett swallowed hard and accepted that BH would pay $2.3bn for the second half of a business for which he had paid only $45.7m for the first half (the price was $70 per share, or $350 per original share if we ignore the five-for-one share split).

Tony Nicely warmly welcomed Berkshire Hathaway's full ownership. Shortly after agreeing the deal, he told *The Washington Post*, "I really believe we probably are in a better position now for faster growth than perhaps we've ever been." With Buffett pushing for a long-term focus, he felt he could pursue growth without hesitating to spend aggressively to build the business in the short run.

Nicely said, "In the insurance business, you tend to lose money in the first year on [new] business. You have higher losses and higher expenses... We won't have shareholders who are concerned with year-to-year [results]. We have a long-term investor who says, 'You folks there grow it to the best of your physical ability and I'll worry about the finances.'"[26]

Under new management

Nicely was very keen to expand the advertising budget, and Buffett encouraged him, thinking that the more people who knew about the low-cost of GEICO's insurance the better – more underwriting profit and more float to invest. But this would only be a good thing so long as GEICO maintained downward pressure on the cost base. Nicely was just the man for this job, because he had been through the school of hard knocks when the company barely survived, and really understood that GEICO's competitive advantage lay with excellent operational efficiency. Expenditure on marketing more than tripled to $100m by 1997. And they didn't stop there; within another two years it was $242m, and $800m by 2009.

Buffett expressed his enthusiasm for more advertising in his 1998 Letter to Berkshire shareholders. "There is no limit to what Berkshire is willing to invest in GEICO's new-business activity, as long as we can concurrently build the infrastructure the company needs to properly serve its policyholders."

He was unconcerned if new ventures made a loss in the first year, as they often did, "We simply measure whether we are creating more than a dollar of value per dollar spent – and if that calculation is favorable, the more dollars we spend the happier I am."

And in his letter the following year: "Tony's foot is going to stay on the advertising pedal (and my foot will be on his)."

He emphasised that the huge hike in advertising spend would enable the business to achieve significant growth, and extend and solidify the promise of the GEICO brand in the minds of Americans. "Personally, I think these expenditures are the best investment Berkshire can make... GEICO is acquiring a direct relationship with a huge number of households that, on average, will send us $1,100 year after year... cash is pouring in rather than going out."

The GEICO Gecko, a cartoon character using surreal humour and satire, with a British accent (not Australian, Warren, as I once heard you say!), made its first appearance during the 2000 television season and quickly became an advertising icon. By 2006, GEICO was spending far more than any of its competitors on advertising because Tony Nicely was doing such a great job of turning advertising money into underwriting profit and float.

> "Last year I told you that if you had a new son or grandson to be sure to name him Tony. But Don Keough, a Berkshire director, recently had a better idea. After reviewing GEICO's performance

in 2006, he wrote me, 'Forget births. Tell the shareholders to immediately change the names of their present children to Tony or Antoinette.' Don signed his letter 'Tony'."[27]

Into the big league

By 2008, GEICO had moved from sixth largest US auto insurer (in 1995), with 2.5% market share, to third largest, with a 7.7% share. Buffett noted that Americans were focused on saving money and as such they were flocking to GEICO.

It only took another four years for it to become the second largest, and by 2015 it had 11.4% of the market. Buffett wrote, "On August 30, 2030 – my 100th birthday – I plan to announce that GEICO has taken over the top spot."[28]

A year of industry-wide losses in 2016 was viewed by Nicely and Buffett as an opportunity for GEICO, because at such times other firms lost their drive to attract business. While they were holding back, GEICO accelerated its new-business efforts. In typical independent-thinking fashion, Buffett said "We like to make hay while the sun sets, knowing that it will surely rise again. GEICO continues on a roll as I send you this letter. When insurance prices increase, people shop more. And when they shop, GEICO wins."[29]

The growth in premium volume (sales of insurance policies) shows that the advertising spend was very worthwhile. Turnover rose ten-fold in 24 years – see Figure 1.5.

As a consequence of turnover growth, the insurance float rose from under $3bn to over $22bn – a lot of money available for shares and other securities. Even a modest return on those securities of, say, 7% (we don't know the true return) would result in over $1.4bn being generated.

Figure 1.5: The Gecko leaps – GEICO premium volume and insurance float ($bn)

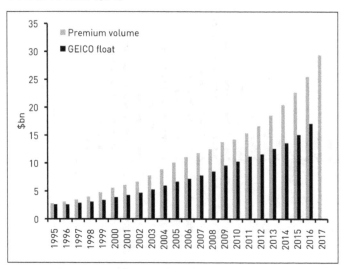

Sources: W. Buffett, letters to shareholders of BH; National Association of Insurance Commissioners.

Figure 1.6: GEICO combined ratio (%)

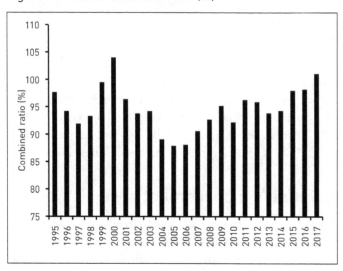

Sources: BH annual reports; W. Buffett, letters to shareholders of BH.

Figure 1.7: GEICO underwriting profit ($m)

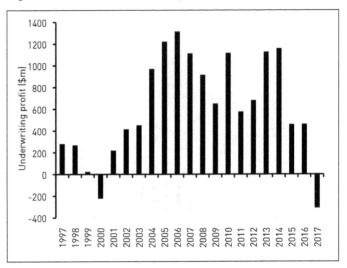

Sources: BH annual reports; W. Buffett, letters to shareholders of BH.

Of course, with most insurance companies, this investment return would be necessary to compensate for losses on underwriting. The second and third charts show that such compensation was not needed for GEICO because Tony Nicely's team produced combined ratios of less than 100%, making underwriting profits sometimes exceeding $1bn.

So a company that BH bought for $45.7m + $2.3bn is today capable of creating money for shareholders of $1bn or more on investments and another $1bn on underwriting in a single year (totalling $15.5bn by the end of 2018). That is a lot of money for Buffett to deploy elsewhere. No wonder GEICO is often regarded as Buffett's greatest investment.

Warren Buffett's management style

The vast majority of managers who come into the Berkshire Hathaway fold never leave, except through illness or retirement (often long-delayed). These people are usually multimillionaires and so do not need to work. However, they feel valued by Buffett and Munger. They feel part of a larger family of like-minded people. They feel that they are doing something worthwhile. Tap-dancing to work, they put in an enormous effort to build something of importance. They want to make their friends, Warren and Charlie, proud of them.

Think like an owner

The case of GEICO illustrates well the approach Buffett takes toward his managers. Tony Nicely thought of GEICO as *his* company, as though he owned it, and accordingly took long-term oriented decisions. This attitude is Buffett's instruction to all his key executives.

It is helped by the enormous amount of freedom each key person is given to run the business the way he/she thinks fit. It is his/her canvas on which to paint; where they can be creative, be a builder of something great with very little, if any, operational input from Berkshire head office, which anyway has only a handful of staff.

Efficient use of time

Being under the Buffett umbrella meant that Tony Nicely didn't have to do what so many CEOs have to: spend vast amounts of time on non-operational activities.

Buffett explained the advantages of being off-market in his 1998 letter to BH shareholders. He wrote that Tony did not need to spend time or energy at "board meetings, press interviews, presentations by investment bankers or talks with financial analysts". And he did not need to "spend a moment thinking about financing, credit ratings or 'Street' expectations for earnings per share." With this operational freedom, Tony and GEICO were free to "convert their almost limitless potential into matching achievements."

A meeting of minds

Nicely told author Robert Miles in 2001, when preparing for his book *The Warren Buffett CEO*, that the greatest thing about becoming part of Berkshire Hathaway was the opportunity to talk to Buffett more frequently. Nicely said that he appreciated the freedom to take a long-term view, running the company so that it would be strong in 30 years' time, not so that it will have a good day tomorrow.[30]

He described Buffett as "the best boss in the world" and praised his wisdom and encouragement. Nicely said that he wanted to make Buffett proud.[31]

The respect was mutual; Buffett wrote in his 1998 letter that there was no better person in the business world than Nicely to run GEICO.

Be motivated by the right things

Buffett encourages decency in business, integrity and service to others. Nicely gains great satisfaction from doing right by the customer, saving them money and giving an excellent service, as well as serving BH shareholders. He says, "It's not material possessions, or wealth, or those type of things that give you satisfaction. It's being part of creating something that is truly worthwhile."[32]

On the key ingredients for a successful operating manager, Nicely said, "I think, certainly, honesty and integrity have to be at the top of the list… the ability to communicate well… to work with people for a common cause."[33]

But financial incentives are also important

Buffett regards selecting the incentive plan for managers as one of his most important tasks. The targets vary from one subsidiary to another, depending on what factors the managers have under their direct control. In the case of GEICO, Buffett focused on two key variables:

1. Growth in number of policies. Insurance is generally unprofitable in the first year under the direct marketing approach, even though it results in longer-term customers who do bring profits. Therefore, GEICO employees should not be penalised by an incentive scheme requiring immediate profits. Thus only volume was a target with first-year policies.

2. Underwriting profitability on seasoned auto business (policies on the books for more than one year).

Each of these factors contributes 50% to bonuses.

Buffett thought it wise to reward all the GEICO staff on the basis of the same criteria through the company's profit-sharing plan. *"Everyone* at GEICO knows what counts," he wrote in his 1996 letter to BH shareholders.

"Berkshire's incentive compensation principles: Goals should be (1) tailored to the economics of the specific operating business; (2) simple in character, so that the degree to which they are being realized can be easily measured; and (3) directly related to the daily activities of plan participants. As a corollary, we shun 'lottery ticket' arrangements, such as options on Berkshire shares, whose ultimate value – which could range from zero to huge – is totally out of the control of the person whose behavior we would like to affect. In our view, a system that produces quixotic payoffs will not only be wasteful for owners but may actually discourage the focused behavior we value in managers."[34]

We have some figures for the extent to which bonuses boosted GEICO employees' take-home pay. In the first year under BH's full ownership (1996), the equivalent of 16.9% ($40m) of salary was handed out in incentive pay. Two years later it was 32.3%, or $103m, and in 2004 it was 24.3% ($191m). With that amount of extra pay on offer, it's no wonder that staff went the extra mile and the number of policies and profitability went up.

Table 1.4 shows that the GEICO team kept underwriting costs in the range of just 14%–20% of premiums taken from customers – often 15 percentage points less than competitors.

Some perspective on the importance of GEICO in the overall scheme of things at Berkshire

GEICO's annual underwriting profits, and the returns on its security portfolio, have allowed Berkshire to grow by directing that cash into investments in both wholly-owned subsidiaries and substantial minority stakes in major US and other companies.

But GEICO wasn't the only insurance company within Berkshire. By the 1990s, National Indemnity had built up a substantial reinsurance and catastrophe business under the leadership of Ajit Jain, adding a very large additional float on top of its personal insurance float.

Table 1.4: GEICO's consistent success at minimising underwriting costs

Year	Underwriting expense (% of premiums)	Year	Underwriting expense (% of premiums)
1995	15.8	2007	18.4
1996	15.8	2008	17.9
1997	16.4	2009	18.2
1998	19.5	2010	17.8
1999	19.3	2011	18.1
2000	18.3	2012	20.0
2001	16.5	2013	17.2
2002	16.8	2014	16.6
2003	17.7	2015	15.9
2004	17.8	2016	15.6
2005	17.3	2017	14.5
2006	18.0		

Sources: BH annual reports; W. Buffett, letters to shareholders of BH.

Other insurance companies have been added over the years, most significantly General Reinsurance (Gen Re) which was taken over in 1998 for $22bn. This contributed a $14.9bn of float which trebled Berkshire's overall float.

Buffett and Charlie Munger put much of Berkshire's success down to the effective investment of low-cost or no-cost float, as well as investing the cash set aside for deferred taxes.

Not only have these sources of cash grown to over $170bn but they come free. They are still *liabilities* but, unlike other sources of capital, they bear no interest and come without covenants or due dates.

In Berkshire's 2017 annual report, Buffett wrote, "In effect, they give us the benefit of debt – an ability to have more assets working for us – but saddle us with none of its drawbacks."

Figure 1.8: GEICO's float and Berkshire's total float from all insurance subsidiaries ($bn)

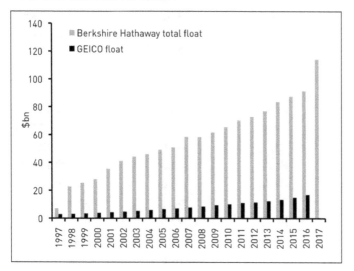

Source: BH annual reports.

You can see in Table 1.5 that it is only in a minority of years (18 out of 51) that the float has had any cost at all, because BH has produced underwriting profits in two-thirds of the years since the purchase of National Indemnity.

The amount of profit flowing from underwriting has been phenomenal. For example, in the 16 years to the end of 2018 there was only one year of underwriting loss. For the entire 16-year period, the pre-tax gain totalled $27bn.

Table: 1.5: Berkshire's success at generating underwriting profits and low-cost or no-cost funds

Year	Underwriting loss ($m)	Average float ($m)	Approximate cost of funds (ratio of 1 to 2)
1967	Profit	17.3	Less than zero
1968	Profit	19.9	Less than zero
1969	Profit	23.4	Less than zero
1970	0.37	32.4	1.14%
1971	Profit	52.5	Less than zero
1972	Profit	69.5	Less than zero
1973	Profit	73.3	Less than zero
1974	7.36	79.1	9.30%
1975	11.35	87.6	12.96%
1976	Profit	102.6	Less than zero
1977	Profit	139.0	Less than zero
1978	Profit	190.4	Less than zero
1979	Profit	227.3	Less than zero
1980	Profit	237.0	Less than zero
1981	Profit	228.4	Less than zero
1982	21.56	220.6	9.77%
1983	33.87	231.3	14.64%
1984	48.06	253.2	18.98%
1985	44.23	390.2	11.34%
1986	55.84	797.5	7.00%
1987	55.43	1,266.7	4.38%
1988	11.08	1,497.7	0.74%
1989	24.40	1,541.3	1.58%
1990	26.65	1,637.3	1.63%
1991	119.59	1,895.0	6.31%
1992	108.96	2,290.4	4.76%
1993	Profit	2,624.7	Less than zero
1994	Profit	3,056.6	Less than zero
1995	Profit	3,607.2	Less than zero
1996	Profit	6,702.0	Less than zero

Year	Underwriting loss ($m)	Average float ($m)	Approximate cost of funds (ratio of 1 to 2)
1997	Profit	7,093.1	Less than zero
1998	Profit	22.8bn	Less than zero
1999	1.4bn	25.3bn	5.8%
2000	1.7bn	27.9bn	6%
2001	4.1bn	35.5bn	12.8%
2002	0.4bn	41.2bn	1%
2003	Profit	44.2bn	Less than zero
2004	Profit	46.1bn	Less than zero
2005	Profit	49.3bn	Less than zero
2006	Profit	50.9bn	Less than zero
2007	Profit	58.7bn	Less than zero
2008	Profit	58.5bn	Less than zero
2009	Profit	61.9bn	Less than zero
2010	Profit	65.8bn	Less than zero
2011	Profit	70.6bn	Less than zero
2012	Profit	73.1bn	Less than zero
2013	Profit	77.2bn	Less than zero
2014	Profit	83.9bn	Less than zero
2015	Profit	87.7bn	Less than zero
2016	Profit	91.6bn	Less than zero
2017	3.2bn	114.5bn	3%
2018	Profit	122.7bn	Less than zero

Source: BH annual reports. Figures in $m unless stated.

A Buffett mistake, $50m lost

Despite Buffett's standard non-interventionist stance when it comes to interacting with his managers, he can sometimes become so excited by an idea that he encourages his managers to implement it. Such was the case with credit cards for GEICO customers. After all, the company already had contact with millions of car owners, data on the behaviour of these people and an efficient distribution method. Why not just sell a credit card alongside insurance? Thus the Geico Platinum MasterCard was born.

The problem is that the credit card business is notoriously treacherous for new entrants. There is a behavioural phenomenon called *adverse selection*, assisted by asymmetric information: the customer knows more about their creditworthiness and reliability than the credit card company and so, given the chance, the least creditworthy people will accept an offer from a new entrant. Thus the new entrant ends up with a portfolio of customers who are, on average, a poor risk.

I'll let Buffett acknowledge his business sin:

> "And now a painful confession: last year your chairman closed the book on a very expensive business fiasco entirely of his own making... GEICO's managers, it should be emphasized, were never enthusiastic about my idea. They warned me that instead of getting the cream of GEICO's customers we would get the – well, let's call it the non-cream. I subtly indicated that I was older and wiser. I was just older."[35]

Naturally, suitably chastened by this harsh lesson, Buffett reinforced his vow to be a hands-off boss, allowing his managers to just get on with the job – at least most of the time:

> "We tend to let our many subsidiaries operate on their own, without our supervising and monitoring them to any degree. That means we are sometimes late in spotting management problems, and that both operating and capital decisions are occasionally made with which Charlie and I would have disagreed had we been consulted... We would rather suffer the visible costs of a few bad decisions than incur the many invisible costs that come from decisions made too slowly – or not at all – because of a stifling bureaucracy."[36]

Learning points

Now that we are up to date with the GEICO story – not the end, because it still has a great future – it is useful to remind ourselves of the key lessons Buffett learned or reinforced through this experience and, by extension, what we can take away from the saga and make use of in our own investment approach.

1. **Focus on the franchise.** When a company seems down and out due to recent managerial errors, this is the time to conduct your own analysis to see if its once-triumphant economic franchise has survived in some form, and whether it can be revived and strengthened.

2. **Understand the quality and characters of the key people.** Make sure the senior individual(s), (a) understand the nature of the economic franchise, (b) will intelligently and energetically pursue profits, and (c) will act with high integrity regarding shareholders.

3. **Do not sell early.** Buffett could have sold at a multiple of the initial share price any time, but he held on. If the franchise remains intact, generating high rates of return on capital and controlled by good managers then, even if your initial investment has multiplied 50-fold (1976 to 1996) it might be worth buying more, not selling.

4. **Look for virtuous circles.** In particular, search for operating virtuous circles, either already up-and-running or likely to be created in the near future.

5. **Encourage investment within the business.** But only so long as each dollar spent creates more than one dollar of shareholder value. Any cash generated above this should be given to shareholders to obtain better returns in other businesses.

6. **Identify and use float wisely.** Many businesses enjoy large cash balances as they receive customer's payments up front, giving managers the comfort blanket of idle money giving a paltry return. Buffett prefers to allocate such money to double digit return investments.

Investment 2

THE BUFFALO EVENING NEWS

Summary of the deal

Deal	The Buffalo Evening News
Time	1977–present
Price paid	$35.5m
Quantity	100% of the share capital
Sale price	Part of Berkshire Hathaway today
Profit	At least 15-fold
Berkshire Hathaway in 1977	Share price: $90–$138
	Book value: $151m
	Per share book value: $155

To understand the beauty of the Buffalo Evening News investment, you need to imagine a world before the internet. In this world, if a town had only one newspaper, then that business could be an excellent economic franchise. This local monopoly was in a position to charge extra on the cover price and, more significantly, raise rates for advertisements.

The problem is that everyone in the investment community knew that one-paper towns were rich-seamed goldmines, and therefore when a paper came up for sale it fetched a high price. In many cases, the price was so high that buyers suffered the winner's curse – they won the auction but regretted it ever afterwards.

Buffett and Munger looked and looked, examined and rejected potential newspaper acquisitions. A small number of shares were bought in four newspaper companies, but the stakes couldn't be built up without paying too much.

Then The Buffalo Evening News came on the market. It was not priced exceptionally high, but there were good reasons for that:

- First, it was one of two newspaper companies operating in Buffalo. They had hacked at each other for years, lowering each other's profits in their desperate competitive attacks.

- Second, the managers had caved in to union demands to such an extent that it was difficult to determine for whose benefit the company was being run – certainly the shareholders didn't seem to get much.

- Third, it did not publish a Sunday edition, the day most attractive to advertisers because readers tended to loiter longer.

- Finally, it was in Buffalo, a town down on its luck; a rust belt town with a shrinking population.

Already, The Washington Post and *Chicago Tribune* had declined invitations to make offers. But Buffett and Munger could see a path through the immediate difficulties, and they had a vision of what it might become.

As it turned out, getting to those sunny uplands took five years of pain and losses. There were times when Buffett was all for throwing in the towel; he prepared himself to take the punch of a $35.5m loss. But at the darkest moments, Charlie Munger – with the help of others – hauled Buffett back on board to make yet one more push.

It was very tough, but by sticking it out they created a business that, in the 1980s, gave back to Berkshire over three times what was paid for it. It was even better in the 1990s, with nearly $300m sent to Berkshire to invest elsewhere – not bad for a $35.5m investment.

Newspaper economic franchises in the 1970s and 1980s

The ideal business to own is an *unregulated toll-bridge* because, according to Buffett, once the capital cost has been paid you can raise prices to out-pace inflation, so long as you can maintain a local monopoly.

Buffett, over many years, had expressed his thoughts on this to his close friends. One of them, Sandy Gottesman, let the cat out of the bag in an interview for *The Wall Street Journal* in 1977. "Warren likens owning a monopoly or market-dominant newspaper to owning an unregulated toll-bridge. You have relative freedom to increase rates when and as much as you want." [37]

Buffett later expanded on the idea of newspaper market power in his 1984 letter to Berkshire shareholders. He wrote that the:

> "economics of a dominant newspaper are excellent … Owners, naturally, would like to believe that their wonderful profitability is achieved only because they unfailingly turn out a wonderful product. That comfortable theory wilts before an uncomfortable fact. While first-class newspapers make excellent profits, the profits of third-rate papers are as good or better – as long as either class of paper is dominant within its community. Of course, product quality may have been crucial to the paper in achieving dominance... [But] once dominant, the newspaper itself, not the marketplace, determines just how good or how bad the paper will be. Good or bad, it will prosper. That is not true of most businesses: inferior quality generally produces inferior economics. But even a poor newspaper is a bargain to most citizens simply because of its 'bulletin board' value. Other things being equal, a poor product will not achieve quite the level of readership achieved by a first-class product. A poor product, however, will still remain essential to most citizens, and what commands their attention will command the attention of advertisers."

The love of newsprint

Buffett had taken a keen interest in newspapers ever since he filed his first income tax return as a 13-year-old paperboy (he paid $7 in tax that year). He reckons he delivered 500,000 papers as a teenager, giving him plenty of time to think about the pull of newspapers for 20th century consumers, and therefore the importance of them to advertisers.

Even today he is an excellent thrower of newspapers. In the early morning before the Berkshire AGM, he takes on all comers in a newspaper throwing competition, which he calls, "The Newspaper Tossing Challenge". Buffett knows just how to fold a paper and throw it from a distance so it does not come undone. He's still pretty good – don't take him on unless you've practised a few thousand times. Bill Gates's attempt was embarrassing!

Early on, Buffett also developed a love of good journalism and an appreciation of the crucial importance of independent, informed analysis and reporting for a healthy democracy. Writing in 2006, Buffett looked back fondly on the good old days for papers:

> "For most of the 20th Century, newspapers were the primary source of information for the American public. Whether the subject was sports, finance, or politics, newspapers reigned supreme. Just as important, their ads were the easiest way to find job opportunities or to learn the price of groceries at your town's supermarkets.

> The great majority of families therefore felt the need for a paper every day, but understandably most didn't wish to pay for two. Advertisers preferred the paper with the most circulation, and readers tended to want the paper with the most ads and news pages. This circularity led to a law of the newspaper jungle: *survival of the fattest*. Thus, when two or more papers existed in a major city (which was almost universally the case a century ago), the one that pulled ahead usually emerged as the stand-alone winner. After competition disappeared, the paper's pricing power in both advertising and circulation was unleashed. Typically, rates for both advertisers and readers would be raised annually – and the profits rolled in. For owners this was economic heaven."[38]

This is the context in which Buffett and Munger sought investments in newspapers in the mid-1970s.

Buying the Buffalo paper

By 1976, Berkshire Hathaway was already a substantial shareholder in The Washington Post – holding about a tenth of the shares – and Buffett had become a close friend of the dominant shareholder and publisher, Katharine Graham. He was also a director of the company.

Graham tells us in her biography that in the mid-1970s she was focusing on how to make the company grow, but lacked expertise in analysing possible purchases or negotiating with targets. She turned to Buffett for help, who seemed to carry around in his head "almost every deal that was taking place or had taken place in the previous ten years."[39]

In December 1976, they were considering a Buffalo television station purchase. Buffett, however, suggested that The Buffalo Evening News, also up for sale, was a better buy. According to Graham, he added that "if we didn't want it, he did."[40]

The Washington Post's board looked at The Buffalo Evening News – henceforth I'll call it 'The News' – but were put off by the strong competition in Buffalo newspapers, formidable unions and the lack of a Sunday edition, and so they decided not to pursue it.

Note the sequence of events: Buffett, displaying his usual high integrity, had wanted to buy the Buffalo paper all along but gave Graham first refusal – she was a friend, and as a director of The Washington Post, Buffett had a fiduciary duty to its shareholders to give honest advice. Now they had turned it down, the way was clear.

Buffett quickly contacted the broker instructed by *The News'* owners to find a buyer, Vincent Manno. He had recently cut the asking price from $40m to $35m when Buffett asked for a meeting. It was only earning $1.7m pre-tax and potential buyers were clearly not interested at $40m.

Buffett and Munger travelled to Manno's home in Connecticut on the freezing first Saturday of 1977. After a little haggling, they settled on a price there and then of $35,509,000, of which $34,076,000 was to be paid in cash, with the balance representing assumption of certain pension obligations. Buffett and Munger took control of 100% of the shares on 15 April 1977.

At the time, the managing editor was Murray B. Light. In his book on the history of *The News, From Butler to Buffett,* he wrote:

> "Buffett was attracted to *The News* because the paper had reached a higher percentage of local households than other big-city dailies in the United States. He was also impressed by the fact that *The News* had almost twice the daily circulation as *The Courier-Express* and 75% more advertising revenue. He was aware that the paper was publishing only six days a week, leaving a void in its publishing cycle on Sundays, and he knew he would have to move to fill that void quickly."[41]

A short history

The paper was born in the recession that followed the Civil War, in the muddy-streeted, saloon-packed (93 of them) and crime-ridden Buffalo, New York, of 1873. It was begun by a 23-year-old entrepreneur, Edward H. Butler, who produced the first Sunday paper for Buffalo's 120,000 or so residents – there were already ten weekday dailies in various languages.

Edward H. Butler Sr. eventually passed the running of the business to his son, Edward H. Butler Jr. Edward Junior's wife, Kate Butler, ran the business after her husband's death in 1956. She was strong-willed and worked six days a week in the News office, making sure her views were known.

She stubbornly refused to listen to those who advised her to gift assets in the years before her death to reduce the impact of inheritance taxes. When she did die in 1974, there was a large bill to pay and no obvious family successor, so estate executors thought there wasn't much option but to put the business up for sale.

Murray Light had become managing editor of The News in 1969, by that time a six-day afternoon publication. Henry Urban was appointed president and publisher in 1974, following Kate Butler's death. He was a gentleman of the old school. Here is an example of him putting greater value on what he regarded as fair-dealing rather than profit-maximising:

> "Urban had a moral compunction against seeking to buy newsprint at a negotiated discount. He said the paper was steadfast in charging all its advertisers fixed rates for their ads…

and given that, it would not be fair to ask *News* suppliers to sell product to us at a discounted price."[42]

Blue Chip Stamps is the buyer

In spring 1977, Buffett controlled three main funds to undertake deals of this kind. The first two, Berkshire Hathaway and Diversified Retail, did not have cash available, and so it was the third, Blue Chip Stamps (BCS), which bought The Buffalo Evening News.

Blue Chip was the ugly duckling in Buffett's collection back in 1969–1970 when he pulled apart the Buffett Partnership, sold its shareholdings and sent the proceeds to his partners (or gave them shares in Berkshire or Diversified Retail). He tried to sell all the shares in Blue Chip but, frustratingly, couldn't do it at a decent price. So he reluctantly held onto the holding – about 7.5% of BCS equity – which the partnership had bought for $3m–$4m in 1968–1969.

As the months passed, Buffett and Munger came to appreciate Blue Chip Stamps' attractive balance sheet. It was ideal for a pair of investors who could see the potential of switching from boring cash and bond investments (vulnerable to inflation) to shares in attractive companies.

At the time, Blue Chip's float – the revenue from selling stamps which had not yet been redeemed – was $60m–$100m. In early 1972, Buffett and Munger arranged for the company to buy 99% of See's Candies for $25m. This was an immediate success. See's profit after taxes was only $2.3m in 1972, but grew to $5.1m in 1976 and then $5.75m in 1977. The West Coast candy company required little capital investment and so the income it threw off could be moved to BCS headquarters for deployment elsewhere. The ugly duckling was growing into a swan.

Another $30m or so of BCS's balance sheet was put into Wesco shares in 1973–74 and it, too, produced a great flow of cash to BCS headquarters. Blue Chip's share of the cash dividend paid by Mutual Savings, the main part of Wesco, was $1.9m in 1975, $3.2m in 1976 and $3.8m in 1977.

Blue Chip produced income from other activities: $2.1m in 1976 and $5.2m in 1977 (its old stamp business generated around $1.1m, and its float earned $4.1m from interest, dividends and realised capital gains from stock market investments). All told, by 1977, BCS was producing an after-tax income of $17m.

So, despite The Buffalo Evening News being the largest investment Buffett and Munger had made to that point, Blue Chip had the wherewithal to comfortably take it whole.

Buffett and Munger were now real enthusiasts for Blue Chip. Berkshire Hathaway had been busy buying more shares in the company and, by the end of 1974, held more than one-quarter of BCS's equity. The holding was increased to 36.5% by the end of 1976. Also, Susie and Warren Buffett owned 13% of BCS shares, and Charlie Munger's fund had one-tenth, with Diversified Retail holding about one-sixth. (After the 1978 merger of Berkshire and Diversified, BH held 58% of Blue Chip. It wasn't until 1983 that it owned all of it.)

A loss-maker, where the news just gets worse and worse

Buffalo may have been a town down on its luck but, for newspaper publishers, it had one major virtue: a great deal of stability in the population. People born and bred in Buffalo were loyal to the place and its institutions, such as its historic newspapers.

Another virtue, for an afternoon paper producer, was the industrial nature of the town. Many of its blue-collar workers got to work early and then read their papers in the late afternoon or evening. A large proportion of them read *The News*. In fact, no other newspaper in a major US city was bought by a higher percentage of local households than *The News*.

Charlie Munger pointed to another factor giving *The News* an advantage – its reputation for high-quality journalism. In his 1977 letter to shareholders of Blue Chip Stamps, he wrote:

> "Our investment decision was based on the belief that the existing journalistic merit of *The News*, encouraged and nourished, will eventually prosper in the marketplace and that inflation will eventually make a prosperous newspaper company a safer asset than any other company which we could then buy

at the price paid for The News. Experience and reconsideration have made us more confident than ever that we were right in our original appraisal of the journalistic merit of *The News*. *The News* is a meritorious newspaper partly because it was dominated and molded for decades by a legendary editor, Alfred Kirchhofer who, although retired, still comes to The News every day at age 83. Mr. Kirchhofer had and has a passion for accuracy, fairness and service. Present management had continued these standards before our purchase, and we have encouraged their perpetuation."

Its strong reputation meant that *The News* was able to outsell the *Courier-Express* during the week – with Monday to Friday circulation of 270,000 compared with 125,000.

Room for improvement

But, as the chairman of Blue Chip Stamps went on to write in his 1977 letter, there were "problems and uncertainties inherent in this sort of newspaper investment". He expressed frustration that when they took over The News, the competing *Courier-Express* published seven days a week whereas, for over 60 years, *The News* had only published on six days. The *Courier-Express*, with its comfortable monopoly, was selling 275,000 on a typical Sunday; the day for which advertisers paid the most.

To Munger, who had studied the financial performance history of city newspapers across the USA, it was essential for a leading paper to have a Sunday edition in order to survive long term. Thus, even before the purchase of The News was complete, Buffett and Munger discussed with the managers the creation of a Sunday paper.

To give the Sunday edition a big launch in November 1977, they knew they had to offer readers an incentive to change habits. So, they began a pre-launch advertising blitz, with its highlight being that home subscribers would, for the first five weeks, pay for seven papers what they currently paid for six ($1.05). That is, Sunday's issue would be free. After the first five weeks, the price would rise to just $1.20.

The counter-attack

The *Courier-Express* bosses were not going to take the competitive threat to their lucrative Sunday market lying down. They first mounted a propaganda onslaught with articles warning the good people of Buffalo about the out-of-town carpetbagger – the 'big brother from Omaha' – about to wreck their beloved *Courier-Express*. Second, they filed a lawsuit alleging that The News was deliberately trying to destroy a competitor by subsidising a Sunday paper in violation of antitrust laws.

Their court application asked for a prohibition on the planned introductory promotional programme, the proposed low price of the Sunday edition at 30c, and the low advertising rates The News was to charge. On top of that, they wanted the award of damages – trebled under the antitrust law – plus attorneys' fees and costs.

Much to the dismay of Buffett and Munger, a preliminary injunction was granted just before the paper's launch. The incumbent company had blatantly pleaded to keep its monopoly position. Even though the Courier-Express did not get everything it wanted, the court hamstrung *The News*. The special-offer price period was cut from five to two weeks; advertisers could not be offered guarantees of Sunday circulation; the reduction in the future price of the paper was limited; no free sampling was allowed; and, very time-consumingly, they had to show a signed customer order authorising each Sunday delivery.

Survivors, ready for a fight

This was harsh. Munger, the lawyer, was determined to fight back and instructed his old Californian legal team to prepare robustly for the full trial. It was many months before this took place and, in the meantime, even with the draconian injunction restrictions, the Sunday paper managed to sell about 160,000 a week in the winter of 1977–1978. While fairly impressive, this was only two-thirds that of the *Courier-Express* and, discouragingly, *The News* had lost around 45,000 of its Saturday circulation. More importantly, the *Courier-Express* held 75% of Sunday advertising. It also spent serious amounts of money on modernising its machinery and adding newspaper features, supplements and reporters to try to outcompete *The News*.

Munger defiantly wrote in February 1978 (in the 1977 BCS annual report) that their commitment to a Sunday paper was "total". They would not back out, even though "because of the expense of litigation and other unexpected problems, the near-term profits of The News at times may be low or nil". Despite the removal of the legal restrictions in an April 1979 appeal, the continued head-to-head competition between the two papers led to years of pain, as you can see in Table 2.1.

Table 2.1: The Buffalo Evening News losses and Sunday circulation figures

	Net income ($m)	Sunday circulation (February)
1977	0.34	
1978	−1.43	160,000
1979	−2.41	156,000
1980	−1.47	173,000
1981	−0.53	178,000
1982	−0.60	183,000

Source: Blue Chip Stamps annual reports. Monday–Friday circulation figures did not move much over this period from the 1977 number of 270,000. In 1982, The News climbed to 40% of the Sunday market.

Hard graft

Buffett, Munger and their team worked unstintingly to try to bring the company to profit. They cut the number of mills supplying newsprint and negotiated better prices. They faced up to the 13 unions at the company in 1980, basically telling them that if the workers continued to strike, holding the company to ransom, it would be closed down. A massive loss would be realised by Blue Chip Stamp shareholders if it did close but, at that time, the owners couldn't see how they could make a return if they had to cope with intransigent unions. It was a credible threat. Buffett and Munger make a point of never bluffing. Fortunately, the union leaders got the message and backed off.

In 1980–1981, recession struck Buffalo particularly hard – sharply reducing the number of retailers in the town, and making others think twice about advertising budgets. In the early 1980s, things looked bleak. But Munger kept faith, writing to BCS shareholders in February 1982:

> "Because we own what we believe to be one of society's best service institutions and much the better of Buffalo's two major newspapers, we still hope and expect that *The News* in due course will earn annual profits consistent with its value to Buffalo and appropriate to our level of investment."[43]

But there was a note of regret at having committed so much money to this company. At this darkest hour, Munger thought a lot of value within Blue Chip, and therefore Berkshire, had been destroyed given that the same money allocated elsewhere would have earned much more. There was a high opportunity cost, which Munger argued was just as important as conventional reported losses from an investment. He wrote:

> "If we hadn't purchased The News in 1977 but had simply earned returns on the unspent purchase price comparable with the average earning power of the rest of our shareholders' equity, we would now have about $70m in value of other assets, earning over $10m per year, in place of Buffalo Evening News and its current red ink.

> When other capital is sprinting, remaining in the starting blocks for a long time prevents one from ever catching the field. Of course, we can't now relive the past but must simply adopt the correct business strategy for the present situation."

Munger believed that strategy was for The News to continue doing the best job it could for its city, its employees, its readers and its advertisers, until its long-term future looked hopeless – caused by some combination of their principal competitor's relative strength, their losses, or trouble with the unions.

This resigned acceptance of a judgement error is just the sort of rational, calm and honest analysis we expect from Buffett and Munger. But what we are not so familiar with is the presence of losses over a prolonged period. Of course, we know how the story ends – with a return of at least 15-fold on the original $35.5m investment. But, in early 1982, this looked far from inevitable.

Buffett and Munger's management style at The Buffalo Evening News

Buffett and Munger inherited two sound managers at The Buffalo Evening News. First, there was Henry Urban who served as president and publisher from 1974 until his retirement in 1983. Urban provided a steady, conservative approach during a particularly tumultuous period. He had no problem switching his allegiance to Blue Chip stamps.[44]

Buffett said of Urban, in his 1983 letter to BH shareholders, that "Henry never flinched during the dark days of litigation and losses following our introduction of the Sunday paper… Henry is admired by the Buffalo business community, he's admired by all who worked for him, and he is admired by Charlie and me."

The second key person was Murray B. Light, who had been with the paper since 1949. He gave every appearance of being the archetypal Hollywood movie newspaper editor: strutting around the newsroom, backslapping and barking orders, as he molded the paper's content and editorials. While hard-driving, he was considered fair-minded and ethical, with a passion for the free press.

Urban and Light respected and wholeheartedly backed Buffett's enthusiasm for quality journalism, and saw in him a supportive boss. Light wrote in his history of the paper that Buffett was, of course, interested in the profitability of the business. Buffett would provide direction on matters related to circulation and advertising rates and, as we have come to expect, he was involved with capital allocation and compensation of management. But beyond that, and particularly in relation to the editorial direction of the paper, Buffett left this to Light and his team.[45]

There you have the main elements of Buffett's approach to managing his companies.

- First he does not have the time nor the expertise to deal with day-to-day matters, or even to make major operating decisions.

And besides which, if he interfered he would deprive proud and capable managers of the autonomy and trust that they deserved; the autonomy and trust that brings loyalty and diligence. Many people are motivated to give of their best if there is a tangible indicator of respect shown by the boss; giving almost complete control to the people on the ground is the ultimate display of respect.

- Second, it is made very clear that Buffett has an overriding purpose in owning the company – to make a high rate of return on capital devoted to it. The information he is most keen to receive regularly is about the key performance indicators contributing to earnings, such as circulation figures or the cost of newsprint.

- Third, he takes responsibility for finding the right remuneration package for the leaders such that their interests are aligned with Buffett's long-term, profit-focused interest. And rewards extend beyond the pecuniary, with his praise for work well done being highly prized by his managers.

- Finally, if the marginal dollar generated by the business will, if left in the business, produce less than a satisfactory rate of return, then it must be sent to head office for Buffett to allocate elsewhere – helping to buy another company or shares on the market.

Buffett was so hands-off that he never asked the editors of *The News* to follow his political philosophy – most of the journalists didn't even know what it was. His instructions to the editors were to support those politicians likely to be most effective for Buffalo readers.

While Buffett was reluctant to interfere, he did make himself available, in the early tough days, to act as a sounding board, or to come up with ideas to somehow beat the competition and bring the enterprise to profit. Light and he would frequently discuss ideas for an hour or more on the telephone. Light was always impressed by Buffett's depth of knowledge about newspapers.

Charlie Munger

Munger was a rock in the dark days of the late 1970s and early 1980s, with his steadfast focus on the long-term prospects for a newspaper which he believed could, if it stuck to its principle of producing an outstanding product with great journalism, make a satisfactory profit. He was particularly proud that over 50% of the paper was news rather than advertisements – most other papers worked on a 40% newshole proportion.

In his 1981 Blue Chip annual report, he wrote that he was not even slightly tempted to sell The News, which was a demonstration of his conviction about the future of Buffalo and about the team at the company. He had confidence that the "fine people who work at The News" could "succeed in making it a sound business for its owners and employees."

Apart from dedication, diligence, and fair and accurate reporting, there was one other thing Munger asked of his managers: that they brought bad news to him as soon as was feasible. Good news will take care of itself, he said, but he needed to know what was going wrong, and quickly, so that he could do something about it, to at least mitigate its effects. He emphasised this approach of facing up to things in the 1981 BCS annual report, where he wrote that he did not want managers to gloss over difficulties, and that he would not do so himself in his annual letters. He believed in "practicing what we preach" in telling shareholders the truth about difficult times in Buffalo. Accordingly:

> "If the litigation continues and if the competing paper succeeds in somehow changing the law ... obtaining the kinds of injunctions it is seeking, or if any extended strike shuts down the Buffalo Evening News, it will probably be forced to cease operations and liquidate."

Stanford Lipsey

The third key manager at The News was Stanford Lipsey. The relationship between Stan Lipsey and Buffett went way back, to at least 1965 when Buffett first offered to buy the *Omaha Sun* newspaper. Lipsey, owner-publisher of the tiny *Sun*, was persuaded to stay on to manage the paper after its sale in 1969. He did a fine job in terms of probing and campaigning journalism – even winning a Pulitzer Prize – but the paper was not a financial success and was sold in 1980. The two of them were close friends and spoke regularly.

When things were going badly with the Buffalo paper in late 1977, Buffett asked if Lipsey would move to Buffalo to improve matters. He was reluctant. Buffett was so keen to get Lipsey's input that he asked if he would at least go up once a month and "do whatever you think needs to be done... The place will just run better if you're there."[46]

Thus a 34-year association with Buffalo was started with a one-week-a-month job as a consultant to the publisher, Henry Urban, concentrating on the circulation and advertising departments. This outsider from Omaha quickly gained the approval of the Buffalo team. Light wrote that "His quick, inventive mind and ability to think problems through carefully and logically won the confidence of everyone."[47] Lipsey ended up staying for the rest of his career, becoming a pillar of Buffalo society, and a major benefactor.

In 1980, Lipsey was free to move to Buffalo full-time. He had become fascinated by, and determined to win, the battle against the *Courier-Express*. A friendly, good-humoured man, Lipsey saw himself not as a businessman but as "a newspaperman... That's what I'm devoted to... [newspapers] are a vital institution in society."[48] He was determined to get the paper through.

When Urban retired in 1983, Lipsey took over as publisher. He had glorious years to look forward to. In the Lipsey era, too, Buffett's input was limited. The one crucial area Buffett liked to discuss was pricing for advertising and charging for the paper. He told Carol Loomis, in a *Fortune* article, that the chief executive (or owner) has a different perspective on pricing than the manager of a particular business:

> "The manager has just one business. His equation tells him that if he prices a little too low, it's not that serious. But if he prices too high, he sees himself screwing up the only thing in his life. And no one knows what raising prices will do. For the manager, it's all Russian roulette. For the chief executive, with more than one thing in his life, it really isn't. So I would argue that someone with wide experience and distance from the scene should set prices in certain cases."[49]

Buffett lavished public praise on Lipsey. Here's an example from his 1986 letter to Berkshire shareholders:

> "Operating results at The Buffalo News continue to reflect a truly superb managerial job by Stan Lipsey. For the third year

in a row, man-hours worked fell significantly and other costs were closely controlled. Consequently, our operating margins improved materially in 1986, even though our advertising rate increases were well below those of most major newspapers. Our cost-control efforts have in no way reduced our commitment to news. We continue to deliver a 50% 'news hole'."

Lipsey said that the best things about working with Buffett were that "he is totally moral and honest, that you know when he is talking to you he is thinking about you, and that he is accessible... we've been working together for more than 30 years and we've never had a disagreement."[50]

Lipsey's approach to his associates aligns perfectly with fellow Omahan Buffett's approach: "treat them like you want to be treated. That's what Warren has done. You go out of your way for your key people, and think hard and creatively about how you can keep an individual happy."[51]

Lipsey retired in December 2012, which prompted Buffett to reflect on his contribution. He wrote that The News could well have been extinct if not for Lipsey. Lipsey's knowledge of the newspaper business – including "circulation, production, sales and editorial" – was "extraordinary". Lipsey had persevered through the difficult years, working with Murray Light, and then managed The News to exceptional performance in the following years. "As both a friend and as a manager, Stan is simply the best."[52]

Survival of the fattest

In the years 1978–1982, both The Buffalo Evening News and *Courier-Express* suffered large losses as they lowered prices in attempts to attract readers and advertisers in an over-supplied market. The outlook was bleak for both. Until, that is, the breathtaking announcement on 19 September 1982 by the owners of the *Courier-Express* that they were quitting, leaving *The News* as the only metropolitan daily paper in Buffalo.

The *Courier-Express*'s owners had simply had enough, and they could see that The News's owners had deep pockets capable of supporting losses for many years yet. Not only did Blue Chip have income from See's Candies and Wesco flowing in, but its parent, Berkshire Hathaway, could also pump in money at the drop of a hat. What was the point of going on with the banging of heads in Buffalo?

Thus it was that the best resourced, the fattest, company prevailed. Buffalo went from a two-paper town to a one-paper town. The rewards are seen in the terrific jump in after-tax profits flowing to Berkshire Hathaway. After the withdrawal of the *Courier-Express,* it only took another three years or so before Berkshire received back the full $35.5m it had put into The News back in 1977. And the profits grew until they were receiving almost as much on an annual basis.

Figure 2.1: The Buffalo News profits after tax attributable to Berkshire Hathaway ($m)

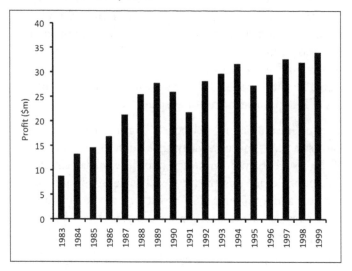

Source: W. Buffett, letters to shareholders of BH (data unavailable after 1999).

In 1983, The News recruited many former *Courier* newsroom and other journalistic staff, and started a morning paper. Also the name was changed to simply *The Buffalo News.* Sunday circulation quickly doubled to over 360,000 and weekday circulation was a much improved 323,000. In January 1983, *Forbes* had a stab at valuing The News – they reckoned $400m.

A decline, but not a fall

By the middle of the noughties, the internet had changed the economics of the newspaper business, as it did with many other industries. Buffett lamented the effect, writing that fundamentals were eroding in the newspaper industry, causing profits at The Buffalo News to decline. He wrote that "When an industry's underlying economics are crumbling, talented management may slow the rate of decline. Eventually, though, eroding fundamentals will overwhelm managerial brilliance."[53]

Despite the deterioration, Buffett vowed to maintain *The News*:

> "Unless we face an irreversible cash drain, we will stick with *The News*… Charlie and I love newspapers – we each read five a day – and believe that a free and energetic press is a key ingredient for maintaining a great democracy. We hope that some combination of print and online will ward off economic doomsday for newspapers, and we will work hard in Buffalo to develop a sustainable business model. I think we will be successful. But the days of lush profits from our newspaper are over."[54]

The advent of online journalism, web advertising and specialised sites – such as house sale sites – caused Sunday circulation to halve in the first 15 years of the 21st century, down to 174,000. Its weekday circulation fell to just 111,000. Despite this, the News still made an operating profit – $10.9m in 2015 and $7.3m in 2016 – assisted by the development of other income streams such as printing for *The New York Times*. Also, expenses were slashed.

The Buffalo News remains a part of Berkshire Hathaway today, and is the primary newspaper of the Buffalo-Niagara region, published every morning (the afternoon edition was dropped in 2006). But the battle to maintain the position is a tough one. At the time of writing in 2018, even editorial posts were being lost to rein in costs.

Learning points

1. **It's not always about the numbers you can see.** A good investment is often identified by thinking through the qualitative potential in terms of strategic position, rather than by looking at recent

accounting figures. The News had the potential to become an unregulated toll-bridge (a dominant economic franchise), even though recent trading had been tough and trading for the immediate years ahead were likely to be unprofitable.

2. **Concentrate on quality of product and quality of managers.** When buying, Buffett and Munger satisfied themselves that the product was held in high esteem and the editors were excellent. And, even in the early painful days, when the paper was losing money week by week, the owners and the editors refused to compromise on quality.

3. **Think long-term.** Buffett and Munger say their holding period for a share is "forever". Such a horizon helps put near-term losses into perspective.

4. **Stick to it when you are hardest hit.** "When things go wrong, as they sometimes will, When the road you're trudging seems all uphill, When the funds are low and the debts are high, And you want to smile, but you have to sigh, When care is pressing you down a bit, Rest! if you must; but don't you quit, Life is queer with its twists and turns, As everyone of us sometimes learns, And many a failure turns about, When he might have won had he stuck it out." ('Don't give up', Anonymous.)

5. **Reserves.** It helped that when Munger made pledges to continue the battle for *The News*, Blue Chip had many sources of income and cash reserves to add credibility to his words. This must have helped to rally The News troops and demoralise the *Courier-Express* owners.

6. **Trust your managers and help them where you can,** without micro-managing.

Investment 3

NEBRASKA FURNITURE MART

Summary of the deal

Deal	Nebraska Furniture Mart
Time	1983–present
Price paid	$55.35m
Quantity	90% of the share capital
Sale price	Part of Berkshire Hathaway today
Profit	At least ten-fold
Berkshire Hathaway in 1983	Share price: $775–$1,345 Book value: $1,118m Per share book value: $975

One of the great traditions for those attending Berkshire Hathaway's shareholder meeting in Omaha each May, is enjoying the evening barbeque and country music at Nebraska Furniture Mart. It's an opportunity to chat with fellow shareholders, wonder at the size of the store and the brilliance of this 1983 investment.

When Berkshire Hathaway bought NFM, it had only one outlet. But it was the biggest furniture store for hundreds of miles. Since then it has grown even bigger, now covering 1,689,000 square feet on 77 acres only two miles from Buffett's home. It sells not just furniture, but over 85,000 items including computers, TVs and household appliances.

In terms of geographical expansion, it has grown modestly – opening giant stores in Kansas City, Dallas-Fort Worth and Des Moines. That's it – only three new stores in four decades. As always, Buffett and Munger allowed large capital investment only where they thought it would create or enhance a competitive advantage, where they could build an economic franchise. No empire-building for its own sake has been permitted; no assumption that what is working in one location could be replicated in hundreds of other places. Only thoroughly thought-through plans to capture customer interest, where competitors could be beaten, and a good return on capital employed obtained.

The success of NFM is all the more remarkable if you consider that it was created by a lady who came to the US an almost penniless 24-year-old, with precious little English, and who never spent a day in school. Mrs Rose Blumkin, or Mrs B as she was known in Omaha, escaped from Belarus during the Russian revolution, bribing guards as she went. It wasn't until 1937 that she set up a tiny shop in a basement, juggling four children with running the store. The motto she adopted has become famous: *sell cheap and tell the truth*. There were tough times; she even had to sell furniture from her own house to pay off debts. However, the decades-long struggle eventually led to the store enticing people to travel hundreds of miles to obtain that special bargain.

When she was 89-years old, Buffett finally managed to persuade her to sell a 90% stake in the business (later reduced to 80%). The deal was done on a smile and a handshake, now known as the 'Historic Omaha Handshake', and a 1¼ page contract drafted by Buffett. He felt no need to check the inventory, or titles on the real estate, or do any kind of due diligence. Indeed, the accounts weren't even audited. He had better insight than that: he knew the people, he knew they could be trusted, and he was very familiar with the quality shopping experience given to the people of Omaha.

Mrs B so loved working at NFM that she carried on until she was 103, perhaps by then doing a little less than her customary 70-hour working week. Buffett said that top business school graduates, or those running the largest corporations, were no match for her. She could run rings round them. There is much to learn from her story and her ideas. Here's what Buffett said in an NBC interview shortly after buying NFM:

> "If I could start a business, and I had first draft-pick, like in the NFL, of the 25 top graduates of the top business schools in the country, and the 25… top CEOs of the Fortune 500, or I could take Mrs B to run the business, I'd take Mrs B. There aren't any other Mrs Bs."[55]

In the same documentary, Mrs B said, "I don't know education books. I used the old-fashioned way: tell the truth, buy right, sell cheap."

Buffett believes in holding onto a talented founding family, with the ethos and team spirit that they bring. For many years after BH's purchase, Mrs B's son, Louie, and, later, his sons Ronald and Irvin, ran the firm alongside Mrs B, until her death in 1998 at the age of 104. Today, Ron and Irv lead with the fourth generation working with them.

Before looking at the NFM deal itself, I'd better fill in the time between the 1977 purchase of The Buffalo Evening News and the 1983 NFM deal. There were no great long-lasting investments, if you exclude some preliminary purchases of Capital Cities shares (the subject of the next chapter). But there was a steady building of economic franchises and some shrewd stock market purchases, as well as a great deal of contemplation on how this growing collection of apparently disparate businesses was to be managed by Buffett and Munger in the future. This was a period of brushing on the foundational background to the great canvas they were painting.

The five years leading up to the Nebraska Furniture Mart purchase

As well as building up the operating businesses, Buffett and Munger were particularly interested in obtaining minority stakes in firms that might have some protection against the ravages of high inflation – which reached a worrying 14% in 1979. In an environment like that, even if you bought a share that gave a pre-tax return of 20%, after deduction of tax your money bought less at the end of the year than at the beginning. Companies that could raise prices by at least the inflation rate, and which did not require large capital investment as they grew, were to be favoured.

Berkshire had income flowing in at a tremendous rate over these five years. In 1977, the operating businesses supplied $39.2m for Buffett and Munger to deploy elsewhere. By 1981, this amount had risen to $62.6m.

Table 3.1: Net earnings after tax attributable to Berkshire Hathaway from operating businesses

	1978 ($m)	1979 ($m)	1980 ($m)	1981 ($m)	1982 ($m)
Insurance underwriting	1.6	2.2	3.6	0.8	−11.3
Insurance investment income (dividends and interest)	16.4	20.1	25.6	32.4	35.3
Realised security gains	9.2	6.8	9.9	23.1	14.9
Associated Retail Stores	1.2	1.3	1.2	0.8	0.4
See's Candies	3.0	3.4	4.2	6.3	6.9
Blue Chip Stamps – Parent	1.4	1.6	3.1	2.1	2.5
Illinois National Bank	4.3	5.0	4.7	-	-
Wesco (Parent and S&L)	3.7	4.2	3.0	3.1	3.7
Other	0.9	1.0	2.6	0.6	1.0
Interest on debt	−2.3	−2.9	−4.8	−6.7	−7.0
TOTAL EARNINGS	39.2	42.8	53.1	62.6	46.4

Source: W. Buffett, letters to shareholders of BH (1978–1982).

Profits from insurance underwriting were no great shakes, but the flow in the form of dividends and interest from securities purchased with insurance float was terrific, rising from $16.4m in 1978 to $35.3m in 1982. No wonder Warren and Charlie tap-danced to work – all that money flowing in was available to finance their latest investment ideas. And that wasn't all that was coming from the insurance float (and Blue Chip's float): from time to time, share holdings were sold producing a capital gain. The annual amounts from this source ranged from $6.8m to $23.1m.

See's Candies more than doubled its profits over those five years to $6.9m. Furthermore, it didn't need the money it was generating for additional capital investment. So the cash was sent up the chain for Buffett and Munger to invest. See's' parent company, Blue Chip Stamps, was also producing a nice flow of income, mostly from its float.

Some money was coming from Associated Retail Stores but, instead of the amount increasing over time, it was in a downward trend. It was just as well that Buffett, years before, had diversified away from dress shops as well as his Berkshire textile manufacturing.

The Rockford-based Illinois National Bank was going from strength to strength, adding over $4m–$5m annually to Buffett's cash pile for reinvestment. Ideally, this excellent company would have been kept in the fold, but the regulators did not like a bank being owned by a non-bank commercial organisation, for fear of conflicts of interest. So, it was separated from Berkshire through the mechanism of handing shares in the bank to BH shareholders on the last day of 1980.

Wesco was building up a head of steam. It was still making money from its savings and loans business in the late 1970s. In addition, it had substantial assets outside of the S&L, earning money from interest on bonds, dividends and capital gains on shares. This pot of money for investment was greatly boosted by the cleverly-timed sale of most of the S&L business in March 1980. The rump S&L continued to make money, even during the national S&L crisis.

The non-controlled businesses

The list of significant shareholdings bought in this period is long (see Table 3.2), but these were not held for the long term. They were all sold, or became relatively small holdings, by the end of 1987. This accumulation of non-controlled holdings was funded mainly by the cash being thrown off by the majority-controlled (operating) businesses, and boosted by the expansion of the insurance business which piled up more float to be invested. Average float in 1977 was $139m, and this grew to $220m in 1982.

Table 3.2: Shareholdings 1977–1982 sold or insignificant by end 1987

	Amount paid ($m)
Affiliated Publications	3.5
Aluminium Company of America (Alcoa)	25.6
Amerada Hess	2.9
Arcata	14.1
The Cleveland-Cliffs Iron Company	12.9
Crum & Forster	47.1
Gatx	17.1
General Foods	66.3
Handy & Harman	27.3
Interpublic Group	4.5
Kaiser Aluminium and Chemical	20.6
Kaiser Industries	0.8
Knight Ridder	7.5
Media General	4.5
National Detroit	5.9
National Student Marketing	5.1
Ogilvy & Mather	3.7
Pinkerton	12.1
R. J. Reynolds Tobacco Company	142.3
Safeco	32.1
Time	45.3
The Times Mirror Company	4.4
F. W. Woolworth	15.5

Source: W. Buffett, letters to shareholders of BH (1978–1982).

Table 3.3: Total value of equities held by Berkshire Hathaway (1977–1982)

	Cost ($m)	Market value at year end ($m)
1977	107	181
1978	134	221
1979	185	337
1980	325	530
1981	352	639
1982	424	945

Source: W. Buffett, letters to shareholders of BH (1978–1982).

Shares in Capital Cities/ABC were accumulated in this period as well. In 1983, the number of Berkshire Hathaway shareholders jumped from 1,900 (up from around 1,000 in the late 1970s) to about 2,900. Most of the increase was due to BH paying for the purchase of Blue Chip Stamps shares with newly issued shares in itself. After this there were 1,146,099 BH shares (only 1% more than in 1965). Now, 18 years later, its shareholders collectively owned great companies such as National Indemnity, See's and The Buffalo News, as well as stakes in American giants like R. J. Reynolds and Time. Berkshire Hathaway shares had risen from under $20 each to over $1,000.

Buffett and Munger's principles

In this period – a decade or so after breaking up the partnership – Buffett and Munger contemplated fundamental principles for managing the collection of businesses and shareholdings they had gathered, and for the way in which they were to treat shareholders. These ideas formed the foundation stones for the creation of the greatest company ever created.

From Buffett's summary of principles (below), published with his 1983 letter to BH shareholders, you can detect that he saw shareholders in the same light as those who had trusted him when he was a twenty-something enthusiast collecting together the savings of a few Omahans. Whatever the rather limited legal obligations he had to shareholders, he was determined to go further. He was also determined to build trust-based friendships with the managers of his operating companies.

These principles are a timeless guide for would-be builders of a diversified business, or a diversified portfolio of shares. I reproduce them in full:

Although our form is corporate, our attitude is partnership. Charlie Munger and I think of our shareholders as owner-partners, and of ourselves as managing partners. (Because of the size of our shareholdings we also are, for better or worse, controlling partners.) We do not view the company itself as the ultimate owner of our business assets but, instead, view the company as a conduit through which our shareholders own the assets.

In line with this owner-orientation, our directors are all major shareholders of Berkshire Hathaway. In the case of at least four of the five, over 50% of family net worth is represented by holdings of Berkshire. We eat our own cooking.

Our long-term economic goal (subject to some qualifications mentioned later) is to maximize the average annual rate of gain in intrinsic business value on a per-share basis. We do not measure the economic significance or performance of Berkshire by its size; we measure by per-share progress. We are certain that the rate of per-share progress will diminish in the future – a greatly enlarged capital base will see to that. But we will be disappointed if our rate does not exceed that of the average large American corporation.

Our preference would be to reach this goal by directly owning a diversified group of businesses that generate cash and consistently earn above-average returns on capital. Our second choice is to own parts of similar businesses, attained primarily through purchases of marketable common stocks by our insurance subsidiaries. The price and availability of businesses, and the need for insurance capital, determine any given year's capital allocation.

Because of this two-pronged approach to business ownership, and because of the limitations of conventional accounting, consolidated reported earnings may reveal relatively little about our true economic performance. Charlie and I, both as owners and managers, virtually ignore such consolidated numbers. However, we will also report to you the earnings of each major business we control, numbers we consider of great importance. These figures, along with other information we will supply about the individual businesses, should generally aid you in making judgments about them.

Accounting consequences do not influence our operating or capital-allocation decisions. When acquisition costs are similar, we much prefer to purchase $2 of earnings that *is not* reportable by us under standard accounting principles than to purchase $1 of earnings that *is* reportable. This is precisely the choice that often faces us, since entire businesses (whose earnings will be fully reportable) frequently sell for double the pro-rata price of small portions (whose earnings will be largely unreportable). In aggregate, and over time, we expect the unreported earnings to be fully reflected in our intrinsic business value through capital gains.

We rarely use much debt and, when we do, we attempt to structure it on a long-term, fixed-rate basis. We will reject interesting opportunities rather than over-leverage our balance sheet. This conservatism has penalized our results but it is the only behavior that leaves us comfortable, considering our fiduciary obligations to policyholders, depositors, lenders, and the many equity holders who have committed unusually large portions of their net worth to our care.

A managerial 'wish list' will not be filled at shareholder expense. We will not diversify by purchasing entire businesses at control prices that ignore long-term economic consequences to our shareholders. We will only do with your money what we would do with our own, weighing fully the values you can obtain by diversifying your own portfolios, through direct purchases in the stock market.

We feel noble intentions should be checked periodically against results. We test the wisdom of retaining earnings by assessing whether retention, over time, delivers shareholders at least $1 of market value for each $1 retained. To date, this test has been met. We will continue to apply it on a five-year rolling basis. As our net worth grows, it is more difficult to use retained earnings wisely.

We will issue common stock only when we receive as much in business value as we give. This rule applies to all forms of issuance – not only mergers or public stock offerings, but stock-for-debt swaps, stock options, and convertible securities as well. We will not sell small portions of your company – and that is what the issuance of shares amounts to – on a basis inconsistent with the value of the entire enterprise.

You should be fully aware of **one attitude Charlie and I share that hurts our financial performance:** regardless of price, we have no interest at all in selling any good businesses that Berkshire owns, and are very reluctant to sell sub-par businesses, as long as we expect them to generate at least some cash, and as long as we feel good about their managers and labor relations. We hope not to repeat the capital-allocation mistakes that led us into such sub-par businesses. And we react with great caution to suggestions that our poor businesses can be restored to satisfactory profitability by major capital expenditures. (The projections will be dazzling – the advocates will be sincere – but, in the end, major additional investment in a terrible industry usually is about as rewarding as struggling in quicksand.) Nevertheless, gin rummy-style managerial behavior (discard your least promising business at each turn) is not our style. We would rather have our overall results penalized a bit than engage in it.

We will be candid in our reporting to you, emphasizing the pluses and minuses important in appraising business value. Our guideline is to tell you the business facts that we would want to know if our positions were reversed. We owe you no less.

Moreover, as a company with a major communications business, it would be inexcusable for us to apply lesser standards of accuracy, balance and incisiveness when reporting on ourselves, than we would expect our news people to apply when reporting on others. We also believe candor benefits us as managers: the CEO who misleads others in public may eventually mislead himself in private.

Despite our policy of candor, we will discuss our activities in marketable securities only to the extent legally required. Good investment ideas are rare, valuable and subject to competitive appropriation, just as good product or business acquisition ideas are. Therefore, we normally will not talk about our investment ideas. This ban extends even to securities we have sold (because we may purchase them again) and to stocks we are incorrectly rumored to be buying. If we deny those reports, but say "no comment" on other occasions, the no-comments become confirmation.

What Rose brought into bloom

Very early in the 20th century, in the family's two-room log cabin in a village near Minsk, a young Rose woke one night to find her mother already hard at work making bread. She told her mother that she couldn't bear "that she had to work so awfully hard", adding that when she grew up she would go to a big town, find a job, make money and go to America. Her mother looked after her eight children as well as running a grocery store; her father was a rabbi. Rose started work, aged six, in her mother's store. But when 13, she felt duty-bound, with so many siblings, to walk from shop to shop looking for a job. Her persistence paid off, and by the time she was 16, despite never attending school, she was a manager – overseeing the work of six men.

Four years later, in 1914, the 20-year-old Rose married Isadore Blumkin, a shoe salesman. She remembers her mother bringing two pounds of rice and two pounds of cookies on her wedding day; "that was the wedding feast". The war came, and Isadore avoided conscription with the "hated Cossacks" by journeying to America. He went without Rose because they did not have enough money for both of them.

With the stirrings of the Russian revolution of December 1916 as a backdrop, the four-feet-ten-inch Rose made her way across Siberia, on the Trans-Siberian Railroad, with no ticket or passport. A border guard on the Russia-China frontier let her pass after she told him that she was buying leather for the Army, and that she would bring him a big bottle of *slivovitz* on her return. "I learned all the tricks" she said. On she went to Japan and Seattle with a tag around her neck saying 'Fort Dodge, Iowa'.

Rose Blumkin was forever grateful for the warm welcome she received: "The people who were born in this country don't appreciate all these wonderful things, like those who came from out of the darkness. I love the United States since the day I come here."[56]

After two years in Fort Dodge, the young couple moved to Omaha, and Isadore opened a second-hand clothing store cum pawnshop. It wasn't until Frances, her eldest daughter, started school that Rose learned English; Frances taught her mother what she had picked up each day.

A major preoccupation was saving her Belarusian family; she would work hard selling clothing, save up 50 bucks and send it home. This was enough to get one of them to America. She brought her parents and five siblings over, one at a time, by the end of 1922.

Finally settled with her four children, aged 43, Mrs B began her business career with $500. She got on a train to Chicago in 1937, then the centre of the nation's wholesale furniture activity. There she found the American Furniture Mart. So impressed was she with the huge building and business, all neatly laid out, that she decided to grandly call her new business the Nebraska Furniture Mart. She bought $2,000 worth of merchandise for the store she was to open, in the basement of the building where her husband's business was located, in downtown Omaha.

She worried all the way home because she only had $500 of equity and $1,500 of debt. So concerned was she that she sold the furniture from her own home – refrigerator and all – to get the money to pay on time.

Mrs B was up against the toughest of competition – large entrenched department stores and specialists – and a basement was hardly the best location. But, along with her $500, she started with the notion: "If you have the lowest price, customers will find you at the bottom of a river".[57] She was correct, people did find her.

But her discounted prices annoyed the carpet and furniture giants. The manufacturers and retailers had a cosy arrangement whereby each got a large margin, if they all maintained high prices. Her rivals first convinced manufacturers to boycott her. She responded by buying from suppliers elsewhere in the country, or by getting other people to buy carpet and other items for her on the quiet. Thus, she was able to continue to sell at low prices.

Mrs B was hauled before a court, not once but on four occasions, on the charge of 'violation of Fair Trade laws'. She said to a judge: "I pay $3 a yard [for carpet], Brandeis [main competitor, now defunct] sell it for $7.95. I sell it for $3.95. Judge, I sell everything 10% above cost, what's wrong? I don't rob customers." Not only did the judge acquit her, he bought $1,400 worth of carpet the next day. Best of all, the papers wrote it up which boosted sales tremendously.

You can gauge the extent of the low margin/high turnover approach from the 1946 accounts, reproduced in Berkshire Hathaway's 2013 annual report (Figure 3.1).[58] Starting the year with a mere $57,460 of net assets, she turned over $575,096 in the next 12 months – an amazing asset turn for that type of product. Cost of sales (mainly payments to suppliers) was a lot more than the figure you might generally expect for furniture retailers. It was $472,891, leaving a gross profit of $102,206, a mere 17.77% gross margin (but not quite the 10% she would frequently quote when anyone was listening). But cost control was so tight that expenditure on everything else – from advertising and salaries to rent and truck fuel – came to only $81,521, leaving an operating profit of $20,685, and a net profit of $29,884 after some additional income.

In 1945, NFM moved out of the basement to a bigger store at 2,205 Farnam St. in downtown Omaha. Louie, her son, joined her there after his second world war service (which included landing on Omaha beach in Normandy, winning a Purple Heart at the Battle of the Bulge, and liberating Dachau concentration camp). It was Louie who took the founding philosophy of his mother and built the company from the base she had created. The combination of her common sense and drive, and his wisdom, even-temper and excellent human skills, meant that the business grew by leaps and bounds in the 1960s and 1970s. He had a natural talent for merchandising, putting much of it down to his mother: "I could have gone through five public schools and four colleges but never got the education that I got from my mother."[59]

While Mrs B was very tough – frequently scolding and sacking staff – Louie was a renowned gentleman; very kind, often rehiring the same people. He recognised his mother was in the habit of criticising to the point of humiliation, whereas he liked "to smear the honey". While she couldn't stand laziness, or employees being "a dummy" or "a golum", she could be kind in many ways. For example, she had a great empathy for the poor (hence her drive to keep margins very low) and the oppressed: "Many immigrants came from the concentration camps. Some needed jobs. We hired them… What class. Those are the people we appreciated."[60] In the mid-20th century she hired many recent Russian immigrants. "I got one girl – I put her in furniture sales and she beats any American college graduate. So friendly. When she makes a sale she's in seventh heaven."[61]

A large out-of-town store was added to the downtown one in 1970, on the site of the current sprawling giant. Things were going well, and then a devastating tornado ripped through it in 1975. Strangely enough, in strategic terms this proved to be a blessing. The response to the roof being torn off the giant warehouse-type store was naturally to take everything back to the one remaining outlet. They discovered that people preferred to shop where there is a very large range concentrated in one place, and with low prices; and they are prepared to travel to obtain bargains. Omaha didn't need more than one very large store selling carpet and furniture. Louie's son, Irv (now CEO) explained the lightbulb moment: "We found out that we could do more out of one [store] than we could out of two in the same city. It gave us the vision to build one big store and, eventually, close our downtown store." The site at 72nd Street was chosen because it had a massive car park and could be extended. By the 1980s, Nebraska Furniture Mart was the biggest home furnishing store in the US.

Figure 3.1: Nebraska Furniture Mart accounts (1946)

```
                        NEBRASKA FURNITURE MART
                   STATEMENT OF ASSETS & LIABILITIES
                         DECEMBER 31, 1946

                              ASSETS

   CURRENT ASSETS
      Cash on Hand                             $      50.00
      Accounts Receivable        $67,007.01
      Less-Reserve for Bad Debts   6,162.58      60,844.43
      Inventory                                 34,650.00   $ 95,544.43

   FIXED ASSETS
      Furniture & Fixtures                    $     42.85
      Leasehold Improvements                    22,787.90
      Truck                                      1,565.35
                                              $24,396.10
      Less-Reserve for Depreciation             5,590.98   $ 18,805.12

   OTHER ASSETS
      Loans Receivable - Simons Jewelry Co.                $  2,000.00

         Total                                             $116,349.55


                           LIABILITIES

   CURRENT LIABILITIES
      First National Bank - Overdraft         $  9,730.54
      Accounts Payable                          20,612.55
      Accrued Taxes                              2,742.05
      Loans Payable -
         Cynthia Schneider        $ 3,000.00
         Norman Batt                2,000.00
         Ben Magzamin               2,000.00
         Omaha National Bank        4,000.00   $11,000.00  $ 44,085.14

   PARTNERS' CAPITAL & UNDIVIDED PROFIT
      Balance, January 1, 1946                 $57,460.27
      Net Profit for Year 1946                  29,884.42
                                              $87,344.69
      Less - Withdrawals                        15,080.28
      Balance, December 31, 1946                           $ 72,264.41

         Total                                             $116,349.55
```

```
                    NEBRASKA FURNITURE MART
                    PROFIT & LOSS STATEMENT
                   YEAR ENDED DECEMBER 31, 1946
                                                                    %
NET SALES                                      $575,096.47    100.00%

COST OF SALES
    Inventory, beginning        $  22,789.00
    Purchases                      457,834.81
    Freight                         17,186.27
    Fabrication & Installation       9,730.72
                                  $507,540.80
    Inventory, ending              34,650.00

      Cost of Sales                            $472,890.80     82.23%

      Gross Profit                             $102,205.67     17.77%

Less - EXPENSES
    Accounting & Legal           $     548.29                    .10%
    Advertising                      5,750.19                   1.00
    Provision for Bad Debts          3,777.63                    .66
    Bank Charges                        40.43                    .01
    Car & Truck Expense              2,000.54                    .35
    Commissions                        434.74                    .08
    Depreciation                     3,770.36                    .66
    Donations                        1,087.50                    .19
    Drayage                             57.17                    .01
    Dues & Subscriptions                49.00                    .01
    Fuel                             1,175.10                    .20
    General Expense                  2,836.75                    .49
    Insurance                        1,543.49                    .27
    Interest                           630.52                    .11
    Light, Power, Water              1,384.09                    .24
    Maintenance & Repair               222.25                    .04
    Postage                            256.83                    .04
    Rent                             9,294.00                   1.62
    Salaries                        40,288.00                   7.00
    Sign Rental                        600.00                    .10
    Stationery & Supplies              659.57                    .11
    Taxes                            1,062.60                    .18
    Payroll Taxes                    1,042.78                    .18
    Telephone & Telegraph            1,141.25                    .20
    Travel                           1,887.60                    .32

      Total Expenses                           $  81,520.68     14.17%

      Operating Profit                         $  20,684.99      3.60%

Add - OTHER INCOME
    Purchase Discounts            $   5,409.33
    Carrying Charges                  3,790.10  $   9,199.43      1.60%

      Net Profit                               $  29,884.42      5.20%
```

Source: Berkshire Hathaway Annual Report (2013).

The deal with Warren Buffett

In 1970, the investment writer 'Adam Smith' (George Goodman) received a letter from Benjamin Graham about an investor he'd never heard of who lived in Omaha. Graham suggested Smith go and talk to him. When the 'Dean of Wall Street' tells you it's worth listening to a talented investor, Adam Smith realised that he would be stupid not to travel to Omaha. Buffett was a gracious host and they spent some time together.

> "We are driving down a street in Omaha and we pass a large furniture store. I have to use letters in the story because I can't remember the numbers. 'See that store?' Warren says. 'That's a really good business. It has *a* square feet of floor space, does an annual volume of *b*, has an inventory of only *c*, and turns over its capital at *d*.' 'Why don't you buy it?' I said. 'It's privately held.' Warren said. 'Oh.' I said. 'I might buy it anyway.' Warren said. 'Someday.'
>
> That phrase – 'That's a really good business' – I heard several times, always applied to something solidly managed, with a secure niche, plenty of capital, and a respectable return on invested capital."[62]

So there we have it: at least 12 years before Berkshire purchased it, Buffett was observing the business economics of NFM, and was impressed. In the decade after the drive around with Adam Smith, NFM grew to take two-thirds of the furniture sales in Omaha. Old competitors closed and potential new ones simply shied away, fearing slaughter.

The problem for Buffett was that NFM was 100% owned by the family, and they showed no sign that they wanted to sell. So, he could only admire from a distance – and let them know that he would like to buy it one day. It was easy to maintain contact as Susan Buffett was friendly with the Blumkins, especially Fran, wife of Louie.

By 1983, Louie's sons, Ronald, Irvin and Steve, had spent many years with the business. But there was tension. Mrs B was just as tough on family members as she was on others around her. This led to periods of moody non-communication. She complained that *she* was being bossed around by "the kids". So if the business was sold, the new owner would be boss, and he could sort out "the bums". Her three daughters (and, therefore, sons-in-law) each had 20% equity stakes in the business, but she wanted them to sell their shares, leaving the business in the hands of Louie. On top of that, she was 89-years old and she didn't want the family fighting over inheritance of the business. And, of course, there were estate tax considerations. Thus, she became open to the idea of selling most of it – turning a single illiquid asset into liquid money that could be allocated to family members, who could then go their own ways.

Buffett approached Louie to discuss an acceptable price. To bolster his chances, he made the point that, if the business was sold to one of the big chains, then sooner or later they would send in their own managers to run things – and they might leverage up and sell at the first opportunity. Under Berkshire's wing, on the other hand, Louie and his sons would retain operational control, and the business would be run for the long term, benefitting staff, customers and Omaha. What they had spent their lives creating would live on, with its extraordinary ethos and culture.

It was only once Louie was on board that they went to see Mrs B in the store. She made up her mind about people very quickly. Fortunately, she liked and trusted Buffett, and the deal was made there and then. Forever afterward she would (jokingly?) say that Buffett tricked her into selling by begging her to name a price. When she did so, he immediately said yes. "He bought for cash and never took inventory. He told me he trusted me with his life – more than the Bank of England. He's plenty smart. He bought a bargain."[63]

Buffett put the encounter like this: "I went out on my birthday, August 30th, 1983. And had that contract … And I gave it to Mrs. B. She didn't read, but Louie, her son, told her what was in it. And I never asked her for an audit. I just asked her if she owed any money. And I asked her if she owned the building. And she said yes. And we made the deal. But it was not a bargain purchase."[64] The contract for the deal was reproduced in the 2013 BH annual report, which you can read online.[65]

Regardless of whether they could agree on who got the better bargain, there was a great deal of mutual respect. Here is what Mrs B said about Buffett: "Warren Buffett. He's a genius. I respect him a lot. He is very honest, very plain and his word is as good as gold. I think there's not another one in the city who is so gentle, so nice, so honest, and so friendly."[66]

For $55.35m, Berkshire Hathaway purchased 90% of the shares (I like the way it is hand written into the contract), leaving 10% with Louie and his three sons. Share options for another 10% were granted to certain key young family managers. Thus, after a period, Berkshire Hathaway ended up with 80%. Notice that the contract was also signed by Mrs B's three daughters.

Mrs B continued to be chairman, and ran the carpet operation, while Louie continued as president and main driver of the business.

The franchise

Why did Buffett value the business at over $60m? Let's start with profit. In 1982–1983, on a turnover of about $100m, pre-tax margin was about 7%. After tax, that was roughly $4.5m[67] for shareholders to take away as owner earnings. So, the one-year price to earnings ratio was about 13. Looking at that data in isolation, Buffett would not declare it to be bought on the cheap: "So, it was not a bargain purchase."[68]

Thus we see that the quantitative facts were inadequate to justify the price. With all investments, we need to add the qualitative to the quantitative. The qualitative factors he had observed over decades meant there was a firm foundation for a growing stream of cash. "It was a great business. It was a wonderful opportunity to join as fine a family as I've ever met."[69] Let's expand on that. Its 200,000 square-foot store sold by far the largest volume of furniture, carpets and appliances in the country. The key to the strength of the economic franchise was:

- First, they could offer customers a huge selection across all price ranges.

- Second, they had a reputation for selling at low mark-ups, resulting in very high volume as people flocked to pick up a bargain. This led to very high sales per square foot ($500).

- Third, they had enormous buying power because of the volume.

- Fourth, they had very low expenses for running the operation. They owned the building and so had no rent; nor did they have any debt. Also, high sales per square foot meant low overhead per unit of revenue.

- Fifth, the above factors formed a positive feedback loop resulting in passing on much of the benefit of low costs to customers, which attracted greater volume which, in turn, boosted range, reputation, buying power and lowered costs.

Figure 3.2: Strengths of the economic franchise

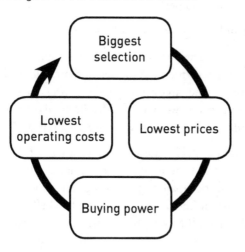

Shortly after buying the company, Buffett wrote: "One question I always ask myself in appraising a business is how I would like, assuming I had ample capital and skilled personnel, to compete with it. I'd rather wrestle grizzlies than compete with Mrs. B and her progeny. They buy brilliantly, they operate at expense ratios competitors don't even dream about, and they then pass on to their customers much of the savings. It's the ideal business – one built upon exceptional value to the customer that, in turn, translates into exceptional economics for its owners."[70]

Charlie Munger, with his great intellectual span, could see the type of business mould NFM fitted into:

"Extreme success is likely to be caused by some combination of the following factors:

Extreme maximization or minimization of one or two variables. Example, Costco or our furniture and appliance store [NFM].

Adding success factors so that a bigger combination drives success, often in nonlinear fashion, as one is reminded by the concept of breakpoint and the concept of critical mass in physics. Often results are not linear. You get a little bit more mass, and you get a lollapalooza result.

An extreme of good performance over many factors.

Catching and riding some sort of big wave."[71]

Nineteen months after the purchase, Buffett marvelled at the edge NFM had over rivals. In his 1984 letter to shareholders, he noted that Levitz Furniture – the largest independent specialty retailer of home furnishings in the country – which prided itself on offering lower prices than most, still operated at a gross margin of 44.4%.

The gross margin at NFM was only about a half of that. NFM's low mark-ups were possible because of its exceptional efficiency: operating expenses (payroll, occupancy, advertising, etc.) were about 16.5% of sales, versus 35.6% at Levitz. By this unparalleled efficiency, and astute volume purchasing, NFM was able to earn excellent returns on capital, while saving its customers at least $30 million annually based on what, on average, it would cost them to buy the same merchandise at stores maintaining typical mark-ups. Such savings enabled NFM to constantly widen its geographical reach and thus enjoy growth well beyond the natural growth of the Omaha market.

Remarkably, by 1990, NFM was found to be the third (out of twenty) most popular furniture retailer in Des Moines. And it didn't even have an outlet there. Des Moines is 130 miles from Omaha and yet customers made the journey, driving past local retailers, drawn by "an irresistible magnet that employs price and selection to pull in the crowds."[72]

A fine family

A good economic franchise on its own is insufficient to justify an investment. Reassurance is needed that the people in charge are both capable and exhibit high integrity.

Buffett had admired the Blumkin family for decades, headed by its smart and inspirational matriarch and her son Louie, "widely regarded as the shrewdest buyer of furniture and appliances in the country."[73] And then there were Louie's three sons, who "all have the Blumkin business ability, work ethic, and, most important, character. On top of that, they are really nice people. We are delighted to be in partnership with them."[74] These three had each attended the best business schools but all agreed the best business school of all was the one run in Omaha by Mrs B and Louie.

An important Buffett and Munger principle is to clearly define your circle of competence and stay within it. The Blumkins could see where they had a knowledge advantage, and they always operated in that territory. They stuck to furniture and carpets, in one location, for decade after decade.

Asked what secrets the Blumkins brought to their business, Buffett said:

> "All members of the family: (1) apply themselves with an enthusiasm and energy that would make Ben Franklin and Horatio Alger look like dropouts; (2) define with extraordinary realism their area of special competence and act decisively on all matters within it; (3) ignore even the most enticing propositions falling outside of that area of special competence; and, (4) unfailingly behave in a high-grade manner with everyone they deal with."[75]

What happened after the purchase?

First, Mrs B, Chairman of the Board, had no intention of retiring for a long time, and Buffett had no intention of asking her to do so. Her salary was raised and she worked her customary seven days a week selling carpet. She was quoted in the local paper as saying, "I come home to eat and sleep, and that's about it. I can't wait until it gets daylight so I can get back to the business."

When Buffett and Munger buy a business they look for people who don't lose an ounce of passion for running it, even after someone else owns most or all of the shares. They certainly struck lucky on that score with NFM because Louie, Ron, Irv, Steve, and other grandchildren of

Mrs B, had a great passion for the business, and showed no inclination to pull back on effort. They were excited about the potential to do great things with the business. Looking at the numbers in Table 3.4, I think we can conclude that they did well. In the ten years after purchase, revenue doubled, as did profits. Most of the cash thrown off was available for Buffett to invest elsewhere.

Table 3.4: Berkshire's share of Nebraska Furniture Mart's earnings after tax and sales

	Earnings after tax ($m)	Sales ($m)
1983 (4 months only)	4.5 annualised	100
1984	5.9	115
1985	5.2	120
1986	7.2	132
1987	7.6	143
1988	9.1	n/a
1989	8.4	153
1990	8.5	159
1991	7.0	n/a
1992	8.1	n/a
1993	10.4	200
2011	Earnings record in 2011, netted more than ten times what it did in 1983	

Source: W. Buffett, letters to shareholders of BH (1984–2011).

After 1993, the publicly available data gets sketchy. As Berkshire Hathaway bought more retailers, its annual report showed the revenue and profit numbers of NFM lumped-in with other companies, thus I'm unable to show the profit growth thereafter. However, Buffett did say that in 2011 NFM's earnings were more than ten times what they were in 1983.

We can do a little inferring: after opening the stores in Des Moines (1993), Kansas City (2003) and Texas (2016), NFM revenue rose to around $1.6bn. From the table we can see that, in the 1980s, earnings were usually in the ballpark of 5–8% of sales. By making a big assumption, we might conclude that NFM is now making something over $80m after tax per year, but that number could be even higher if you allowed for even more efficiencies gained with greater size. Whatever the true number, it is likely that the annual income is much more than the total paid for the 80% stake in 1983.

For six years after Berkshire bought into her company, Mrs B continued to out-sell and out-hustle those around her: "She runs rings around the competition. It's clear to me that she's gathering speed and may well reach her full potential in another five or ten years. Therefore, I've persuaded the board to scrap our mandatory retirement-at-100 policy. (And it's about time: with every passing year, this policy has seemed sillier to me.)"[76]

But, in 1989, she had a big falling out with her grandsons. They wanted to remodel the carpet department and make alterations to its operations. She did not agree and so quit. For a while she stayed at home but soon found that intolerable, so, at the age of 95, she started a new business selling carpets and furniture. Where did she set up? On a piece of land right opposite the NFM. She was competing with her family, working seven days a week.

It wasn't until 1992 that there was sufficient reconciliation for her to sell her building and land to NFM. This time around, Mrs. B graciously offered to sign a non-compete agreement.

For another four years, until she was 103, she ran her carpet business. More than 1,000 attended her funeral, in August 1998, including three siblings she had rescued from the Soviets in 1920–1922, 12 grandchildren and 21 great-grandchildren. The store didn't close for the funeral because the family thought she would disapprove of such a missed opportunity to sell.

Ron and Irv still run the business today (Steve is in California running a different business) and are very proud to be associated with Buffett. Irv said of Buffett's approach: "He never ever will tell us this is what you ought to do, but by the time he tells a story it's pretty clear what we ought to be doing. He, like my Dad, is an incredible role model."[77]

"You struggle, you work hard, you hope, sometimes your wishes come true, sometimes not... My wish came true."[78]

Mrs Rose Blumkin

Nebraska Furniture Mart – Learning points

1. **If you spot a good business it might be worthwhile following its fortunes over many years,** even if you are prevented from buying, either because it is too expensive or the owners don't want to sell.

2. **Low-cost producers can be good investments.** Low cost and low margin combined with extensive range can lead to great customer benefits and high returns on capital once the company is dominant in its area (geographical or product area).

3. **Look beyond this year's earnings when valuing a company.** Reported earnings must be seen in the context of potential for profit growth together with capital investment requirements. This, in turn, depends on whether there is a protective moat around the economic franchise, leading to a durable competitive advantage; and whether managers are competent and of high integrity.

4. **Enjoy your time with the directors and senior managers.** Encourage and praise them when the opportunity arises.

5. **Don't assume a successful formula offering high returns on capital employed can be repeated.** It's most likely that it cannot, so great caution is needed in geographical or product line expansion. NFM has opened only three stores in 40 years.

Investment 4

CAPITAL CITIES-ABC-DISNEY

Summary of the deal

Deal	Capital Cities – ABC – Disney
Time	1986–2000
Price paid	$517.5m
Quantity	18% of the combined Capital Cities and ABC. Then 3.5% of Disney.
Sale price	Over $3.8bn
Profit	Over 600%
Berkshire Hathaway in 1986	Share price: $2,440–$3,170 Book value: $2,073m Per share book value: $1,808

This investment was founded on a relationship. The friendship and deep respect came first, followed by confirmation of business nous – evidenced by terrific profits and return on capital employed at Capital Cities. Then there were years of Buffett frustration at not being able to invest in that talent and quality business franchise. Only after 15 years did Buffett finally find a way to enjoy the financial benefits of being a business partner (if we ignore a temporary loss-making investment in 1977). He did so by committing the largest amount Berkshire Hathaway had ever put into a company. Berkshire had come so far from its $22m foundation, when Buffett took control only two decades before, that it could, in 1986, allocate $517.5m to just one investment.

Just look at that length of time between recognising Capital Cities as an excellent company, and Buffett actually committing money to it – 15 years. How is that for patience and discipline? A decade and a half had to pass before it made sense to invest wholeheartedly in an identifiably wonderful company – it was simply too expensive before then. In that time, Buffett's understanding of the business grew, as did his trust and admiration in the principal manager. He saw both competence and integrity.

The Berkshire–Capital Cities deal is the first I'll cover in this case study. The second is very much linked to the first. Berkshire bought 18% of Capital Cities' newly created shares in 1986, providing it with the extra cash needed to complete, what was then, the second biggest takeover in American history, that of ABC for $3.5bn. Thus, in short order, Buffett bought into one giant broadcaster and brought a second under the same managerial wing.

Then there is the third deal: Disney bought all the shares in Capital Cities/ABC in 1996, allowing BH to walk away with $1.3bn of cash to invest elsewhere, and $1.2bn of Disney shares. This is on top of the amount Berkshire had gained from earlier sales of Capital Cities shares.

From small acorns

The relationship started in the late 1960s when a mutual friend invited Buffett and Thomas S. Murphy to lunch in New York. They hit it off immediately and Buffett's admiration of Murphy as "the top manager in the US" began.[79]

Murphy was a second world war naval veteran and Harvard Business School graduate. In 1954, aged 29, he went to work for a tiny company called Hudson Valley Broadcasting, of Albany NY. The company started with less than $1.5m, had only one television station and one AM radio station. Television was in its infancy and was generally loss-making. Murphy was given the grand-sounding title of chief operating officer – actually, he was the first employee.

Murphy attributed much of his future success to the fact that he learnt the ropes in a small company going through hard times. The tight-knit team had to cope with serious financial problems – three years of losses. They almost went broke twice and were forced to approach the original shareholders to bail them out. They learned how to run a parsimonious operation, with not one person or item of equipment more than was absolutely necessary.

Sticking with it through the hard times was worth it because the industry was poised to take off, as households up and down the land bought TVs. There were a fixed number of licences to operate a TV station; if you had one of those, to a certain degree, you were protected from competition. Also, the business was not capital-intensive. And, while the government had a small degree of involvement, it did not dictate prices charged to advertisers.

The Albany business grew its revenue and, because it had relatively fixed costs, could grow its margins rapidly once the break-even point was exceeded. After the company had paid for the studio, the cameras and antenna, the business was pretty much set – costs were much the same whether it served 300,000 households or three million. As viewer numbers rose, however, advertisers paid more.

Murphy and his inspirational boss, Frank Smith, saw the potential flowing from the economics in this business sector, with its characteristic disproportionate rise in profits following sales growth. Other station owners didn't grasp the full extent of the profit potential, and so were willing to sell their businesses at low prices to what was renamed Capital Cities after its first merger in 1957. Dozens of acquisitions were to follow.

Cash continued to flow without the need for much in the way of capital expenditure. Owner earnings were about the same as reported after-tax profits, because capital expenditure was generally the same as depreciation, and working capital increases were minimal. Thus, a reported after-tax profit of say $8m was all available for shareholders. They could take it in dividends, or – if they trusted it would be invested well – leave it with the managers to buy more stations. Trust they did, and richly rewarded they were.

In 1964, Murphy was appointed president, and in 1966, after the sad early death (at 56) of Murphy's mentor and friend, Frank Smith, he was promoted to chairman and CEO. At that point, the business consisted of five television stations and half a dozen radio stations.

Style

Murphy said he "always ran the company, for better or for worse, as if I owned 100 percent of it. We really thought about our stockholders. We ran the company to do the best job for our stockholders. We never ran it to get big. We ran it, if we could, to get our stockholders rich."[80]

Already we can see why Buffett and Murphy got along at that fateful first meeting:

1. He understood that cost control matters, even when a business grows; it was instinctive to him.

2. He recognised that he ran a business generating high rates of return on capital employed, because it had licences permitting rapidly increasing profits as sales grew. Clearly he had a good grasp of strategic positioning, perceiving an economic franchise with a deep and dangerous moat, and knew how to deepen and widen that moat.

3. He ran it for the benefit of shareholders – that was in his character; he felt he was there to serve those who had trusted him with their money.

There is a fourth factor Buffett admired: Murphy understood the concept of *circle of competence* and made sure he stayed well within it. "I stayed as long as I could in the businesses we understood, which were television and radio."[81]

Having said that, it wasn't long before Capital Cities had collected the maximum number of broadcasting licences allowed by the regulator. Then, Murphy went looking elsewhere for profits and found them in a related field of enterprise, an arena where he reasoned he had a good knowledge. "When we got as big as the FCC [the regulator] would allow, I went into another business that I could understand, which was the newspaper business. In a sense, it's a monopoly business like broadcasting and is advertiser supported."[82] A major magazine publisher, Fairchild, owning *Women's Wear, Daily Trade Record* and other well-loved magazines, was bought in 1968.

Murphy was able to concentrate on strategy, and in finding new companies to come into the fold, because he had a brilliant manager, Dan Burke, looking after operations. Buffett praised the pair:

> "I've been on record for many years about the management of Cap Cities: I think it is the best of any publicly-owned company in the country. And Tom Murphy and Dan Burke are not only great managers, they are precisely the sort of fellows that you would want your daughter to marry. It is a privilege to be associated with them."[83]

And in 2015:

> "These two were the best managerial duo – both in what they accomplished and how they did it – that Charlie and I ever witnessed."[84]

Buffett praised Murphy and Burke on a wider stage in an interview for a *Fortune* article in 1985:

> "In Buffett's admiring phrase, Murphy and Burke are 'models of pleasant rationality' who know how to motivate managers without often brandishing bludgeons or setting specific financial goals. Their low-key management style, grounded in decentralization and cost control, is imbued with the notion that each manager has the confidence of superiors, and is expected to realize his or her full potential."[85]

If only Berkshire could have it

The growth potential of Capital Cities was widely recognised by the stock market and so the share price remained high. Indeed, Capital Cities shares had risen by an average of well over 20% a year since it went public in 1957, a rich valuation that precluded Buffett from buying shares.

Shortly after their first meeting, Murphy tried to recruit Buffett to be a board member of Capital Cities. But Buffett explained, "I can't be a director of your company because your multiple is too high. I would want a big position."[86] At the time, Buffett was hoping to be invited to join the The Washington Post board, and he was forbidden by the media regulator to be on the boards of two powerhouses in publishing, TV and radio.

Despite Buffett having no financial stake in Capital Cities, he committed to help his friend. Buffett told Murphy, "If there's any way I can be of help to you, please feel free to call me."[87] They would regularly talk on the phone and Murphy became part of Buffett's inner circle. They sought each other's counsel. Murphy was particularly keen on asking Buffett what he thought about his ideas for the business, and his latest potential deal. "Warren was the best director I had, even though, technically, he wasn't directing. Whenever I was going to make a deal, I'd call Warren and talk with him about it. He was very free with his time and his advice."[88]

Figure 4.1: Capital Cities/ABC split-adjusted share price

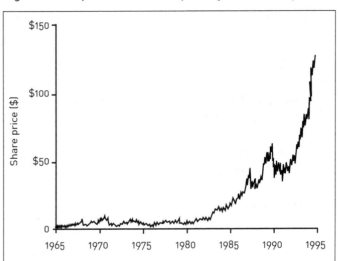

In 1977, there was a stock market window in which Buffett judged that Capital Cities shares were reasonable value, so Berkshire bought 220,000 for $10.9m ($49.48 per share). By 31 December 1977, they were priced at $59.20 but, ultimately, turned out to be a poor investment as Buffett sold them at just $43 in 1978–1980. Six years later, after buying three million shares at a much higher price, he publicly flogged himself for getting out:

"Of course, some of you probably wonder why we are now buying Cap Cities at $172.50 per share given that your Chairman, in a characteristic burst of brilliance, sold Berkshire's holdings in the same company at $43 per share in 1978–1980. Anticipating your question, I spent much of 1985 working on a snappy answer that would reconcile these acts. A little more time, please."[89]

Where did Berkshire Hathaway get all that money?

Before examining the deal itself, it's instructive to consider where the $517.5m came from. What had the rest of Berkshire Hathaway been doing to generate such a vast amount of money?

Initially, Buffett was not expecting great inflows of cash in the 1980s. Between August 1983, when he bought Nebraska Furniture Mart, and the end of 1985, Buffett was warning his shareholders/partners that they would have to get used to much lower returns than in the past. In the 1984 letter to shareholders, he was adamant:

"I have told you in the past of the drag that a mushrooming capital base exerts upon rates of return… Our historical 22% rate is just that – history (over 22 years). To earn even 15% annually over the next decade… we would need profits aggregating about $3.9bn. Accomplishing this will require a few big ideas – small ones just won't do. Charlie Munger, my partner in general management, and I do not have any such ideas at present, but our experience has been that they pop up occasionally." (How's that for a strategic plan?)

Of course, we now know that Buffett and Munger far exceeded their target. The general movements in the stock market in the mid-1980s (see chart) helped a little but hardly account for the near doubling in net book value over this period.

Figure 4.2: Dow Jones Industrial Average
(October 1982–December 1985)

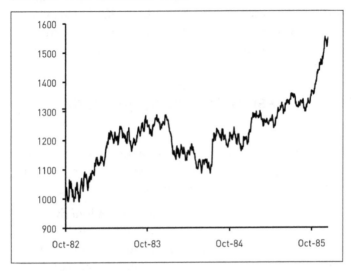

Source: ADVFN.com

What really counted were the extraordinary capital gains made on the shares bought and sold by the insurance subsidiaries, together with the large flow of associated dividend and interest income. Add to this the rising profits of The Buffalo News, Nebraska Furniture Mart, See's Candies and Wesco (see Table 4.1).

Table 4.1: Net earnings after taxes attributable to Berkshire Hathaway from operating businesses

	1983 ($m)	1984 ($m)	1985 ($m)
Insurance underwriting	–18.4	–26.0	–23.6
Insurance investment income (dividends and interest)	39.1	62.1	79.7
Realised security gains	45.3	71.6	325.2
The Buffalo News	8.8	13.3	14.6
Nebraska Furniture Mart	1.5	5.9	5.2

	1983 ($m)	1984 ($m)	1985 ($m)
Associated Retail Stores	0.4	-0.6	0.1
See's Candies	12.2	13.4	14.6
Blue Chip Stamps – parent	-0.4	-0.9	2.8
Mutual Savings & Loan	1.9	3.2	4.0
Wesco Financial	3.4	4.8	4.2
Other	27.2	11.3	18.4
Interest on debt	-7.3	-7.5	-7.3
Charity donations by BH shareholders	-1.7	-1.7	-2.2
TOTAL EARNINGS	112.2	148.9	435.8

Source: W. Buffett, letters to shareholders of BH (1984–1986).

All told, those three years produced after-tax income of $697m. The lion's share came from an investment in General Foods, sold in 1985, which was mostly purchased in 1980 "at far below what we felt was their per-share business value."[90] The pre-tax realised gain from selling the company to Philip Morris was $338m.

> "We thus benefitted from four factors: a bargain purchase price, a business with fine underlying economics, an able management concentrating on the interests of shareholders, and a buyer willing to pay full business value. While that last factor is the only one that produces reported earnings, we consider identification of the first three to be the key to building value for Berkshire shareholders. In selecting common stocks, we devote our attention to attractive purchases, not to the possibility of attractive sales."[91]

Another boost to future profits, although small, was the closure, over the period July to December 1985, of the loss-making textile operation. After years of trying to keep it alive, for the sake of the loyal and hard-working employees as much as anything, Buffett finally concluded that it offered the prospect of "unending losses".[92]

In 1965, all $22m of Berkshire net accounting worth was in textiles. But the movement of capital, first into insurance in 1967 (National Indemnity), and then a host of other businesses, resulted in a company that could report after-tax income of over $400m for one year.

Reflecting on the textile business, and the shift of resources, Buffett wrote in his 1985 letter:

> "Some years ago I wrote: 'When a management with a reputation for brilliance tackles a business with a reputation for poor fundamental economics, it is the reputation of the business that remains intact.' Nothing has since changed my point of view on that matter. Should you find yourself in a chronically-leaking boat, energy devoted to changing vessels is likely to be more productive than energy devoted to patching leaks."

Following that philosophy, and putting it to work with enormous skill, Buffett and Munger were in a position to find $517.2m to back their friend Tom Murphy in his biggest ever acquisition, while still holding onto some excellent whole-controlled companies, as well as a first-class portfolio of marketable securities.

The deal

The 1980s was the era of corporate raiders – fed by junk bonds and egged on by investment bankers – buying up companies, playing financial games and then selling, often causing great disruption to the operating businesses and their previously loyal managers.

ABC was being eyed by these marauders, and the man who had built this company into the most respected TV empire, Leonard Goldenson, was concerned for its future. He was 80-years old and thought that the circling vultures would rip apart all that he had created. He looked inside the company for a successor but didn't find anyone ready to take the leading role.

The rules on ownership of TV stations had loosened (the FCC had recently increased the number of VHF television stations that any one firm could own from five to 12). Encouraged by this, Tom Murphy approached Goldenson in January 1985. There was already a strong relationship between the two companies because Capital Cities' stations broadcast ABC's output. "We were the biggest ABC affiliate that was not owned by ABC" said Murphy.[93]

Goldenson had known and admired Murphy for many years, and was open to discussing the idea of a business combination. Murphy recalls, "I went to him and I said, 'Leonard, I'd like to see if we can make a deal together.' I thought he'd throw me out of the 39th floor, but he didn't. As a matter of fact, we very quickly made a deal."[94]

But Goldenson immediately foresaw a problem: those nuisance corporate raiders, with their high borrowing and short-term mindset, could swoop down at any time, buy up a large proportion of the shares – if not bid for the entire combined company – and ruin the long-term performance by destroying the strategic and cultural strength Murphy and his team would try to build after the merger.

While Goldenson trusted Murphy to keep the business together and make it thrive, he did say "Tom, you'll need a 400-pound gorilla to prevent someone from coming in and trying to take both of us over."[95] Murphy would need a large stockholder who could block any takeover approach. "As a result, I got mixed up with my pal Warren Buffett. I had known Warren for fifteen years. When I called him up, he was a director at Washington Post. I told Warren, 'I think I have a deal with Leonard Goldenson and I would like your advice.'"[96]

The kingmaker

Berkshire already owned over $46m of ABC shares and Buffett had taken a keen interest in both companies. He instantly recognised the logic of the deal, with its numerous sources of potential synergy, and the value of Murphy and Burke's cost-cutting brilliance. He had also figured that for the managers to feel safe and get on with running the business for long-term shareholder wealth creation, they would need a large shareholder who would refuse to sell, regardless of tempting short-term gains offered by Wall Street financial players. Murphy recollects:

> "[Buffett] came up the next day and we discussed it. I told Warren that I really wanted to make a deal with him, if he wanted to make a deal with me. He thought about it and said,

'OK, I think that's a good idea. I'd like to do that...' Then he said, 'I'll put $500m in...' The deal was $3.5bn, and Warren offered $500m [actually $517.5m]. I suspect Warren thought I was being rash. ABC was so much bigger than Capital Cities was, but I told Warren that Capital Cities made an awful lot of money and the margins were great, so I convinced him."[97]

Both knew the process of acquisition would take many months due to the need to satisfy the regulator, e.g. by agreeing to sell overlapping TV and radio stations. Buffett was concerned that the shares would appreciate during that period, as the market absorbed the idea that value was going to be created for Capital Cities shareholders. He therefore insisted that the $172.50 to be paid for each of the three million shares was a fixed amount, even if it wasn't to be paid until 1986, and even if the market price of Capital Cities shares had rocketed by then. Murphy was quick to agree because Berkshire's cash was vital to make the deal happen. The total paid for ABC was $3.5bn but Capital Cities had to borrow $2.1bn of that – to borrow more would have been reckless. There was a plan to raise another $0.9bn by selling TV stations.

On the announcement of a merger, the normal market response is for the target shares to rise and the acquirer's to fall (because the market often thinks that executives are over-optimistic and end up paying too much). On this occasion, both shares advanced when the information was released to the market. ABC's share price soared by 42% to $106 within a week, and Capital Cities went up by 22% to $215 a share. An article in *Fortune* explained:

> "The market's thundering approval denotes an almost reverential confidence in the management of Capital Cities, which will run the surviving company."[98]

Commitment, but The Buffalo News was sacrosanct

There were two complications to be cleared away. First, Capital Cities had a TV station in Buffalo which would have to be sold because Buffett was not allowed to have influence over both the station and the newspaper. Murphy agreed.

Second, Buffett had to resign from the board of The Washington Post if he was to be a director of Capital Cities, which he duly did – after all, he could still advise Katharine Graham without having a seat at the table.

To show his confidence and trust in Murphy and Burke, Buffett went much further. He gave Murphy voting rights over Berkshire Hathaway's Capital Cities' shares, and handed over the right to decide if the shares were to be sold.

> "One of the interesting things that happened is that Warren put his 18% ownership of the company in my hands for 11 years. I never would have thought of asking him for it, but he told me to vote his share of the stock. He put me in absolute control of the company. He showed great confidence in me and my partner Dan Burke. We had a wonderful, wonderful relationship for all the years we ran ABC. And there's no question that Warren Buffett gave me a great deal of security. He was my 400-pound gorilla, so to speak."[99]

A measure of Murphy and Burke's managerial brilliance: Capital Cities shares were sold on the stock market in 1957 at $0.72 (adjusting for splits). By December 1985, they were quoted at $224.50. Over 28 years that is a compound annual rate of return of 22.8%. On top of that, there were dividends. (There was a ten for one share split in 1993, and so a chart of its share price shows a mere $22.45 for 1985, but it represents a price of $224.50 in pre-1993 terms. They rose to over $1,000 in pre-1993 split terms, before being bought by Disney.)

Why the deal with ABC was worth doing

In his March 1986 letter to Berkshire shareholders, Buffett said that the January purchase of three million shares in Capital Cities, enabling it to acquire ABC, would result in "economics that are likely to be unexciting over the next few years." This was not exactly what Berkshire shareholders wanted to hear but Buffett offered a little comfort. "This bothers us not an iota; we can be very patient. (No matter how great the talent or effort, some things just take time; you can't produce a baby in one month by getting nine women pregnant.)"

So, the returns were not going to be quick, but he was sure it was a good investment, despite him saying in a newspaper interview that Benjamin Graham would not be applauding him on this one.

> "Our Cap Cities purchase was made at a full price, reflecting the very considerable enthusiasm for both media stocks and media properties that has developed in recent years (and that, in the case of some property purchases, has approached a mania). It's no field for bargains. However, our Cap Cities investment allies us with an exceptional combination of properties and people – and we like the opportunity to participate in size."[100]

Prior to the merger, in early 1985, both Capital Cities and ABC had market capitalisations around $2.2bn, despite ABC having much higher revenue ($3.7bn) than Capital Cities (under $1bn). But the profit numbers were much closer together (see Table 4.2).

Table 4.2: Capital Cities and ABC earnings after tax

	Capital Cities		ABC	
	Total ($m)	Per share ($)	Total ($m)	Per share ($)
1982			160	5.54
1983	114	8.53	160	5.45
1984	143	10.98	195	6.71
1985	142	10.87		

Capital Cities bought all the 29.1m shares outstanding in ABC for $3.5bn ($118 per share) plus a tenth of a warrant (worth $3 or so). A warrant gave the holder the right to buy Capital Cities shares at $250 for a period of two and a half years following completion of the merger. Ten ABC shares were required to obtain one warrant.

Price versus value

We might start thinking about price versus value from the 1985 perspective, by assuming that the combined company would produce earnings of about $300–350m, a rough estimate of what they earned as separate businesses.

But that would be to forget the massive debt this enterprise carried – over $2bn. In 1986, corporate bonds offered at least 9% interest, and so this company had an interest burden north of $180m, leaving earnings at under $200m per year. This is for a company which was priced by the market at $3.6bn (16.08m shares × $224.5) so the shares were trading on a high earnings multiple. (There were 13.08m shares before Berkshire's purchase of an additional 3m.)

But the analysis so far fails to allow for the potential of the company's business franchises – in an expanding media market – its excellent management, and some great synergies.

First, look at the assets it held

In those days, the majority of viewers tuned in to watch the three giant networks through TV station affiliates – cable was around, but was pretty small. The ABC network reached just about every American. As well as the network, Capital Cities/ABC owned eight stations, each ranked one or two in their markets. Advertisers spent more as each year passed, competing for TV slots to reach mass audiences.

ABC Radio Networks had over 2,000 affiliates, as well as 17 radio stations, and a broad range of paper publications – including *Institutional Investor* and *The Kansas City Star/Times*. It also owned a motion pictures studio.

ESPN, the sports cable business, was the hidden jewel – ABC held 80% of its shares. Its numbers looked pretty bad in the 1980s, but it was destined to be of great interest to Disney in the 1990s. Murphy recalls Goldenson telling him that one day ESPN would be really valuable:

> "ESPN is unbelievably successful. When we bought it in 1985, it was losing $40m a year. Leonard Goldenson said to me, 'Tom, someday that's going to be worth as much as one of your big television stations.'... Capital Cities bought ABC because we thought we could run the television stations and make more money, which we did. But the thing that has actually been a huge break for us is the continual growth of ESPN. It has gone from

losing $40m, to losing $20m, to breaking even, to making $50m, to making $100m. Now, it's in the stratosphere."[101]

Second, look at the return on equity capital

Because media businesses in the 1980s needed only minor additional capital as they added customers, these two companies, when separate, regularly churned out returns on equity in the range 15–22%. There were good reasons to expect that this level would be at least maintained.

Third, look at the ability to cut costs

Murphy's managerial style was that of decentralisation of operating decisions to the local level. Managers were told to operate their businesses as though they owned them for the long term. Managers must focus on costs; those with long experience of working under Murphy knew what they had to do. Some of the recently acquired had to learn that ratings are important, but only so far as high ratings fed profits – they are not the end goal. If they failed to achieve good profits then Murphy intervened. Over 1,500 redundancies were made and frivolous expenses such as florist bills of $60,000 a shot, and limousine rides, were stopped. Buildings in prime locations were sold.

Murphy explained his approach in an interview in 2000. He felt that a company's responsibilities extended not just to its employees, audience and shareholders, but also to the communities it served.

> "…we told our employees that we hire the smartest people we can find, and that we have no more of them around than necessary. We also told them that we would be highly decentralized and give them a lot of responsibility… For most employees, we'd give them a ticket on the horse race, which means we'd give them options… We told employees that the one thing they could not do was anything that would embarrass the company. They could not do anything that was improper or unethical because there would be no second chance."[102]

Murphy believed that if the company did well by its community and its employees, then shareholders would do well.

Fourth, look at the ability to pay down debt

Murphy was able to raise $1.2bn in pretty short order by selling overlapping TV stations.

In the five to six years following the acquisition, cash flow beyond that needed for capital investment and additional working capital accumulated to over $2bn.

Despite having built Capital Cities through a series of acquisitions in the 1960s and 1970s, in the late 1980s he looked at what was available and thought the prices too high. Instead, the cash generated by the business was used to reduce debt and build up cash reserves. By 1991, debt and cash holdings were about the same; in 1992, cash holdings actually exceeded debt, which by then had fallen below $1bn.

Profits rose

It wasn't long before Capital Cities/ABC's profits after tax were above $400m (see Table 4.3). Berkshire's share of these earnings was 18%, between $67m and $87m. Admittedly, not all of this was paid out in dividends because it made more sense to plough most of it back into the business – to make it even stronger.

Table 4.3: Capital Cities/ABC profits after tax (1986–1992)

	$m
1986	181.9
1987	279.1
1988	387.1
1989	485.7
1990	477.8
1991	374.7
1992	389.3

Source: R. G. Hagstrom, *The Warren Buffett Way* (John Wiley & Sons, 1995).

Capital Cities/ABC also bought back shares during these years, because Murphy regarded his company's shares as underpriced relative to other attractive companies. In December 1993, Berkshire sold one-third of its shares at $630 per share to Capital Cities/ABC Inc., receiving $297m after tax. This left Berkshire with 13% of the outstanding shares.

The following year saw a ten-for-one share split resulting in Berkshire's remaining holding of two million becoming 20m, with a market value totalling $1.7bn.

Look-through earnings

Buffett reported the following 'look-through earnings' in his annual letters (see Table 4.4). Look-through earnings consisted of:

- the cash dividend paid to Berkshire

- Berkshire's share of the retained operating earnings that, under GAAP accounting, were not reflected in Berkshire's profits

- an allowance for the tax that would be paid by Berkshire if these retained earnings of investees had instead been distributed to Berkshire.

Table 4.4: Capital Cities owner earnings attributable to Berkshire Hathaway (1990–1994)

	Dividends ($m)	Berkshire's share of undistributed operating earnings ($m)	Tax ($m)	Total look-through earnings ($m)
1990	0.5	85	−11.0	75
1991	0.5	61	−8.0	54
1992	0.5	70	−9.9	61
1993	0.5	83	−11.5	72
1994	0.5	85	−11.7	74

Source: W. Buffett, letters to shareholders of BH (1991–1994).

Thus, an original investment of $517.5m generated look-through earnings of between $54m and $75m a year, which is a perfectly acceptable level. And then it got even better. After the cost of the investment was reduced to $345m, by selling one-third of the shares in 1993, Capital Cities/ABC continued to make over $70m of look-through earnings a year for Berkshire – a *very good* performance.

Buffett's advice to investors

Buffett recommends that all investors work out the owner earnings on their portfolios. This requires the investor to determine the underlying earnings attributable to the shares held in their portfolio and to total them. The goal of each investor should be to create a portfolio (in effect, a *company*) that will deliver the highest possible look-through earnings in a decade's time.

> "An approach of this kind will force the investor to think about long-term business prospects rather than short-term stock market prospects, a perspective likely to improve results. It's true, of course, that, in the long run, the scoreboard for investment decisions is market price. But prices will be determined by future earnings. In investing, just as in baseball, to put runs on the scoreboard one must watch the playing field, not the scoreboard."[103]

The big reward – Disney's valuation of Capital Cities/ABC

On buying into Capital Cities, Buffett wanted to reassure Murphy and Burke that he would not cut and run. He said that handing over voting control, and the decision on when to sell Berkshire's shares, was intended to motivate his managers to give of their best for the long-term benefit of shareholders. With Buffett's self-imposed restrictions in place:

> "the first-class managers with whom we have aligned ourselves can focus their efforts entirely upon running the businesses and maximizing long-term values for owners. Certainly this is much better than having those managers distracted by 'revolving-door capitalists' hoping to put the company 'in play'... We

don't want managers that we like and admire – and who have welcomed a major financial commitment by us – to ever lose any sleep wondering whether surprises might occur because of our large ownership."[104]

Buffett went further after the merger, declaring that Capital Cities was one of only three permanent holdings for Berkshire's insurance subsidiaries. "Even if these securities were to appear significantly overpriced, we would not anticipate selling them, just as we would not sell See's or The Buffalo Evening News if someone were to offer us a price far above what we believe those businesses are worth."[105]

In his 1987 letter to shareholders, Buffett admitted that his and Munger's determination to hold for the long-term might seem eccentric to some on Wall Street. He claimed that the two of them subscribed to David Ogilvy's advice: "Develop your eccentricities while you are young. That way, when you get old, people won't think you're going ga-ga."

> "Our attitude, however, fits our personalities and the way we want to live our lives. We would rather achieve a return of X while associating with people whom we strongly like and admire, than realize 110% of X by exchanging these relationships for uninteresting or unpleasant ones. And we will never find people we like and admire more than some of the main participants at the three companies – our permanent holdings."

You can see, in Table 4.5, the degree of concentration in the portfolio in the mid-1980s, as Buffett found few opportunities to purchase minority interests at low prices, and kept to his commitment not to sell The Washington Post, GEICO or Capital Cities/ABC. Capital Cities/ABC alone accounted for up to 43% of the marketable securities.

Table 4.5: Berkshire Hathaway common stock shareholdings (1986–1988)

	Number of shares (m)	Cost ($m)	Dec 1986 market value ($m)	Dec 1987 market value ($m)	Dec 1988 market value ($m)
Capital Cities/ABC	2.99 in 1986 and 3.00 thereafter	515.8 in 1986, 517.5 in 1987 and thereafter	801.7	1,035.0	1,086.8
GEICO	6.85	45.7	674.7	756.9	849.4
Handy & Harman	2.38	27.3	47.0	n/a	n/a
Lear Singer	0.49	44.1	44.6	n/a	n/a
The Washington Post	1.73	9.7	269.5	323.1	364.1
The Coca-Cola Company	14.17	592.5 in 1988	n/a	n/a	632.4
Federal Home Loan Mortgage Corporation Preferred stock	2.40	71.7 in 1988	n/a	n/a	121.2
Other common stockholdings		12.8 in 1986	36.5	n/a	n/a
Total common stock			1,874.0		

Source: W. Buffett, letters to shareholders of BH (1986–1988).

Buffett complained that in 1987–1988 he was unable to invest in stock market-quoted companies at prevailing high prices, saying that he and Charlie had had little to do with stocks during the recent few years. Thus, by the end of 1987, Berkshire had no share investments over $50m other than the Permanent Three (or some arbitrage holdings). He parked money in medium-term bonds ($900m) and bought $700m of Salomon Inc. 9% preferred stock.

From franchise to mere 'business'

In the early 1990s, the writing was on the wall for old media companies. New technology threatened their ability to charge a high price relative to cost; advertisers were presented with a proliferation of alternative ways to attract attention.

Writing in his 1991 letter to shareholders, Buffett expressed the view that television, newspaper and magazine properties had begun to resemble *businesses* more than *franchises* in their economic behaviour.

He defined a franchise as providing a product or service which is: needed or desired; thought by customers to have no close substitute; and not subject to price regulation. These conditions enabled a company to price its product or service aggressively, generating a high return on capital.

Franchises, he said, could tolerate mismanagement for a while; poor managers could diminish the franchise's profitability but could not seriously damage the business model.

A business, on the other hand, could earn exceptional profits only by beating its competitors on price, and attracting volume, or if the supply of its product or service is limited. Superior management could maintain these conditions for longer but, ultimately, both are susceptible to competition. Poor management, however, could kill a business at any time.

Buffett felt that media properties had lost their strength as franchises. Customers now had more choice. "Unfortunately, demand can't expand in response to this new supply: 500m American eyeballs and a 24-hour day are all that's available. The result is that competition has intensified, markets have fragmented, and the media industry has lost some – though far from all – of its franchise strength."[106]

Buffett offered an illustration of the impact, on corporate values, of the switch from franchise to business. A franchise might be reporting $1m of owner earnings this year but could reasonably be expected to increase that number by 6% in each future year, due to its ability to raise prices. The growth rate makes a big difference to the valuation.

If we assumed a required rate of return of 10%, with a growth rate of 6%, then the present value (intrinsic value) would be $1m/(0.10 – 0.06) = $25m.

If, however, the franchise had evaporated, so that zero growth in earnings might be expected, the present value (intrinsic value) would be a mere $10m, i.e. $1m/(0.10 – 0) = $10m.

Buffett said that the intrinsic value of Capital Cities/ABC (and The Buffalo News and The Washington Post) had "declined materially because of the secular transformation that the industry is experiencing". But he wasn't planning on selling his core media assets, because the intrinsic value losses had been moderated by excellent management at The Buffalo News, Capital Cities and The Washington Post; they had low debt and still "continue to have far better economic characteristics than those possessed by the average American business. But gone are the days of bullet-proof franchises and cornucopian economics."[107]

And then... Disney pounced

The obvious logic of combining the world's number one content provider and the world's number one distribution company was discussed by many analysts in the 1990s. There was enormous potential in expanding, outside of the USA, the geographical area where their products could be offered – particularly for sports and animated entertainment.

Despite talks, Tom Murphy and Michael Eisner of Disney could not come to an agreement. Eisner was willing to offer a generous $19bn for Capital Cities/ABC, but he did not want to exchange shares in Disney – he insisted on a cash purchase. There were two problems with cash.

First, capital gains taxes would have to be paid by many shareholders (e.g. Berkshire). Secondly, Capital Cities/ABC shareholders would not be participating in the future success of the combined enterprise. Thus, Murphy rejected the offer.

Every July, there is a gathering of media moguls and other high-powered people from around the world in Sun Valley, Idaho (organised by Herb Allen). It was there that a deal was finally agreed. In his 1995 letter to shareholders, Buffett related how a chance meeting had helped the deal happen.

After the meeting, on 14 July 1995, Buffett is invited to lunch at Allen's house. Leaving afterwards, to meet Tom Murphy for a game of golf, he bumps into Michael Eisner walking along the same street.

Buffett congratulates Eisner on a great presentation at the meeting that morning. They get chatting and the subject of a merger between Capital Cities and Disney crops up. It wasn't the first time a merger had been discussed, but progress had never been made, partly because Disney was insistent on a cash deal and Capital Cities desired stock.

When Murphy arrived, the three of them had a brief chat in which both Eisner and Murphy indicated that they might be prepared to bend on the make-up of the deal. Within a few weeks, agreement had been reached and a contract drawn up in three days.

> "The Disney/Cap Cities deal makes so much sense that I'm sure it would have occurred without that chance encounter in Sun Valley. But when I ran into Michael that day… he was heading for his plane so, without that accidental meeting, the deal certainly wouldn't have happened in the time frame it did. I believe both Disney and Cap Cities will benefit from the fact that we all serendipitously met that day."[108]

For each Capital Cities/ABC share, Eisner offered one share in Disney plus $65 cash. Shareholders were free to ask for a preponderance of Disney shares, or predominantly cash, if preferred.

On 5 March 1996, Buffett took two envelopes to the Manhattan bankers handling the sale. The first envelope contained Berkshire's $2.5bn shares in Capital Cities/ABC (20m), to be handed over to Disney. The second envelope was sealed, with the following written across it 'Do not open until 4.30pm on 7 March'.[109] Up to that point, he had told neither Murphy nor Eisner whether he wanted cash or shares. When the envelope was opened, it read that Berkshire wanted shares only.

That wasn't to be. So many Capital Cities/ABC shareholders desired shares in Disney that they had to compromise and accept a mixture, because Michael Eisner insisted on half in cash and half in shares overall. Thus, Berkshire ended up with $1.2bn in cash and $1.3bn in Disney shares – not bad for an investment of a mere $345m only 10 years before.

What happened next

At first, Buffett was enthusiastic about Disney, and even added to Berkshire's 21m shareholding. He was particularly enthused about the 'Mouse' not having an agent; an animated character, unlike a star actor, could not demand a high proportion of the value created by a movie – because they were 100% owned by Disney.

But as the bubble of 1998–2000 progressed, he sold Disney shares into that market strength, raising about $2bn before capital gains tax deduction (this number is to be treated with caution; the exact number is not in the public domain, and I've had to piece it together from scattered data). By then, the evidence of the effect of the internet, satellite TV and cable competition was building, and Disney was selling on a price earnings multiple of over 40.

In sum, Berkshire Hathaway paid $517.5m for its Capital Cities/ABC shares. In 1993, the pre-tax receipts from selling one-third of those shares was $630m. In 1996, $1.2bn was received from Disney (before tax) plus Disney shares, and between 1998 and the end of 2000, about $2bn was received from the sale of the Disney shares.

Tom Murphy, then in his seventies, continued at Disney for a while until, in 2003, aged 78, he joined the board of Berkshire Hathaway. And he is still there in his nineties, advising Buffett and Munger.

Figure 4.3: Disney's share price (1995–2003)

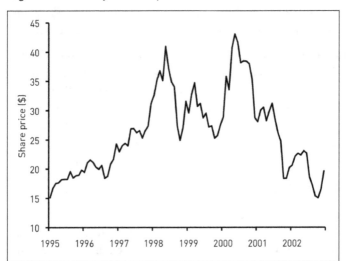

Learning points

1. **Knowing the people running a business can be very important.** Because Buffett trusted Murphy to manage the business well, and in the interests of shareholders, he looked for an opportunity to invest at a later date.

2. **Patience and discipline.** Following a first-class company is wise – getting to know the business and the managers – but accumulation of such knowledge only leads to an investment when there is a good margin of safety between intrinsic value and market price.

3. **Economic franchises can be great investments.** But only if the price is not too high. Characteristics of a franchise: (a) a product or service needed or desired; (b) no close substitutes available; (c) not price regulated.

4. **Circle of competence only.** Business managers must recognise and keep within the boundaries of their circle of competence.

5. **Get into the right business boat.** Put energy into changing vessels rather than patching leaks.

6. **Loyalty and non-confrontation.** Investors can reap a dividend if they are loyal and non-confrontational with managers (if they deserve it). Buffett was an attractive 400-pound gorilla ('white squire')[110] compared with voracious short-termist Wall Street players.

7. **Look-through earnings thinking gives a valuable perspective.** For portfolio constituents, calculate the underlying earnings attributable to your shares, whether these sums are paid as dividends or retained. Aim for the highest look-through earnings a decade from now.

8. **To put runs on the scoreboard one must watch the playing field [business performance] not the scoreboard [stock market].**

Investment 5

SCOTT FETZER

Summary of the deal

Deal	Scott Fetzer
Time	1986–today
Price paid	$315.2m
Quantity	100% of the equity
Sale price	Still held
Profit	$2bn, and counting
Berkshire Hathaway in 1986	Share price: $2,440–$3,170
	Book value: $2,073m
	Per share book value: $1,808

The Scott Fetzer purchase is remarkable, firstly, because it was a conglomerate. Until that point, Buffett and Munger focused on companies engaged in one line of business, and which were expected to continue in that line for decades to come. See's Candies stuck to manufacturing and retailing its goodies; the Illinois National Bank only undertook banking in a small geographical area; National Indemnity and GEICO were insurers. Even Capital Cities/ABC's various businesses were related to entertainment.

But Scott Fetzer had over 20 businesses with few commonalities. Its biggest subsidiary sold encyclopaedias door-to-door ($600 per set). Its vacuum cleaner division also sold door-to-door, at up to $900 per machine, but otherwise was totally different. Scott Fetzer had subsidiaries making and selling products as wide ranging as air compressors, electric motors and trailer hitches.

This investment is also remarkable because the leader of the company pursued a leveraged managerial buyout only a few months before, which would have made him undisputed boss of his own company, a corporation big enough to be a member of the Fortune 500. And there he was, accepting Buffett and Munger as overlords.

Thirdly, the managerial team must have been incredibly enthusiastic after selling out to Berkshire Hathaway because they went on to achieve outlandishly good returns on capital employed. Returns of over 50% per year were the norm. And because Scott Fetzer didn't need much additional investment, in capital items and working capital, amazingly high dividends flowed to Buffett and Munger to invest in other companies. In the first 15 years alone, $1.03bn was sent to head office in Omaha. And this from a company bought for only $315.2m.

This case study is very useful in illustrating Buffett's method of calculating owner earnings. In an appendix to his 1986 letter to shareholders, he sets out the components required to estimate Scott Fetzer's owner earnings. He further explains why this is the best method for forecasting annual flows to shareholders in order to value a company. This is the only public example of Buffett illustrating this most important technique.

A little history

George Scott and Carl Fetzer started a machine shop in Cleveland, Ohio in 1914. In 1922, they partnered with a fellow Clevelander, Jim Kirby, who had invented a new type of vacuum cleaner. They ran a very successful business until the 1960s, focused almost exclusively in that product area. At this point, flush with cash, the company went on an acquisition splurge – ending up with 31 businesses by 1973.

In the mid-1970s, Ralph Schey was appointed chairman and CEO. He set about reducing the sprawling conglomerate to a mere 20 divisions, but held onto those with good brands in consumer markets.

After the experience of the 1973–1975 recession, he figured consumer brands would have more resilience in any future downturn. Also, this approach matched the skill set of the senior managers who were less manufacturers and more marketers.

Schey set about broadening the consumer product offering. He started, in 1978, with the acquisition of Wayne Home Equipment – a producer of oil and gas burners, pumps for space heaters and boilers, and water pumps. The bigger deal of 1978 was the $50m purchase of World Book, the market-leading direct seller of encyclopaedias. World Book operated in an oligopoly, with Encyclopaedia Britannica a distant second. In the days before the internet, World Book was a mainstay of American middle-class life, with annual sales of around 200,000–300,000 sets. Even though hundreds of dollars were required for a full set, parents thought the investment well worthwhile.[111] Encyclopaedias were usually sold on credit and so Scott & Fetzer (as it was called then) made good profits supplying finance.

The takeover craze – and Scott Fetzer under threat

The 1980s was a period of ferocious private equity raids – think of the movie *Wall Street* (1987). Much of this was financed by freshly-minted junk bonds supplied by Drexel Burnham Lambert, resulting in highly-leveraged companies dangerously teetering on a cliff edge of debt; one false move and the company was done for, resulting in devastated employees and towns.

Ivan Boesky, a takeover specialist commanding a $200m fund, began accumulating Scott Fetzer's shares in spring 1984 (it is thought that Gordon Gecko in *Wall Street* is based partly on Boesky – four years later he was to start a three-year prison sentence for insider dealing). On 26 April 1984, Boesky offered to buy Scott Fetzer at $60 per share. This was a total of $420m, but as *The New York Times* noted,[112] "The company's main attraction is thought to be nearly $100m in cash on hand", so the real cost was substantially less.

Ralph Schey anticipated raiders arriving at his door sooner or later. A few days before Boesky made his move, Schey announced that he had put together his own bid in a management buyout (MBO), offering $50 per share ($360m). Schey could see he was now outbid and, besides, he had had problems raising the money, so he withdrew the offer.

But Boesky only had about 5% of the shares so he had a lot of persuading to do if he was to triumph, especially given that the offer was at a low price-earnings ratio of $60/$4.80 = 12.5. Clearly the market remained sceptical as to whether Boesky would be successful, given that the share moved to only $57.50.

On 8 May, the board rejected the offer citing "significant uncertainties and conditions related to the proposal."[113] Schey was dead against it, fearing the worst for his friends and colleagues in the business. "I felt an obligation to our employees to see that they were all treated about as equally as possible. I didn't want any one group of employees… to suddenly find themselves out in a marketplace where nobody wanted them."[114]

There was some toing and froing until, in August 1985, Boesky threw in the towel and started selling his shares. The management plan to buyout the shareholders had already been resurrected, now pitched at $62, or $440m. But there was a major problem: a very significant part of the money was to come from Scott Fetzer's employee stock ownership plan (ESOP). This was to hold 41% of the shares for putting $182m into the new company set up for the takeover (whereas the management paid only $9m for their 29%).

The government objected to only 41% being held by the ESOP, especially given that managers assumed they could take advantage of a tax break to pump an extra $25m into the ESOP. The deal fell apart and, on 5 September, Schey terminated the plan, saying Scott Fetzer was now released "from restrictions preventing solicitation of new proposals and that other possible transactions would be considered."[115] The shares fell to $55.50 which, in October, attracted a bid from another couple of raiders, the Rales Brothers (Steven and Mitchell) at $60. They too had a habit of using junk bonds for acquisitions.

The deal

Warren Buffett followed the Scott Fetzer saga in the press and thought it might be worth writing a letter to Schey, to see if he might be interested in joining the collection of businesses owned by Berkshire – companies which were granted a high degree of managerial autonomy and were encouraged to focus on the long horizon.

Buffett described how the deal came about in a lecture to Notre Dame Faculty MBA students and undergraduate students in spring 1991:[116]

"I'd never met the fellow... I wrote him a letter [October 10], I said 'Dear Mr. Schey: Here's what we are...' I sent him an annual report and said 'If you want to do business with someone whose checks will clear, who won't bother you, here's all the shoes that will drop' (I told him all the bad things about us – a one-page letter)... I said 'If you want to talk about it, I'll meet you, and if you don't, throw the letter away.' He called me up, we met on a Sunday in Chicago [22 October], made a deal that night and, in a week, the deal was done. That was five or six years ago – I've been to Cleveland twice, not because I needed to. He runs that business exactly like he [owned it himself]."

Schey told *Fortune,* in 1988, that Buffett's speed and waving of the due diligence rigmarole illustrated the lack of bureaucracy when working with him. "If I couldn't own Scott Fetzer myself, this is the next best thing."[117] He added that it was even better than running a public company, having had his fill of institutional investors questioning and second-guessing him. And he was frustrated with the board's excessive caution in authorising major moves. "Schey's prize example is his current [1988] intention to decentralize the World Book organization, which has been hunkered down at Chicago's Merchandise Mart forever. Schey's old board, he says, would probably have resisted the risk of restructuring; Buffett waved him ahead."[118]

One week after that Chicago meeting, Scott Fetzer's board approved the sale. The day after the announcement (29 October 1985), *The New York Times* described the attraction of Scott Fetzer as its steady cash generation and its pile of cash. However, said an analyst, it was a 'modest' growth business, but this was compensated for by low volatility.[119] It reported earnings in 1984 of $40.6m ($6.01 a share), a 26% increase from $32.2m, or $4.80 a share, in 1983. Sales in 1984 were $695.4m.

Buffett saw much more than *The New York Times* writers: a set of strong economic franchise moats and strong businesses. He particularly liked World Book as "something special", expressing in his 1985 letter to Berkshire shareholders the attachment that many felt to the books:

> "Charlie and I have a particular interest in the World Book operation because we regard its encyclopedia as something special. I've been a fan (and user) for 25 years, and now have grandchildren consulting the sets just as my children did."

He added that World Book was regularly rated the most useful encyclopedia by teachers, librarians and consumer buying guides, yet it sold for less than any of its major competitors. This combination of exceptional products and modest prices, he said, helped persuade them to pay the price demanded for Scott Fetzer – despite declining results for many companies in the direct-selling industry.

The company as a whole was seen by Buffett and Munger as "understandable, large, well-managed, a good earner… [with many of its businesses] leaders in their fields."[120] Best of all "return on invested capital is good to excellent for most of these businesses."[121]

In January 1986, Berkshire paid $60 per share, or $315.2m after taking account of the spare cash sitting within the company (which could be transferred to Berkshire shortly after acquisition). The fact that Ralph Schey was willing to continue as CEO was crucial to its attraction:

> "When Ralph took charge, the company had 31 businesses, the result of an acquisition spree in the 1960s. He disposed of many that did not fit or had limited profit potential, but his focus on rationalizing the original potpourri was not so intense that he passed by World Book when it became available for purchase in 1978. Ralph's operating and capital-allocation record is superb, and we are delighted to be associated with him."[122]

Who needs a strategy department?

Buffett makes light of his incredible understanding of corporate strategic positioning, and his highly attuned instincts regarding business qualities. "The Scott Fetzer purchase illustrates our somewhat haphazard approach to acquisitions. We have no master strategy, no corporate planners delivering us insights about socioeconomic trends, and no staff to investigate a multitude of ideas presented by promoters and intermediaries. Instead, we simply hope that something sensible comes along – and, when it does, we act."[123]

And yet that approach seems superior – in the right hands – to relying on highly-paid investment bankers to do your thinking for you, as illustrated in Buffett's 1999 letter to shareholders:

> "In 1985, a major investment banking house undertook to sell Scott Fetzer, offering it widely – but with no success. Unfortunately, Scott Fetzer's letter of engagement with the banking firm provided it a $2.5m fee upon sale, even if it had nothing to do with finding the buyer. I guess the lead banker felt he should do something for his payment, so he graciously offered us a copy of the book on Scott Fetzer that his firm had prepared. With his customary tact, Charlie responded: 'I'll pay $2.5m not to read it'."[124]

Berkshire's acquisition strategy, Buffett claimed, was simply to wait for the phone to ring. When it did, it was usually because a manager who had sold to them in the past had recommended to a friend that they think about doing the same.

Great returns

Scott Fetzer is one of Buffett and Munger's greatest ever investments. For only $315.2m, Berkshire Hathaway bought a company producing more than $35.6m after-tax in the first year. And it just kept rising, to more than $56.5m in 1990 and more than $83m in 2002 (see Figure 5.1). After that, we lack publicly available information, but it is reasonable to surmise that it is doing at least as well today despite the slowdown at World Book. You can see a list of Scott Fetzer's companies at the end of the chapter.

I've written 'more than' in the last paragraph because on top of the numbers shown there was a profitable Scott Fetzer Financial Group, a credit company holding both World Book and Kirby receivables; BH included the profits from this unit within a separate subsidiary. Initially, this also included Mutual Savings but was joined by other finance operations as Berkshire bought more companies.

Buffett extracted the numbers for Scott Fetzer's finance operations in 1990 to write that $12.2m pre-tax was made. So, the total 1990 after-tax profit from Scott Fetzer was $56.5m + $8.1m = $64.6m. From other data we can figure that, in the late 1980s, the Scott Fetzer finance operations produced annual after-tax profits of the order of $3–4m; and in the early 1990s $8–10m (see Table 5.1 on next page).

In the chart, Scott Fetzer Manufacturing Group comprises the businesses other than World Book, Kirby and the finance operation. There were no additions or disposals of subsidiaries over these years. In the late 1980s, the companies under Ralph Schey's command were contributing about 40% of Berkshire's non-insurance earnings.

Figure 5.1: Berkshire's share of Scott Fetzer net earnings ($m) after taxes

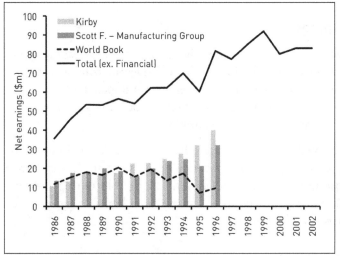

Source: BH annual reports (1986–2002).

World Book's progress

In the 1980s, World Book was a real jewel; unit volume grew 45% between 1982 and 1986. Profits generated for Berkshire were $11.7m in 1986 and rose rapidly to almost double that in 1990. There were four more good years to follow, but then the disruptive technology of the internet with its free information made an increasing impact. At first, the company tried to compete using CD technology, but that was soon superseded. By the mid-1990s, profits were below $10m and since then the company has struggled to find its place in this era of near-infinite information access.

Today, World Book concentrates almost exclusively on selling its 22-volume paper edition to schools and libraries. It also supplies a range of online subscriptions to its encyclopaedias (monthly payments). Its selling pitch – to differentiate it from the general internet – is that the material is accurate, trustworthy and tailored to be age-relevant and grade-relevant. It has also established itself as a general non-fiction book supplier to schools and libraries, with offerings from atlases to colourful animal factbooks for children.

Kirby's progress

Kirby vacuum cleaners are sold as the Cadillac's of the cleaning world, high-performance and lasting for decades. Despite coming at a hefty price, unit sales rose one-third between 1982 and 1986. Profits after-tax in 1986 were an impressive $10.5m, but much better was to come – over the next 11 years they almost quadrupled.

Becoming much more significant to Berkshire than World Book, Kirby sells approximately 500,000 vacuum cleaners a year. This is despite them costing $1,300 or more and still being sold during in-home demonstrations in 50 countries (taking three hours or more – they have persistent salespeople).

Return on capital

The profit numbers for Scott Fetzer are impressive enough, but even more significant are those for return on capital. In 1992, for example, Scott Fetzer was employing only $120.7m of equity capital and yet produced after-tax earnings of more than $70.5m (see Table 5.1). Furthermore, it achieved this with "only minor amounts of borrowed money (except for the debt it employs – appropriately – in its finance subsidiary)."[125] Remarkably, it had reduced both inventory and fixed assets to less than when Berkshire bought it, resulting in more than

100% of its earnings being distributed to Omaha over the seven years to the end of 1992. To do this **and** increase annual profit is spectacular.

Table 5.1: Scott Fetzer net assets, profits and dividends (1986–1994)

$m	Book value (beginning of year)	After-tax income	After-tax profit as a percentage of book value	Dividends to Berkshire Hathaway
1986	172.6	40.3	23%	125.0
1987	87.9	48.6	55%	41.0
1988	95.5	58.0	61%	35.0
1989	118.6	58.5	49%	71.5
1990	105.5	61.3	58%	33.5
1991	133.3	61.4	46%	74.0
1992	120.7	70.5	58%	80.0
1993	111.2	77.5	70%	98.0
1994	90.7	79.3	87%	76.0
TOTAL		555.4		634.0

Source: W. Buffett, letters to BH shareholders (1986–1994). You can gain some insight into the profits from the financial services side of SF from the difference between the earnings numbers in this table and the earlier chart. Finance was making $3–4m after tax in the earlier years, $8–10m in the later years.

Even though Berkshire paid $315.2m to buy Scott Fetzer, the book value of net assets that its managers had to employ was a mere $172.6m, according to the balance sheet that BH absorbed. Despite earning only $40.3m in the first year, Scott Fetzer was able to pay a dividend of $125m by using its surplus cash. This performance was achieved with a balance sheet unflattered by raised debt, nor the result of selling plant then leasing it back, nor by selling receivables ahead of collection from customers. "Throughout our years of ownership, Scott Fetzer has operated as a conservatively-financed and liquid enterprise."[126]

Buffett points out that had Scott Fetzer been included in the Fortune 500 list, as a stand-alone company, its return on equity would have qualified it for fourth place. But that is not the whole story. Those companies ranking above it were emerging from bankruptcy, and most of their so-called earnings were due to debt forgiveness, thus Scott Fetzer would, in fact, have deserved first place among 500 peers.

However, rather than being able to attribute the success of the company to a cyclical peak in earnings, a monopolistic position, or leverage, Buffett was clear that the managerial expertise of CEO Ralph Schey was the key factor:

> "The reasons for Ralph's success are not complicated. Ben Graham taught me 45 years ago that, in investing, it is not necessary to do extraordinary things to get extraordinary results. In later life, I have been surprised to find that this statement holds true in business management as well. What a manager must do is handle the basics well and not get diverted. That's precisely Ralph's formula. He establishes the right goals and never forgets what he set out to do. On the personal side, Ralph is a joy to work with. He's forthright about problems and is self-confident without being self-important."[127]

When considering the return figures in the table, it's important to note that implementing GAAP accounting in 1986, after the acquisition, required Berkshire to switch to *current values* of some assets and liabilities in Scott Fetzer's balance sheet. The value of inventories was increased by $37.3m (they had been distorted by the 'last-in-first-out' method of using up inventory items). Also, fixed assets went up by $68m, and $13m of deferred tax liabilities were eliminated. These, and other, adjustments meant that Scott Fetzer's management was working with around $280m of net tangible assets if measured using values then current. If this number is used as the denominator, rather than $172.6m, the percentage returns on capital fall but are still nevertheless exceptionally high; high enough to pay over $1bn in dividends to Berkshire in the first 15 years of ownership.

How to design a compensation package

An important reason for the exceptionally high returns on capital is that Schey was incentivised, through his compensation deal, to focus on returns on capital rather than total profits. As always, Buffett drew up a simple contract, but it hit the nail on the head when aligning the interests of the manager with those of Berkshire's shareholders.

The first logical step is to ensure that compensation is based on the results at Scott Fetzer rather than those at Berkshire. He wrote in his 1994 letter to BH shareholders:

> "What could make more sense, since he's responsible for one operation but not the other? A cash bonus or a stock option tied to the fortunes of Berkshire would provide totally capricious rewards to Ralph. He could, for example, be hitting home runs at Scott Fetzer while Charlie and I rang up mistakes at Berkshire, thereby negating his efforts many times over. Conversely, why should option profits or bonuses be heaped upon Ralph if good things are occurring in other parts of Berkshire but Scott Fetzer is lagging?"[128]

Second, make sure the rewards are great for great performance. "In setting compensation, we like to hold out the promise of large carrots, and make sure their delivery is tied directly to results in the area that a manager controls."[129]

Third, penalise low rates of return on capital through a charge on use of capital; reward high rates of return and pay a bonus to managers handing over capital to head office:

> "When capital invested in an operation is significant, we both charge managers a high rate for incremental capital they employ, and credit them at an equally high rate for capital they release. The product of this money's-not-free approach is definitely visible at Scott Fetzer. If Ralph can employ incremental funds at good returns, it pays him to do so. His bonus increases when earnings on additional capital exceed a meaningful hurdle charge. But our bonus calculation is symmetrical: if incremental investment yields sub-standard returns, the shortfall is costly to Ralph as well as to Berkshire. The consequence of this two-way arrangement is

that it pays Ralph – and pays him well – to send to Omaha any cash he can't advantageously use in his business."[130]

Following these simple principles, and basing simple one-page contracts on them, Buffett obtained first-class performances from his managers, and allocated capital to best advantage across Berkshire Hathaway.

Other companies take a more complex but less effective approach, as Buffett says:

> "It has become fashionable at public companies to describe almost every compensation plan as aligning the interests of management with those of shareholders. In our book, alignment means being a partner in both directions, not just on the upside. Many 'alignment' plans flunk this basic test, being artful forms of *heads I win, tails you lose.*
>
> A common form of misalignment occurs in the typical stock option arrangement, which does not periodically increase the option price to compensate for the fact that retained earnings are building up the wealth of the company. Indeed, the combination of a ten-year option, a low dividend payout, and compound interest can provide lush gains to a manager who has done no more than tread water in his job…
>
> Our compensation arrangement with Ralph Schey was worked out in about five minutes, immediately upon our purchase of Scott Fetzer and without the 'help' of lawyers or compensation consultants… Our compensation arrangements with the managers of all our other units are similarly simple, though the terms of each agreement vary to fit the economic characteristics of the business at issue."[131]

Owner earnings

In the context of Scott Fetzer, Buffett explained what he meant by owner earnings, which is the best measure of money generated for shareholders, and is the key input to intrinsic value estimation:

(a) reported earnings, plus

(b) depreciation, depletion, amortisation, and certain other non-cash charges, less

(c) the average annual amount of capitalised expenditures for plant and equipment, etc., that the business requires to fully maintain its long-term competitive position and its unit volume. If the business requires additional working capital to maintain its competitive position and unit volume, the increment also should be included in (c).[132]

He hastens to add that this equation will not lead to precise figures, "since (c) must be a guess – and one sometimes very difficult to make". Nevertheless, owner earnings remain the key to establishing valuations for both individual shares and entire companies. He quotes John Maynard Keynes: "I would rather be vaguely right than precisely wrong."[133]

When it comes to Scott Fetzer, Munger and he judged that element (c) was very close to $8.3m which, in this particular case, is exactly the same as the company deducted for 'Depreciation of plant and machinery' in its formal accounts for 1986, i.e. element (b) in the equation. In other words, the using up of capital items (tangible and intangible) roughly matches the expenditure needed on new capital items to maintain unit volume and the quality of the competitive position. Implicitly, they judged that, in this case, there is no need to add to the amount tied up in working capital year on year.

Table 5.2: Buffett's owner earnings estimate for Scott Fetzer (1986)

	$m
Reported earnings	40.2
Plus (b) depreciation, depletion, amortisation, and certain other non-cash charges	+8.3
Minus (c) amount needed to be spent on plant and equipment and incremental working capital the business requires to fully maintain its long-term competitive position and its unit volume	–8.3
OWNER EARNINGS	40.2

Buffett warns that most managers will need to spend more under (c) than is shown under (b) simply to tread water in terms of competitive position and unit volume. In these cases, reported earnings will overstate owner earnings, often substantially so.

See's Candies has different investment needs

Buffett illustrated in his 1986 letter, using See's Candies, the need for thought about expenditure on capital items and incremental working capital. With this company, $0.5m to $1m more per annum is needed to be spent under (c) than is added for depreciation and amortisation under (b), if the firm is to simply hold its ground competitively.

Published cash flow is NOT owner earnings

We must also be suspicious of 'cash flow' numbers produced by companies and analysts. They will routinely include (a) plus (b) but fail to subtract (c).

> "... if all US corporations were to be offered for sale simultaneously through our leading investment bankers, and if the sales brochures describing them were to be believed, governmental projections of national plant and equipment spending would have to be slashed by 90%... To be sure, businesses... may in a given year be able to defer capital spending. But over a five or ten-year period, they must make the investment – or the business decays."[134]

Buffett expresses a cynical view on why these cash flow numbers are promoted by sellers of companies and shares "in attempts to justify the unjustifiable (and thereby to sell what should be the unsalable)."[135] They are useful for spin doctors when reported earnings look inadequate to service junk bond debt, or to justify a foolish share price:

> "The company or investor believing that the debt-servicing ability, or the equity valuation, of an enterprise can be measured by totaling (a) and (b) while ignoring (c), is headed for certain trouble... Accounting numbers... [are] the starting point for us in evaluating our own businesses and those of others. Managers

and owners need to remember, however, that accounting is but an aid to business thinking, never a substitute for it."[136]

Intrinsic value

Intrinsic value is the discounted value of the cash that can be taken out of a business during its remaining life. This number is bound to be highly subjective because the valuer is forced to estimate future owner earnings; the annual sums that can be taken by shareholders without damaging competitive position or unit volume. Estimating the future is never going to be precise; it is going to be fuzzy. Despite this, Buffett urges us to do it as the "only logical way to evaluate the relative attractiveness of investments and businesses."[137]

An education

To help us understand why book value is not intrinsic value, Buffett draws an analogy with a college education: the cost of the education is the book value (ideally, this should include the opportunity cost of attending college, e.g. lost earnings from work).

For intrinsic value, in pure economic terms (where we ignore the aesthetic, social, psychological, etc., benefits of education), we estimate the graduate's lifetime earnings and deduct the amount he/she would have earned without attending college. These annual additional earnings figures are discounted to a present value at an appropriate rate, to give the intrinsic economic value of education.

Some graduates find that book value exceeds the intrinsic value, but in many cases intrinsic value far exceeds book value, confirming a wise allocation of capital at the start of the college course. The most important lesson is that book value is not relevant when it comes to calculating intrinsic value.

Scott Fetzer's intrinsic value

If we want to apply this principle to Scott Fetzer, the key facts are that $315.2m was paid for a business with $172.6m of book value. "The $142.6m premium we handed over indicated our belief that the company's intrinsic value was close to double its book value."[138]

In his 1994 letter, Buffett illustrated the difference by showing declining book value between 1986 and 1994 but rising earnings and dividends (see Table 5.3). Clearly, intrinsic value increased (assuming continued sound strategic positioning and managerial quality and, therefore, good future earnings).

Table 5.3: Contrasting book value and earnings for Scott Fetzer (1986–1994)

$m	Book value (beginning of year)	After-tax income	Dividends to Berkshire Hathaway
1986	172.6	40.3	125.0
1987	87.9	48.6	41.0
1988	95.5	58.0	35.0
1989	118.6	58.5	71.5
1990	105.5	61.3	33.5
1991	133.3	61.4	74.0
1992	120.7	70.5	80.0
1993	111.2	77.5	98.0
1994	90.7	79.3	76.0

Source: W. Buffett, letter to shareholders of BH (1994).

Scott Fetzer had large amounts of excess cash when Berkshire bought it, and so was able to pay its parent company $125m in the first year, $84.8m more than owner earnings.

> "Clearly, the intrinsic value of the business has consistently grown… The difference between Scott Fetzer's intrinsic value and its carrying value [book value] on Berkshire's books is now huge."[139]

An attempt at valuation using owner earnings

Buffett does not provide us with his 1985 estimate of intrinsic value – the discounted value of estimated future owner earnings – in fact, he hasn't published his numbers for any company. Most likely, and I speculate, he thought in terms of a range of values based on his expectation of the following year's owner earnings being $40.2m.

Perhaps he started off being very conservative, and assumed that the $40.2m would not grow over the years. Would he then, he might ask himself, still be content to invest $315.2m?

A perpetual return of 12.8% ($40.2m/$315.2m) per year would still be an OK investment (inflation was under 2% in 1986). We'll take this as our base case and create some other scenarios that Buffett **might** have contemplated.

A modest growth scenario

Buffett may have thought about a more optimistic scenario in which owner earnings grow at, say, the nominal GDP growth rate for the US economy in 1986, i.e. 3.5%, for all future years. This shift in assumption has a large impact on the present value of future owner earnings. The ten-year Treasury bond rate averaged around 7.7% in 1986. If he used this as a discount rate, and assumed 3.5% growth in owner earnings, then the estimate is almost $1bn:

Intrinsic value = next year's owner earnings divided by required rate of return minus growth rate

Intrinsic value = ($40.2m × 1.035)/(0.077 − 0.035) = $991m

(We don't take account of the $84.7m of cash sent to BH because we are comparing with BH's net cost of acquiring Scott Fetzer of $315.2m, i.e., after allowing for the release of cash.)

A scenario using a risk-adjusted discount rate

If we allow for extra risk, because Scott Fetzer shares are riskier than 10-year Treasuries, we can add a *risk premium* to the required rate of return of, say, 7%. Thus, the discount rate is 7.7% + 7% = 14.7%.

The risk premium might have been this high if Buffett was following the finance textbooks of that time (somewhat unlikely, but possible), in which case:

Intrinsic value = ($40.2m × 1.035)/(0.147 − 0.035) = $371m

A fast-growth scenario

Perhaps Buffett tried a scenario in which he anticipated the growth rate on owner earnings to be as it actually turned out over the following nine years, i.e. 8.8% average annual rate (almost doubling owner earnings over nine years).

Intrinsic value = ($40.2m × 1.088)/(0.147 − 0.088) = $741m

Of course, we could go on trying scenarios to build up a picture of what might have happened, e.g. use the average owner earnings over the prior five years, rather than the most recent, to estimate the next year's owner earnings, but the essence of the valuation process has been illustrated.

Whenever undertaking intrinsic value analysis there is one aspect that should always be remembered. Benjamin Graham urged us to allow a good margin of safety, when making a judgement, on the difference between our range of reasoned intrinsic value scenarios and the asking price.

Buffett has not demonstrated the details of his intrinsic value calculations, so we are left to guess how he chose a discount rate, or allowed for growth of earnings in future years. Even Charlie Munger was not privy to the details. He once said, "we have such a fingers-and-toes style about Berkshire Hathaway. Warren always talks about those discounted cashflows [owner earnings] − I've never seen him do one", and Buffett quipped, "There are some things you only do in private."[140]

Buffett is very quick at mental arithmetic and the explanation may lie in the possibility that he can just click off the calculations in his head. A more likely explanation is that it is not necessary to be all that precise − a ball-park figure is all that is required. You can lose yourself in detail and miss the bigger picture. As Buffett says, "If the [value of the company] does not scream out at you, it's too close."[141]

Intrinsic value and capital allocation

Despite the fuzziness, the intrinsic value concept is incredibly important not just for investors but for managers – they must understand it too, as Buffett set out in his 1994 letter:

> "When managers are making capital allocation decisions – including decisions to repurchase shares – it's vital that they act in ways that increase per-share intrinsic value and avoid moves that decrease it. This principle may seem obvious but we constantly see it violated. And, when misallocations occur, shareholders are hurt."

Buffett felt that, when contemplating business mergers and acquisitions, many managers tended to focus on whether the transaction was immediately dilutive or anti-dilutive to earnings per share. This kind of emphasis, he warned, carried great danger. He used the example of a 25-year-old first-year MBA student, considering merging his future economic interests with those of a 25-year-old day labourer. The MBA student, a non-earner, would find that a 'share-for-share' merger of his equity interest in himself with that of the day labourer would significantly enhance his near-term earnings. But that would be mad, as the students potential long-term earnings would be far in excess of those of the labourer.

Berkshire, he said, had rejected many merger and purchase opportunities that would have boosted current and near-term earnings but that would have reduced per-share intrinsic value.

> "Our approach, rather, has been to follow Wayne Gretzky's advice: 'Go to where the puck is going to be, not to where it is.' As a result, our shareholders are now many billions of dollars richer than they would have been if we had used the standard catechism."

At Berkshire, managers looked for ways to deploy their earnings advantageously in their businesses. What's left, they would send to Buffett and Munger to use those funds in ways that built per-share intrinsic value.

The Scott Fetzer businesses

Ralph Schey retired, much to Buffett and Munger's regret, aged 76, in 2000. When he died in 2011, Buffett said, "He was a terrific business person. There wasn't one thing I could have added to the management of Scott Fetzer. What really impressed me was [Schey's] breadth of knowledge about each of the companies. He could have run any or each."[142]

Schey had said of Buffett, "He's a very unique guy, so you just don't find many like him. There are not many guys who are comfortable operating the way he does, or who can affect people the way he does. He makes you want to do well, partly for yourself, but also because you know it will make him proud, and you want to make him proud. And that's a very rare thing."[143]

Table 5.4: The companies within Scott Fetzer

Company	Activity	Number of employees in 2017
Adalet	Explosion-proof and flameproof enclosures; fittings for hazardous and non-hazardous environment markets	164
Altaquip	Repair service for manufacturers of power equipment such as air compressors, generators, paint sprayers, lawn and garden equipment, and chainsaws	166
Campbell Hausfeld (moved from Scott Fetzer to become part of Marmon, another Berkshire subsidiary, in 2015)	America's leading producer of small and medium-sized air compressors	n/a
Carefree of Colorado	Comfort and convenience products for the recreational vehicle and marine industries (e.g. awnings for caravans and motorhomes)	336
Cleveland Wood Products (CWP)	Vacuum cleaner brush rolls, commercial cleaning brushes, floor care products; and sewn bags for vacuum cleaner, food service and military applications	39
Douglas/Quikut/Ginsu	Ginsu knives for the home, gourmet, and professional markets; electric and manual fishing knives	38
France	Electric lighting	95

Company	Activity	Number of employees in 2017
Halex	Fittings for the electrical industry – mostly metal items such as casings	72
Kirby	Vacuum cleaners	344
Stahl	Bodies for trucks, dumps, utility vans and cranes; toolboxes; truck and crane accessories	134
United Consumer Financial Services	Financing for direct sellers' products including home care systems, fire alarm systems, air and water purification systems, cookware, and pet care products	197
Wayne Water Systems	Sump and utility pumps; offers a full line of sewage, well, lawn, pool and pond pumps	101
Western Enterprises	Supplies products for the control, storage and transmission of high-pressure gases to the medical and specialty gas markets	232
World Book	Encyclopaedias, reference sources and digital products for the home and schools	138
Scott Fetzer Financial – absorbed within Berkshire's Finance and Financial Products Business in 1986	Supplies credit to Kirby customers and others	n/a

Company	Activity	Number of employees in 2017
Other Scott Fetzer companies	Arbortech – Manufacturer of chip bodies and utility tree vehicles for line-clearing and tree care	320
	Meriam Process Technologies – Instruments measuring pressure and flow of liquids or gases	
	Powerex Inc. – Compressed air and vacuum systems for medical, laboratory and industrial environments	
	Scot Laboratories – Cleaning products for carpets, floors, autos and homes	
	ScottCare – Telemetric monitoring, diagnostic and rehabilitative systems for cardiovascular patients	
	Scott Fetzer Electrical Group – Electrical power products	
	Wayne Combustion Systems – Oil-fired burners for water heaters, boilers and furnaces; gas burners used in pizza ovens, bakers' ovens, dishwashers and residential gas ranges	

Source: BH annual report (2017).

Learning points

1. **Not all conglomerates are a mess.** Excellent senior managers will be able to handle the complexity.

2. **Being a decent, honourable, intelligent and sensitive owner of businesses gives you an edge in persuading teams of managers/ owners to sell, and subsequently work hard.** Buffett and Munger were a much better prospect than notorious corporate raiders; the latter came with high leverage, ruthlessness, interference and short-term focus.

3. **Owner earnings is the most useful income metric, and discounted owner earnings is the best valuation method for estimating intrinsic value.** Owner earnings are conventional earnings after tax with non-cash items added back, and a deduction for necessary investment in capital items and working capital. 'Necessary' is defined as that needed to fully maintain the business's long-term competitive advantage and its unit volume.

4. **Motivate managers to generate high rates of return on capital.** A simple one-page contract with easy to understand targets for return on capital, and large rewards to managers for achieving high percentages, and penalties for low returns, is required as well as incentives to send surplus capital to the parent for investment elsewhere.

5. **Do the ordinary extraordinarily well.** It is not necessary in investment, or in business, to do extraordinary things to get extraordinary results.

Investment 6

FECHHEIMER BROTHERS

Summary of the deal

Deal	Fechheimer Brothers
Time	1986–today
Price paid	$46.2m
Quantity	84% of the equity
Sale price	Still held
Profit	Not public information, but the cumulative profits attributable to Berkshire exceeded the purchase price after seven years
Berkshire Hathaway in 1986	Share price: $2,440–$3,170 Book value: $2,073m Per share book value: $1,808

The Fechheimer story is unusual because Buffett and Munger chose to buy a controlling stake from private equity sellers who had acquired their shares in a leveraged buyout five years before. These smart cookies cashed-out making a good profit. While there are often good reasons for private equity players to sell – such as raising finance to invest in other high-risk/high-return ventures, or to fulfil obligations to return capital to investors – anyone buying from them always needs to ask two questions. Firstly, why are they willing to part with what they are bound to hawk as a brilliant company? Secondly, have they made the numbers look pretty for the two years prior to the sale by, say, holding back on essential R&D, marketing, management training, etc., and by annoying customers with unjustified price rises, thereby damaging the economic franchise?

To counter these worries Buffett and Munger sought and found reassurance that the business remained strong and that the price being asked was not excessive relative to its earnings power. Yes, this reassurance came partly from the accounting numbers, but more significantly from the character and commitment of the Heldman family who had run the firm since 1941. They possessed the qualities Buffett looked for, i.e. "talented, high-grade, and love what they do."[144] And they still held the remaining 16% of the shares, so director and shareholder alignment of interests was assured.

Advertising works

By 1982, there were thousands of readers of Buffett's annual letters and many of Berkshire Hathaway's shareholders were wealthy business men and women. Collectively, they had a terrific knowledge of businesses across America. Buffett figured that these people might be willing to act as his eyes and ears when it came to finding new businesses worth buying.

So, from 1982, he placed an advertisement in his letters asking shareholders to look out for the following types of opportunity:

- large purchases (at least $5 million of after-tax earnings)

- demonstrated consistent earning power (future projections are of little interest to us, nor are 'turn-around' situations)

- businesses earning good returns on equity while employing little or no debt

- management in place (we can't supply it)

- simple businesses (if there's lots of technology, we won't understand it)

- an offering price (we don't want to waste our time or that of the seller by talking, even preliminarily, about a transaction when price is unknown).

"We will not engage in unfriendly transactions. We can promise complete confidentiality and a very fast answer as to possible interest – customarily within five minutes. Cash purchases are preferred, but we will consider the use of stock when it can be done on the basis described in the previous section [we will not issue shares unless we receive as much intrinsic business value as we give]."[145]

The $5m floor was raised to $10m in 1985, when Berkshire needed to find larger companies to move the dial of Group profits. The lower limit was ratcheted up over subsequent decades – now Buffett speaks of going hunting with an elephant gun because he needs to be buying in the hundreds of millions, if not billions to make much of a difference to a company worth $500bn.

Bob responds

So it was, in January 1986, that long-time Berkshire Hathaway shareholder Robert Heldman, chairman of Fechheimer Brothers, wrote to Buffett explaining that the company in which his family wanted to keep its 16% shareholding met the criteria Buffett had set out. I'm not sure that Buffett was convinced at first because Bob Heldman tells us that he "wrote several times" pointing out his company's virtues before getting a response (Buffett had never heard of it).

They met in Omaha in spring 1986, which gave Heldman a chance to explain the business. Since 1842, it had supplied uniforms to public service organisations and the military. Greatly boosted by the Civil War and the two world wars, by the 1980s it was a trusted supplier of dress uniforms to the US Navy, and it sold to police forces around the country, as well as fire departments, postal and public transport workers. Its uniforms were even precisely specified for baseball umpires.

Fechheimer had a network of three dozen or so company-owned stores as well as arrangements with scores of independent dealers under a variety of trading names. The high street presence provided the opportunity of face to face interaction with customers, building long-term relationships as well as being convenient – something competitors lacked.

Less than half of the merchandise it sold was manufactured at its factories, but that portion was very important because it was a key differentiator:

- First, military and postal uniforms must, by law, be produced in the USA. Also, some police departments have a policy of only buying products produced domestically.

- Second, Fechheimer's manufacturing expertise allows it to find bespoke solutions for customers.

- Third, its Flying Cross brand was recognised and respected in many public service organisations; its logo spoke a heritage of quality and service.

- Fourth, it was the market leader and so had better economies of scale and breadth of offering than competitors.

Any aspiring entrant to this industry would need to spend a considerable amount to build such name recognition and obtain the required operational efficiencies. These barriers to entry suggested some sustainability in its competitive advantages.

Admittedly, there are suppliers of cheaper uniforms but to many they look cheaper, and states, counties and armed forces groups often will not accept anything that looks second-rate and may lack durability.

The deal

Without having visited Fechheimer's offices and plant in Cincinnati, Buffett and Munger agreed to meet Heldman and his team for negotiations in such a small Idaho settlement that it did not have a road in – both sides and their lawyers had to get a plane to Boise and then another, much smaller, plane to take them to Middle Fork on the Snake River.

The deal was completed on 3 June 1986 using only about 2% of Berkshire Hathaway's net worth. About 84% of the stock was purchased for a price that was based upon a $55m valuation for the entire business. The circumstances of the acquisition were similar to those prevailing in the purchase of Nebraska Furniture Mart:

> "... most of the shares were held by people who wished to employ funds elsewhere; family members who enjoyed running their business wanted to continue both as owners and managers; several generations of the family were active in the business, providing management for as far as the eye can see; and the managing family wanted a purchaser who would not re-sell, regardless of price, and who would let the business be run in the future as it had been in the past. Both Fechheimer and NFM were right for us, and we were right for them."[146]

The principal managers were Bob and his brother George Heldman, who by then were in their mid-60s, "spring chickens by our standards" Buffett thought. He likes to keep as many highly competent and trustworthy septuagenarians as possible running his businesses if they had that drive and love of the business he looked for; and besides, Buffett was already 56 and Munger in his early 60s. Bob and George were supported by three members of the next generation of Heldmans – Gary, Roger and Fred – which gave reassurance of continuity.

Buffett's only complaint was the small size of the company relative to Berkshire:

> "As a prototype for acquisitions, Fechheimer has only one drawback: size. We hope our next acquisition is at least several times as large but a carbon copy in all other respects."[147]

What happened after the deal?

Buffett and Munger are strong believers that companies should stay within their circle of competence and not try to stretch themselves by expanding into other product areas. They should also be very careful about trying to replicate success in one geographical area by investing precious money trying to attract customers in other places.

They also like simple-to-understand businesses which occupied a niche subject to little change, be that technological change or social change. Buffett expressed it well in his 1987 letter:

"Severe change and exceptional returns usually don't mix. Most investors, of course, behave as if just the opposite were true. That is, they usually confer the highest price-earnings ratios on exotic-sounding businesses that hold out the promise of feverish change. That prospect lets investors fantasize about future profitability rather than face today's business realities. For such investor-dreamers, any blind date is preferable to one with the girl next door, no matter how desirable she may be."

Experience, however, indicated to Buffett that the best business returns are usually achieved by companies that are doing today pretty much what they were doing five or ten years ago. That was no excuse for managerial complacency; businesses always have opportunities to improve service, product lines, manufacturing techniques, etc. and these opportunities should be seized. Businesses that constantly encounter major change face a higher risk of making errors in strategy.

"Furthermore, economic terrain that is forever shifting violently is ground on which it is difficult to build a fortress-like business franchise. Such a franchise is usually the key to sustained high returns."

Three decades later, uniforms are being made and sold in much the same way. Sure, fabrics and factory machinery might have improved, and the internet has impacted marketing and sales, but the fundamentals are much the same as they were back then.

Buffett points us to evidence outside of Berkshire to support his case that companies which continually improve a straight-forward business – not dashing all over the place in fast-moving markets and technologies – generally perform better. He says that only 25 out of 1,000 companies in a *Fortune* study produced average returns on equity in excess of 20% over the ten years 1977 through 1986, with no year worse than 15%. During that decade, 24 of them outperformed the S&P 500.

These companies were similar in two respects. Firstly, most of them used very little leverage compared to their interest-paying capacity.

Buffett believed that really good businesses usually didn't need to borrow. Secondly, except for one high-tech company, and several others that manufactured ethical drugs, they were businesses that seemed rather mundane. Most sold non-sexy products or services in much the same manner as they did ten years previously (though in larger quantities, or at higher prices, or both). The record of the 25 companies confirmed to Buffett that making the most of an already strong business franchise, or concentrating on a single winning business theme, is what usually produces exceptional economics.

> "Berkshire's experience has been similar. Our managers have produced extraordinary results by doing rather ordinary things – but doing them exceptionally well. Our managers protect their franchises, they control costs, they search for new products and markets that build on their existing strengths and they don't get diverted. They work exceptionally hard at the details of their businesses, and it shows."[148]

He praised the Heldmans for their focus over three generations, consistently building sales and profits:

> "There's nothing magic about the Uniform business; the only magic is in the Heldmans. Bob, George, Gary, Roger and Fred know the business inside and out, and they have fun running it. We are fortunate to be in partnership with them."[149]

Getting Berkshire's money back... and more

We have income data for Fechheimer Brothers for the first ten and half years under Berkshire's ownership – after that the results of this relatively small company were subsumed in a collect-all category. The table shows that it was only seven years before Berkshire had received all that it had paid for its share of Fechheimer. The money was released to Berkshire for Buffett to allocate to investments in other companies.

Table 6.1: The rapid return on investment delivered by Fechheimer to Berkshire

	Berkshire's share of Fechheimer's net earnings (after taxes and minority interests) ($m)
1986 (6 months)	3.8
1987	6.6
1988	7.7
1989	6.8
1990	6.6
1991	6.8
1992	7.3
1993	6.9
1994	7.1
1995	8.8
1996	9.3

Source: W. Buffett, letters to shareholders of BH (1986–1996).

But it's interesting to note the low level of earnings growth. This did not bother Buffett and Munger too much, because they knew that what really counted was return on capital employed rather than fast growth in sales and profits. And Buffett said that Fechheimer's return on invested capital "remains splendid" (1989 letter).

It would seem that capital expenditure and recruitment were put on a tight rein so that Fechheimer invested only where good returns were to be had. For example, it had over 1,000 employees in the 1980s but less than 600 by 2010. Buffett had better uses for that capital.

The Sainted Seven – a lesson in the power of good businesses

In 1987, Buffett dubbed Berkshire's seven largest non-financial businesses the Sainted Seven. They were:

- The Buffalo News

- Fechheimer

- Kirby

- Nebraska Furniture Mart

- Scott Fetzer Manufacturing Group

- See's Candies

- World Book

Leaving aside Berkshire's insurance subsidiaries and its stock market share investments, these seven alone had combined operating earnings of $180m before deduction of interest and taxes. But that wasn't the most exciting aspect – amazingly, this group managed to produce $180m of operating earnings using only $175m of equity. There wasn't much debt, so interest was only a combined $2m, leaving $178m of operating profit.

If they are viewed as a single company, the *after-tax* earnings of that company in 1987 would have been approximately $100m – a return of 57% on equity capital.

To give some idea of how remarkable this is, Buffett notes that *Fortune* compiled data on 1,000 companies (the 500 largest industrials and the 500 largest services companies) and found that only six could manage an average return on equity of over 30% during the decade to 1987. None could get as high as 57%, the best being 40.2%.

Table 6.2: Income of the Sainted Seven

	Pre-tax earnings ($m)	Berkshire's share of net earnings (after taxes and minority interests) plus $2m to allow for minority interests in the earnings of Fechheimer and NFM ($m)	Return (after tax and minority interests) on the $175m of equity capital allocated to these seven in 1987 ($m)
1987	180	100	57%
1988	191	117	67%
1989	195	119	68%
1990	203	123	70%
1991	191	117	67%
1992	218	133	76%
1993	224	136	78%
1994	240	148	85%

Source: W. Buffett, letters to shareholders of BH (1987–1994).

While it is reasonable to assume that, over this period, the amount of capital used by the Sainted Seven did not move far away from the $175m allocated in 1987 (because Buffett generally insisted that earnings from these companies be sent to Berkshire for him to allocate elsewhere), it is also important to remember that $175m is the balance sheet net tangible assets, and not the amount Berkshire paid to acquire the companies. BH, in fact, paid a combined premium to underlying equity capital of $222m.

But, as Buffett says, the managers of these companies should not be judged by the returns they achieve on what Berkshire paid for them, but on the return achieved on the assets they have under their command, i.e. net tangible assets; "what we pay for a business does not affect the amount of capital its manager has to work with" (1987 letter). Buffett marvelled at the wealth-producing power of the Sainted Seven; so little capital was required to run the businesses that they could grow while making almost all of their earnings available for deployment in new opportunities. Much of this success was due to their "truly extraordinary managers". The Blumkins, the Heldmans, Chuck Huggins, Stan Lipsey and Ralph Schey all combined "unusual talent, energy and character to achieve exceptional financial results."

> "For good reasons, we had very high expectations when we joined with these managers. In every case, however, our experience has greatly exceeded those expectations. We have received far more than we deserve, but we are willing to accept such inequities. (We subscribe to the view Jack Benny expressed upon receiving an acting award: 'I don't deserve this, but then, I have arthritis and I don't deserve that either.')"[150]

Of his management style regarding the Sainted Seven, Buffett said he and Charlie's main job is 'applause'. This applause it not that of an indiscriminate Pollyanna, but an informed applause which comes after decades of observing managerial behaviour and business performance.

> "Charlie and I have seen so much of the ordinary in business that we can truly appreciate a virtuoso performance. Only one response to the 1987 performance of our operating managers is appropriate: sustained, deafening applause." (1987 letter)

An example of the extraordinary: at the 1988 gathering of shareholders for the Berkshire Hathaway AGM, Buffett joked that the Heldmans had such a command of the details of their business that when a prisoner entered San Quentin, Bob and George probably knew his shirt size. Throughout the USA, they knew and understood their customers, and knew what was going on in the competition.

A change of guard

It was only two years later that George decided to retire aged 69. Buffett didn't want him to go, but took comfort from the continued attention of Bob, Fred, Gary and Roger Heldman. Buffett said that George was leaving "us with an abundance of managerial talent."[151] But then Bob fell ill and had to leave the company, so Buffett had lost two highly competent managers in short order. Bob's son took over, but as Carol Loomis, a friend and confidant of Buffett, wrote in *Fortune*, he "couldn't cut the mustard and was ousted."[152] There followed a few years with no settled CEO.

In 1997, Patrick Byrne was appointed chief at Fechheimers. He is the son of Jack Byrne of GEICO fame and had experience in insurance – naturally – and a tool-and-die firm. Byrne was once asked what it was like working for Buffett. "It's like drinking from a firehose... one of the highlights of my life to be able to call him up and ask about different business issues... There was a physicist Richard Feynman who died some years ago and another physicist said of him that there are two kinds of geniuses in the world. There's the kind that you and I would be if we were a lot smarter. And there's the kind we'd never be no matter how much smarter we were. They are somewhere off to the side. That's Buffett."[153]

But Byrne departed, in 1999, to take up the CEO position in a small online business, later renamed Overstock.com, in which he held 60% of the shares (bought for $7m). This merchandiser of 'closeout stock' now has a market capitalisation of $420m, and Byrne is still CEO.

In 2000, Buffett felt the need to draft in one of his trusted insurance lieutenants, Brad Kinstler, to take over at Fechheimer Brothers. He quickly put it back on track. Brad stayed until 2006 when he was needed to take over the reins from Chuck Higgins at See's Candies, where he remains to this day. He comments on Buffett's approach:

> "Warren looks at the long-term picture. Because he does not put us in the position of needing to achieve constant revenue and earnings growth in all economic environments, we can shift our attention to the long term... He understands that the road can be bumpy at times. When problems occur, he knows that the best policy is to fix them and move on, but he wants them fixed and not repeated. [The autonomy granted to Berkshire managers] gives us the confidence and passion to manage the business just as if it was ours. Our managers certainly feel that ownership."[154]

Bob Getto took over as President and CEO in 2007 and is still going strong, ably assisted by Fred Heldman, now in his 60s, as senior vice president.

Learning points

1. **Return on capital used in the business is the key metric rather than growth in sales and earnings.** Investors always on the prowl for companies offering growth miss out on some excellent investment bargains in businesses that should not grow much beyond their current size (and should, perhaps, shrink). What matters is how well a business can deploy the incremental dollar of investment in plant, intellectual property, marketing, etc. What is the incremental return on capital?

2. **People make all the difference.** Fechheimer Brothers' competitive advantages gave it some ability to generate good returns, but the crucial element has been excellent managerial talent. As Buffett said in his 1987 letter, "There's nothing magic about the Uniform business; the only magic is in the Heldmans. Bob, George, Gary, Roger and Fred know the business inside and out, and they have fun running it. We are fortunate to be in partnership with them." And of the Sainted Seven he said (1988 letter): "In most cases, the remarkable performance of these units arises partially from an exceptional business franchise; in all cases, an exceptional management is a vital factor. The contribution Charlie and I make is to leave these managers alone."

Investment 7

SALOMON BROTHERS

Summary of the deal

Deal	Salomon Brothers
Time	1987: convertible preferred stock
	1993–1994: common stock
	Held until 1997 (except $140m of preferred redeemed in 1995)
Price paid	$700m for the preferred stock
	$324m for the common stock
Quantity	Maximum total voting power was 20% of Salomon
Sale price	Preferred and common sold for $1.8bn, plus $140m of the preferred redeemed, plus dividends of more than $592m
Profit	$1,508m
Berkshire Hathaway in 1987	Share price: $2,675–$4,250
	Book value: $2,840m
	Per share book value: $2,477

The Salomon Brothers case study is fascinating because it is probably the most significant failure of Warren Buffett's career. That's not to say he didn't make some money on it – so the failure does not lie there. This is a failure of analysis of the culture he bought into. Buffett invested in a sector he had long criticised for its profligate ways; for its socially useless game-playing, and incentives which sometimes sideline integrity. He placed one-quarter of Berkshire's net worth into Salomon, largely on the strength of his assessment of the character of one man. It was presented to Berkshire shareholders as a low-risk deal providing a solid income flow, with the potential to share in the upside should the investment bankers perform well.

In the event, he very nearly lost everything put into it. And it wasn't just money at stake. Buffett's reputation was flying high in the 1980s but, by the early 1990s, because of unethical behaviour at Salomon, he had to step into the breach, scrabbling around trying to save a business he had backed with his name. He had allowed himself to fall into the trap of becoming closely associated with Salomon, only to find pockets of ethical rottenness within its walls. The behaviour of some of its Wall Street traders was, at the very least, highly questionable, and downright illegal at worst. Following public revelation of laxity in control from the top, and venality of its deal makers, Salomon found its business evaporating as clients simply avoided it for fear that it may not survive the scandal.

Buffett and Munger's original intention was to buy securities allowing them to sleep well at night through a period of market turmoil. As it turned out they both lost a great deal of sleep, worrying whether there would be anything left standing the next day.

A gusher of cash but... where to put it?

In the mid-1980s, Berkshire's controlled subsidiaries and security investments were bringing in hundreds of millions of dollars for Buffett and Munger to invest (see Table 7.1).

Table 7.1: Net earnings after taxes attributable to Berkshire Hathaway from operating businesses

	1985 ($m)	1986 ($m)	1987 ($m)
Insurance underwriting	−23.6	−29.9	−20.7
Insurance investment income (dividends and interest)	79.7	96.4	136.7
Realised security gains	325.2	150.9	19.8
The Buffalo News	14.6	16.9	21.3
Fechheimer	-	3.8	6.6
Kirby	-	10.5	12.9
Nebraska Furniture Mart	5.2	7.2	7.6
Scott Fetzer Manufacturing Group	0	13.4	17.6
See's Candies	14.6	15.2	17.4
Wesco – other than Insurance	9.7	5.6	5.0
World Book	-	11.7	15.1
Other	19.9	−4.9	4.3
Interest on debt	−7.3	−12.2	−5.9
Charity donations by BH shareholders	−2.2	−2.2	−3.0
TOTAL EARNINGS	435.8	282.4	234.6

Source: W. Buffett, letters to shareholders of BH (1986-1987).

But there was a problem for any value investor at that time; the stock market had been zooming away. The Dow, a mere 800 in the early 1980s, more than tripled in five years to reach 2,709 in August 1987 (see Figure 7.1).

Figure 7.1: Dow Jones Industrial Average (January 1980–August 1987)

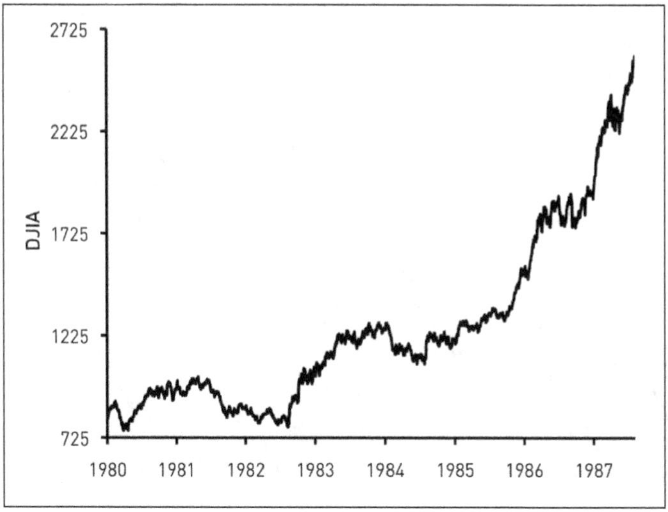

Source: www.advfn.com

Investors had been so pessimistic in 1980 and 1981 that they priced the typical American share at a mere 7–9 times the previous years' earnings. Then, as recession was put behind them, companies and shareholders gradually grew in confidence, and price to earnings (PE) ratios rose to double figures (see Figure 7.2).

Things started to get out of hand in 1986, and more so the following year. By August 1987 US shares were on an average price earnings ratio of over 20, with many stock market darlings on much higher multiples than that.

While Mr Market was busy getting carried away, Buffett and Munger had great difficulty identifying equity investments at sensible prices. In fact, Buffett went so far as to state that during 1986 "we had no new ideas in the marketable securities field."[155] He wistfully reminisced about the days when "we could readily employ large sums in outstanding businesses at very reasonable prices."[156]

Figure 7.2: S&P 500 PE ratio (1980–1990)

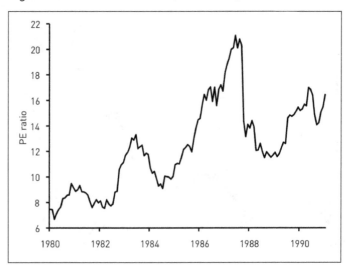

Source: www.macrotrends.net/2577/sp-500-pe-ratio-price-to-earnings-chart

The principal course of action was a boring and frustrating one: "to pay off debt and stockpile funds."[157] In 1986, the insurance companies bought $700m of tax-exempt bonds with maturity dates 8–12 years hence. Buffett was glum, "You might think that this commitment indicates a considerable enthusiasm for such bonds. Unfortunately, that's not so: at best, the bonds are mediocre investments. They simply seemed the least objectionable alternative at the time we bought them, and still seem so. (Currently liking neither stocks nor bonds, I find myself the polar opposite of Mae West as she declared: 'I like only two kinds of men – foreign and domestic')."[158]

When writing this, in February 1987, he couldn't see the outlook getting better so long as widespread enthusiasm for the stock market persisted: "under current stock market conditions, we have little hope of finding equities to buy for our insurance companies."[159]

A manifestation of Buffett's unwillingness to buy common stock in an irritating bull market is shown in Table 7.2 – the number of large equity commitments fell from 11 companies in 1982 to only three in 1987. He had been busy selling down to only the three 'permanent' ones – GEICO, Capital Cities/ABC and The Washington Post – plus a few small arbitrage positions.

The rise in market value of the Permanent Three makes it appear that Buffett was buying during 1987, but the truth is the number of shares held by Berkshire stayed the same (apart from a very small increase in Capital Cities) while the market value of the three holdings jumped from $1,746m, in December 1986, to $2,115m in December 1987. The jump in value the year before is largely accounted for by the $517.5m paid for the holding in Capital Cities.

Table 7.2: Berkshire Hathaway net holdings of marketable equities

	1982	1983	1984	1985	1986	1987
Total number of separately identified companies	11	10	10	7	5	3
Total market value of separately identified companies, ($m)	912	1,288	1,232	1,170	1,838	2,115
Total market value of common stocks, including small investments ($m)	946	1,306	1,269	1,198	1,874	See note.*
Identified company						
Affiliated Publications	✓	✓	✓	✓		
American Broadcasting Companies			✓	✓		
Beatrice				✓		

The Deals of Warren Buffett: Volume 2, The Making of a Billionaire

	1982	1983	1984	1985	1986	1987
Capital Cities/ABC					✓	✓
Crum and Forster	✓					
Exxon			✓			
General Foods	✓	✓	✓			
GEICO	✓	✓	✓	✓	✓	✓
Handy & Harman	✓	✓	✓	✓	✓	
Interpublic	✓	✓	✓			
Lear-Siegler					✓	
Media General	✓	✓				
Northwest Ind.			✓			
Ogilvy & Mather	✓	✓				
R. J. Reynolds	✓	✓				
Time	✓	✓	✓	✓		
The Washington Post	✓	✓	✓	✓	✓	✓

Source: W. Buffett, letters to shareholders of BH (1982–1987).

* Buffett wrote: "At yearend 1987 we had no major common stock investments (that is, over $50m) other than those we consider permanent or arbitrage holdings." (1987 letter)

Stick to principles through thick and thin

Ever since he was a 19-year-old student of Benjamin Graham (1950–1951), Buffett knew he would have to accept long periods when it didn't make sense to buy, years when Mr Market is full of vim and irrationality. By the same token, he knew that exuberance would eventually pass and opportunities to buy at reasonable prices would appear again. In the meantime, iron discipline was required not to submit to the urge to *do something*. Sir James Mackintosh (and Winston Churchill) had a term for it: "masterly inactivity". That does not mean doing nothing. Charlie Munger advises four actions are required of investors:

1. Preparation

2. Discipline

3. Patience

4. Decisiveness

The actual act of buying or selling shares/companies – the **decisiveness** element – is less than one-quarter of what is required. Before that there is weeks of hard **preparation.** For example, examining company after company to find one or two gems per year. Peter Lynch refers to this as looking for grubs under rocks: "If you turn over 10 rocks, you'll likely find one grub; if you turn over 20 rocks, you'll find two."[160] In 1986–1987, Buffett and Munger were looking under hundreds of rocks, but not finding *any* grubs. Still, the work had to go on. The act of looking is valuable in itself: even if a good company is over-priced at the time of analysis, and therefore not a good investment, perhaps it's worth continuing to follow its progress in the hope that the price will one day fall to a reasonable level, one with intrinsic value above market price by a comfortable margin of safety.

Discipline is required to stick to a sound investment philosophy. This is especially hard when people around you are making seemingly easy profits, despite being ill-informed speculators jumping on the latest craze. Your mind starts to waver: should you join with them, going with what is currently in vogue?

Months, even years, go by when following intelligent investment principles means that you underperform, or simply can't invest. These moments call for a great deal of **patience**; waiting for the tide to turn.

Munger also advises us to "commit more time to learning and thinking than doing" and "the only way to win is to work, work, work, work, and hope to have a few insights." You can see why Buffett regards Munger as a great help for staying on the straight and narrow path.

With this intellectual grounding, Buffett's attitude to the situation he found himself in was that his turn to bat would come again. But, that spring, Buffett and Munger could see little of value in the markets. Buffett told shareholders that they had no idea when markets would change, but change they would. The two diseases of *fear* and *greed* would forever break out in the investment community. The timing of these epidemics would be unpredictable, as would the magnitude of the market aberrations they caused. Therefore, they weren't going to try and predict when they might happen.

> "Our goal is more modest: we simply attempt to be fearful when others are greedy and to be greedy only when others are fearful."[161]

So where did he put the money?

A great deal of the Berkshire cash flow went into long-term bonds which, although often earning over 10% per year in interest, were a worry because Buffett feared inflation might go to double figures – causing bond prices to fall.

He was also interested in short-term arbitrage purchases of equities. These were usually during corporate events such as following a takeover/merger bid. "We restrict ourselves to large deals that have been announced publicly and do not bet on the outcome. Therefore, our potential profits are apt to be small; but, with luck, our disappointments will also be few."[162] The Lear-Siegler investment shown in Table 7.2 above is an example of one of these temporary holdings.

> "Arbitrage is an alternative to Treasury Bills as a short-term parking place for money – a choice that combines potentially higher returns with higher risks. To date, our returns from the funds committed to arbitrage have been many times higher than they would have

been had we left those funds in Treasury Bills. Nonetheless, one bad experience could change the scorecard markedly."[163]

An investment instrument which offers the prospect of debt-like returns if the company does not perform as expected, but also has the possibility of participating in its success, is the convertible preferred stock. When the Salomon investment opportunity arose, Buffett insisted that he would not buy common stock – that would be too risky given the nature of the business – but he would buy preferred shares on an exceptionally high fixed dividend. This deal was the start of a pattern of investing in preferred stocks.

Salomon in 1987

Salomon (Brothers or Inc) was a creature of, and helped create, modern Wall Street. Indeed, so typical of the breed, and so dominant did it become in the 1980s, that if Hollywood had wanted a model of a hard-bitten, tough-trading scene, with floors of Masters-of-the-Universe, take-no-prisoners dealmakers then Salomon was the place to go.

It had always been a dealmaker, but the early days were much more about steadily building long-term relationships and a reputation for integrity. Before the first world war, it had a modest business arranging loans for Wall Street securities brokers, and dealing in bonds for financial institutions. Its big break came during the war when the government invited Salomon to market some of the large number of bonds it was selling.

Its corporate bond underwriting business was expanded aggressively in the 1960s, as it gained a name for taking significant risks upon itself to ensure companies walked away with the promised cash. One example of extreme risk was the underwriting of $76m of convertible preferred stock for a small insurance company in 1976. This company was GEICO. Eight Wall Street institutions had already turned the company away, thinking it was destined for complete failure (see Investment 1). Buffett admired the way that John Gutfreund (pronounced good-friend), then second-in-command at Salomon, was willing to put the firm's reputation and money on the line to guarantee that GEICO got the full $76m – even though no other bank would take a part of the deal. In the end, Berkshire offered to take the whole lot, but that wasn't necessary, because the backing of both Buffett and Salomon reassured other investors and they piled in. Berkshire ended up with only 25%.

Growing in confidence, in the 1970s Salomon developed its merger and acquisitions wing, and opened in London and Hong Kong. When John Gutfreund took over as CEO in 1978, Salomon was already the second largest underwriter, and largest private brokerage house, in the US. It grew in new directions, e.g. earning a reputation as an enthusiastic participant in the leveraged buyout craze of the 1980s. It was also a pioneer in selling mortgage-backed securities – buying home mortgages from thrifts[164] and repackaging them into bonds tradeable on Wall Street.

By 1987, it offered a wide range of investment banking services, from market-making in corporate bonds and trading foreign exchange, to mergers advice and equity fund raising. Standing atop this giant, John Gutfreund had become the 'King of Wall Street', according to the cover of *BusinessWeek*.[165]

The deal

Buffett and Gutfreund developed a friendship while working together on the GEICO deal. In the years that followed, they regularly discussed pressing issues on the telephone and in person; even the head of an investment bank needs someone he can trust to quickly grasp an issue and talk through ideas. Buffett observed the way that Gutfreund would advise client companies to take actions that were in their best interests, rather than prioritising the fees that Salomon might earn if another course was taken. Gutfreund might have had a Wall Street reputation for being a domineering hardcase, but Buffett perceived a degree of honesty, energy and competence that he liked; and, perhaps, to run an investment bank full of aggressive egos, pulling in various directions, you needed someone capable of cajoling and swearing with the best of them to gain some order.

In mid-1987, Minorco –the overseas investment arm of Anglo American and De Beers group of South Africa – made it plain to John Gutfreund that they wanted to sell their 14% ($700m) shareholding in Salomon.

They hawked it round Wall Street until the aggressive corporate raider Ron Perelman showed an interest. Perelman said that, if he bought the 14%, he would demand two seats on Salomon's board. This put fear into Gutfreund and his executives, and the King of Wall Street decided to ask his old confidant, Warren Buffett, if he would act as a white squire, i.e. a large shareholder friendly to the managers. The plan was that Buffett would inject money into Salomon, which could then buy-in its own shares from Minorco, thus making it difficult for Perelman to gain a large stake.

Buffett regarded Salomon's common stock as far too risky for Berkshire but, nevertheless, wanted to enjoy at least some of the benefit should the bank perform well over the following few years. He thus agreed to buy preferred stock which permitted him to convert into common stock starting three years after the deal, i.e. October 1990 (potentially amounting to 12% of Salomon's common stock). Until converted, the preferreds gave a generous 9% yield. On $700m, that meant sending Berkshire an annual income of $63m.

Overall, he estimated that Berkshire could obtain a satisfactory 15% return per year on the assumption that the common stock rose from the low $30s to more like $50–$60 over the years. If it turned out that the common stock did not rise above the convertible price of $38, Berkshire could always hold on and collect preferred dividends; the company had agreed it would buy back the $700m of preferreds over the five years between 31 October 1995 and 30 October 2000 ($140m per year).[166]

Buffett expressed his inability to predict future profits for Salomon, and so the reason for selecting convertible preferred rather than the common stock, in his 1987 letter to shareholders:

"We, of course, have no special insights regarding the direction or future profitability of investment banking. By their nature, the economics of this industry are far less predictable than those of most other industries in which we have major commitments. This unpredictability is one of the reasons why our participation is in the form of a convertible preferred."[167]

He held firmly to the view he expressed in his *Washington Post* article a few months before,[168] that Wall Street was a "get rich in a hurry" place, where bright graduates encourage clients to be wastefully hyperactive:

> "The Street's income depends on how often prescriptions are changed, not upon the efficacy of the medicine. But what's good for the croupier, taking his bite out of each transaction, is poison for the patron. Turning from investor into speculator, he suffers the same kind of negative financial effects that befall the person who is converted from making a once-a-year bet on the Kentucky Derby to betting all races, every day. Wall Street likes to characterize the proliferation of frenzied financial games as a sophisticated, pro-social activity, facilitating the fine-tuning of a complex economy... It has always been a fantasy of mine that a boatload of 25 brokers would be shipwrecked and struggle to an island from which there could be no rescue. Faced with developing an economy that would maximize their consumption and pleasure, would they, I wonder, assign 20 of their number to produce food, clothing, shelter, etc., while setting five to endlessly trading options on the future output of the 20?"

Gutfreund's fear of Wall Street's corporate raiders was so great that, not only did he grant an outstandingly generous yield for the convertible preferred stock – and allowed the conversion price to be merely a few percent higher than the prevailing common stock price – but he granted two board places, one for Buffett and one for Munger. There was some grumbling within Salomon and its shareholder body that Buffett was being treated in a very special way, but Gutfreund was adamant that it was worth it to gain Buffett's protection from all those marauding corporate raiders fuelled by junk bonds.

In deciding to part with one-quarter of Berkshire's net asset value – the largest investment made to that point – Buffett put a great deal of weight on his assessment of John Gutfreund's character:

> "Charlie and I like, admire and trust John. We first got to know him in 1976, when he played a key role in GEICO's escape from near-bankruptcy. Several times since, we have seen John steer clients away from transactions that would have been unwise,

but that the client clearly wanted to make – even though his advice provided no fee to Salomon and acquiescence would have delivered a large fee. Such service-above-self behavior is far from automatic in Wall Street."[169]

The crash of October 1987

Buffett had a front row seat to observe the stock market crash of October 1987 following his purchase of Salomon preferred a month before. Prior to the crash, he had been told by earnest mathophiles at Salomon that they had got the 'science' of investment sussed. They could see from analysing market movements and a raft of macro and company stock trading data where to place their bets. They had computer programmes selecting shares. And to protect the downside they wrote code instructing computers to automatically sell shares and futures contracts in shares if the market fell by more than a set percentage. Thus, they thought themselves insulated from any downturn.

Figure 7.3: The Dow Jones Industrial Average (August 1987–January 1988)

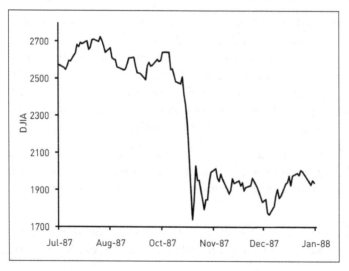

But Buffett and Munger had seen this kind of over-confidence before. These people were not engaged in investment, as defined by Benjamin Graham, at all. That is:

(a) a thorough understanding of the company

(b) a margin of safety

(c) the expectation of merely reasonable returns.

It was the opposite: that shudder-making activity, *speculation*. We can see a result of that speculation in Figure 7.3. In just a few days the market fell 36% from its peak.

Buffett was scolding

Buffett blamed so-called 'professional' investors, those managing many billions of assets, for the crash. He railed against their short-termism. Instead of focusing on the quality of the businesses they invested in, many prestigious money managers now focused on what they expected other money managers to do in the days ahead. For them, stocks had become tokens in a game.

Buffett railed against *portfolio insurance*, a money-management strategy embraced in 1986–1987. This approach dictated that ever-increasing portions of a stock portfolio be sold off as prices declined (similar to a small speculator's stop-loss strategy). Price movement was the only factor that mattered; a down-tick of a given size would trigger a sell order. According to the Brady Report, $60bn to $90bn of equities were poised on this hair trigger in mid-October of 1987.

So, the lower a company's price, the more vigorously it would be sold. The logical, but mad, corollary to this, Buffett declared, was that these shares should be repurchased once the prices had rebounded significantly.

In markets that behaved in such an erratic manner, many commentators concluded that small investors had little chance of success. Not Buffett:

> "This conclusion is dead wrong. Such markets are ideal for any investor – small or large – so long as he sticks to his investment knitting. Volatility caused by money managers who speculate

irrationally with huge sums, will offer the true investor more chances to make intelligent investment moves. He can be hurt by such volatility only if he is forced, by either financial or psychological pressures, to sell at untoward times."[170]

The 1929 decline in the stock market and many other crashes were followed by severe economic events. But the 1987 plunge was distinct, weird even, in that the real economy carried on much as before. See's candy still sold in great volume, and the number of Kirby vacuum cleaners purchased was unchanged. This crash seemed to be almost purely a financial bubble, as reflected in Berkshire Hathaway's share price movements, starting the year slightly under $3,000 and ending it only slightly above that. But this was after the rollercoaster ride, up by over 40% at one point – a remarkably similar pattern to the market as a whole.

Figure 7.4: Berkshire Hathaway share price (1987)

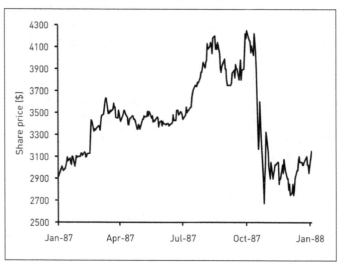

Source: www.finance.yahoo.com

Ignoring Buffett and Munger

While the Wall Street shenanigans of 1987 made little impact on the real economy, they did create winners and losers on Wall Street; and Salomon, being an aggressive player in many risky areas, was affected more than most. It managed to lose $75m after-tax in the month of October. For the year, profits were down around 80% on their peak level of $557m, recorded in 1985. In January 1988, Gutfreund announced he was to take no bonus for 1987. However, he didn't want to be completely empty-handed: he would instead receive 300,000 options for Salomon's stock excisable at $18.125, the then market price – quite a fall from over $30 only weeks before. If the share price rose to $38.125 those options would have intrinsic value of $6m.

Despite the serious errors under his leadership, he remained at the helm in 1988. "John Gutfreund stands out as an imposing figure. Supremely self-confident, intellectual, ferociously competitive, he is a throwback to the days on Wall Street when partnerships reigned and the personality of one man could dominate a firm. 'There are a lot of people here, I mean senior people, who measure their day by whether John smiles at them,' says one senior executive."[171]

In his determination to restore profits, Gutfreund elected to sack 800 people (out of 6,800), in the process closing down those divisions helping state/city authorities sell bonds, and the division which arranged commercial paper sales for corporations (borrowing of a few days or a few weeks).

How can this be going on?

The newly-installed board directors, Buffett and Munger, were astonished. Following a year when profits plunged, along with the share price, the response of the senior management team was to drop the price hurdle set for staff stock options to become valuable – making it easier for them to earn fat bonuses at a time when shareholders had suffered a great deal. Naturally, Buffett and Munger argued against the practice; it was morally wrong. But the Wall Street culture led to a shrug of the shoulders in response to their remonstrations, and the two out-of-towners were ignored.

Without being specific, Buffett says that there were many other things about Salomon that troubled him, "One thing after another would come up that I thought was nutty, but they didn't want me to say anything."[172] Resigning from the board was difficult because it would send a negative signal to the market and probably drive down the shares, thus imposing a cost on Berkshire shareholders. And besides, he still admired and trusted Gutfreund.

In the late 1980s, while Gutfreund *appeared* powerful, Salomon became increasingly fragmented into fiefdoms ruled over by domineering, often buccaneering, characters. Gutfreund was losing control to his earls and barons. He tried to cut poorly performing areas, but when he did so the talent he wanted to keep would often move to competitors. Warlords within the firm would threaten to leave in order to lever from Gutfreund larger bonuses for their team, and yet more autonomy. Gutfreund increasingly acquiesced.

A great mass of opaque derivative deals were accumulated by various chiefs. It was very difficult to establish realistic values for these positions because most were not traded on exchanges, and so mathematical models had to be devised to estimate value based on variables such as standard deviation of movements of the underlying over, say, the previous two years. Remarkably, the very people who carried out these calculations, using rather malleable models, were the people who had set up the derivative deals in the first place, and who could look forward to a large bonus if the model showed an increase in value from one period to the next. Charlie Munger, as a member of the audit committee, protested, but was able to change very little. Salomon's common stock price went nowhere for years, as bonuses jumped. Some kingpins received over $20m in a single year; over 100 traders made more than $1m in annual bonus.

Always in need of credit

While focused on their bonuses, and therefore intent on growing deal volume, the mini-kings of Salomon created a frightening vulnerability for the firm. There was an increasing tendency to finance the purchase of financial assets (bonds, equities, interest rate derivative positions, etc.) through the selling of pieces of paper which stated such things as "in seven days from the date of issue this will be redeemed by Salomon paying $1bn". What was handed over by the lender to Salomon at the outset was slightly less than $1bn, thus providing the purchaser of this commercial paper with an effective interest rate.

This habit was all well and good:

1. if the sums involved were small relative to the net value of the firm, but Salomon had net assets of roughly $3–4bn holding up liabilities headed above $100bn

2. if Salomon did use the money to buy relatively illiquid assets with the raised funds, then confidence in the commercial paper market was maintained, allowing it to regularly roll-over its short term debt. But if, in seven days, no one wanted to replace the $1bn lent by way of commercial paper, Salomon may be forced to sell long-term assets to redeem the $1bn; to do so in a hurry may result in low prices being received.

The near-death of Salomon

In summer 1991, the common stock price almost touched the $38 level, at which it made sense to convert the preferred shares into common ones. It looked like Buffett was finally going to achieve returns greater than the mere fall-back level of 9%, as he enjoyed the rising value of equity-kicker from conversion.

But then, calamity! On Thursday 8 August, Buffett was beside Lake Tahoe, Nevada when he received a message that Gutfreund urgently needed to speak with him. The call was set for that evening when Gutfreund, flying in from London, was expected at Salomon's lawyer's offices. Perhaps it was good news, Buffett thought. Perhaps Salomon was to be sold and Berkshire could walk away with a fine profit?

But the news was appalling. Paul Mozer, Salomon's managing director responsible for bidding for government Treasury securities, had broken the rules repeatedly. To be a **primary dealer** in government notes/bonds was a great privilege; it meant that Salomon was one of the chosen few who could offer to buy securities on its own behalf, or on behalf of other investors, in great volume. These securities could then be sold on to the ultimate investors, after Salomon had taken a cut. It was a position of trust.

Because there were so few primary dealers, it was possible for one or a group of them to corner the market by buying up all or most of an issue and then, say, push secondary market prices up by squeezing the supply coming onto the open market. In response to this incentive, the US Treasury introduced a rule that no primary dealer was permitted to buy more than 35% of an auction. That way there would be a spread of buyers and a healthy after-market.

Paul Mozer chose to get around the rule by openly bidding for the maximum 35% on Salomon's behalf, then, without asking them, bidding for more bonds on behalf of some Salomon customers. These securities were then swiftly transferred from the client's account to Salomon's account, with its clients having no idea that their accounts had been used in this way. Having a very large proportion of the bonds, Mozer was then able to manipulate the market to achieve higher prices from keen buyers unable to pick up their desired bonds from competing dealers.

The cover-up is worse

Buffett, standing at a payphone in Nevada, was informed that Mozer had been suspended and a press release was to go out soon. As so often in cases of breach of trust and scandal, it is not the original act that is the most damaging. Salomon might have got away with blaming the illegal act on a rogue trader, paid a fine, lost some business, but otherwise survive. But it compounded the crime by not being open with the government and the regulators about what the bosses knew, and when they knew it.

Four months before that August phone call, Mozer had told his immediate boss what he had done (only after getting an angry letter from the Treasury). His boss took it up the chain of command to Gutfreund and other senior people. They concluded that, to maintain trust with the Treasury and the financial watchdogs, they must tell the New York Federal Reserve Board. But then, nothing. They procrastinated for four months. And, of course, they had denied most of the directors on the board of Salomon any knowledge of the infraction. And, in May, Mozer had done it again, buying the vast majority of the auction.

Instead of owning up to hiding the truth for four months, in the 9 August press release, Gutfreund and his executive team chose to ignore the point. Munger, the lawyer, was furious. He was told that if they dared to go for full disclosure of their previous obfuscatory behaviour, then the firm might lose both the confidence of the authorities, and the confidence of those it borrows money from, most notably all those buyers of short-term commercial paper. Billions of dollars could flow out from Salomon in days with no way of replacing it, as lenders ran scared that Salomon would be the subject of crippling sanctions from the regulators – including losing the right to bid in the important Treasury auctions which gave Salomon a mark of respectability, and a source of profits. They thought they could get away with telling the authorities, privately, that they had messed up by not confessing to them earlier; and avoid alerting nervous lenders and derivative counterparties by omitting this element from the press release.

On 14 August, the board of Salomon met via telephone and insisted that the firm publicly confess to the cover-up. This went ahead, but by then Gutfreund had erred again. The day before the meeting he had received a letter from the Federal Reserve Bank of New York stating that Salomon's 'continuing business relationship' with the Federal Reserve was now called into question because of the failure to disclose Mozer's behaviour, and the executive directors' knowledge of it, earlier in the year. It gave Salomon ten days to write a comprehensive report setting out all they knew. The regulator, quite rightly, expected the letter to be passed on to all the directors so they could respond; one action might be the sacking of senior executives. But Gutfreund chose to keep the Fed's letter from the other board members.

The directors, kept in the dark, did not act as the regulator, Gerald Corrigan, expected. He took this to be an act of arrogance and defiance. Buffett later said, "Understandably, the Fed felt at this point that the directors had joined with management in spitting in its face."[173] Now, the enraged officials were going to come down on Salomon like a ton of bricks.

Salomon's shares fell to under $27 after the more detailed 14 August press release was sent out. But this was just the start. Confidence among creditors was being badly eroded by both the formal announcements and the rumours. By that summer, Salomon had something like $150bn of liabilities – mostly short-term loans in the form of commercial paper and medium-term notes. The slightest scent of trouble and these lenders stopped answering calls, instead placing their money somewhere else. They started a run on the bank.

Salomon acted as market-maker for the debt issued by many firms, including its own. Usually, few trades would take place in Salomon's notes but, on 15 August, there was an avalanche of sell orders. At first the market-makers coped by lowering the prices at which they would buy but, in the end, they were forced to do something that sent a very worrying signal: they refused to trade. Now, the buyers of Salomon's debt were very nervous because there was no one left who would buy their supposedly 'tradeable' assets (all the other market-makers had also ceased dealing).

Buffett and Munger to the rescue

At 6.45 am the next day, Gutfreund phoned Buffett at home in Omaha and told him he was going to resign. An hour or so later, once Buffett had reached his office in Kiewit Plaza, they had another conversation in which they agreed that Buffett would step into the breach to try and sort things out.

According to his close friend, *Fortune* writer and pro bono editor of Buffett's shareholder letters for 40 years, Carol Loomis, his motives for accepting the extraordinarily difficult job of rescuing Salomon were: first, he wanted to save the $700m Berkshire had put into it, but he also felt, as a director of a company in trouble, a responsibility to help its shareholders as best he could. He glanced around for another candidate, but it was very apparent that he was the logical person. Buffett half-jokingly told Berkshire shareholders, in his letter that year, that his job at Berkshire was not so onerous and therefore he could slip away to New York:

> "Berkshire's operating managers are so outstanding that I knew I could materially reduce the time I was spending at the company and yet remain confident that its economic progress would not skip a beat… My job is merely to treat them right and to allocate

the capital they generate. Neither function is impeded by my work at Salomon. You should note, however, the 'interim' in my Salomon title. Berkshire is my first love and one that will never fade: at the Harvard Business School last year, a student asked me when I planned to retire and I replied, 'About five to ten years after I die.'"[174]

How to choose a manager

The key task for Buffett on that fateful August Friday was to regain the trust of the regulators. To start with, this meant that he should wait in Omaha for a phone call from Gerald Corrigan, president of the Federal Reserve Bank of New York. When it finally came, Corrigan mentioned – assuming Buffett and the other directors knew – that he had required an honest account of what had happened. Buffett was nonplussed: what request had been made? When they met in New York that evening, Corrigan was not in a mood to be cordial, and warned Buffett to be ready for "any eventuality", which is very threatening language for a regulator as it might mean withdrawal of permissions to conduct business.

On the Saturday, Buffett had the task of finding a new chief. He devised a simple but clever plan for this. The top 12 executives in the firm were invited to speak with Buffett individually for 10–15 minutes each. The key question Buffett asked was who they thought should become their boss. Their vote was overwhelmingly for the Brit, Deryck Maughan, who had been head of the Tokyo office – far from the Wall Street shambles. He was regarded as a man of high integrity and competence; and had the advantage of not coming from the sullied trading side of Salomon, being a corporate financier accustomed to developing long-term business relationships based on trustworthiness.

Buffett later recounted his thinking, in a talk to Columbia business students:

> "Whoever went into the foxhole with me could stick a gun to my head. If they wanted to come around and say they got an offer from Goldman Sachs or something, for twice as much money as they were making, or wanted special personal indemnification because of lawsuits – a million things could happen with some people."[175]

He posed them a question: say they won a lottery and the prize was to pick a classmate, 10% of whose income they would recieve for life. Who would they choose? He ventured that they would eventually choose someone they knew they could depend on, whose ego would not get in the way of their career prospects, who was happy to give others the credit for good ideas, and who was consistently good rather than erratically brilliant. He then said that each student in front of him could choose to adopt these voluntary items of character – most of it is habit. And went on to say:

> "Deryck Maughan simply behaves well... He doesn't give up his independence or his ability to think independently or any of those qualities whatsoever. ... Deryck, two or three months after he took the job, had never asked me how much he got paid, let alone had a lawyer around negotiating for him... [he] had one thought in mind, and that was keeping the place initially together, and then building a business that fits his image of what he wanted it to be... He was working 18-hour days. He could have been making more money someplace else... Pick the kind of person to work for you, that you want to marry your son or daughter. You won't go wrong."[176]

The Saturday *New York Times* reported Buffett's appointment to chair of Salomon, referring to his reputation for "brilliant investing and a caustic attitude to the foibles of Wall Street... by turning to Mr. Buffett, whose years of investing have won him a reputation as a 'Mr. Clean' on Wall Street, Salomon signalled the gravity of the unfolding scandal and the threat to its reputation."

Mr Buffett told the directors that he would be very open as he worked to straighten out the firm's status and its reputation for staying just within the bounds of the rules. The perception that a leading force in that market was not honest could damage the credibility of American markets worldwide. " 'The way our business operates is because everybody is completely honest,' a senior Wall Street executive with a background in the Treasury securities markets said. 'You transfer billions of dollars on a phone call, my word to your word. And these people lied.' "[177]

No rest on Sunday

At 10 am on Sunday, the Treasury phoned to say that in a few minutes it would announce that Salomon would no longer be allowed to bid in Treasury auctions, either for its own account or for clients. This would kill the entire corporation. The direct impact was slight because, by then, Salomon was making money in many areas of finance beyond trading in government debt. What really mattered was the perception of the rest of the financial world: Salomon was now regarded as *persona non grata* by the Treasury. If the Treasury wouldn't deal with Salomon, why should anyone else? When the Japanese market opened, late afternoon New York time, Salomon's securities would be slaughtered as lenders/investors ran for the door.

There was no time to lose that Sunday morning. The board had to decide whether to opt for liquidation of assets followed by bankruptcy, thereby spreading the impact of its failure between creditors, after losing everything for common and preferred stockholders.

But there was a slim hope before complete resignation to liquidation – to attempt to persuade the Treasury to rescind or amend the prohibition. While a bankruptcy plan was being worked on, Buffett phoned the Treasury and the chairman of the Federal Reserve, Alan Greenspan. Eventually, the secretary of the Treasury returned Buffett's call (from the horse races). Fortunately for Buffett, the two men knew each other. Nicholas Brady was nephew to Malcolm Chace, a member of the family which had sold Berkshire Fine Spinning to Hathaway Manufacturing. Brady's Harvard Business School MBA thesis on Berkshire (1954) drew such a negative conclusion that he sold his shares. Buffett and Brady had encountered each other over the years and formed a friendship.

By this time, the emotional strain was beginning to tell, and Buffett's voice was cracking as he implored Brady to withdraw the ban. He added that the company was already preparing for bankruptcy and, because of its enormous size and the intertwining of Wall Street's financial obligations, Salomon's failure would bring down many other financial institutions. This would not only be enormously damaging to Wall Street but to the whole financial world, because Salomon had obligations in all the major financial centres.

Brady took some persuading – many phone conversations with Buffett and many consultations with other government and regulatory leaders – but, finally, at 2.30pm, Jerome Powell, assistant secretary of the Treasury (now chairman of the Federal Reserve) phoned Buffett to say that an announcement was going out that Salomon was to be permitted to bid in auctions on its own account but not on customers' accounts. This sent a message that the Treasury thought Salomon was sound, even if it had elements that had behaved badly. The regulators had put a significant amount of weight on the character of Warren Buffett and his commitment to right the ship.

The board quickly formally voted through Buffett's appointment as chairman, and Deryck Maughan as a director and head of operations. These two went down to a packed press conference, a few minutes later, and for more than two hours answered questions. "How will you handle needing to be both here and in Omaha?" a reporter asked. "My mother has sewn my name in my underwear, so it'll be okay." When asked about Salomon's culture, he said that some people might call it macho or cavalier and "I don't think the same things would have happened in a monastery."

It worked. Monday's trading in Salomon's securities was reasonably well-ordered. The months that followed were tough, but Maughan's leadership resulted in a significant reduction in the number of financial instrument exposures it had, and therefore the amount it needed to borrow.

A slow rebuilding

The regulator's fine, when it eventually came, was a relatively light $190m plus a $100m restitution fund. Importantly, there were no criminal charges. The fine had been lowered because of the exceptional level of cooperation Buffett offered, and the credibility of his word on better behaviour in the future.

At first, Buffett spent several days each week in New York (being paid a grand total of $1 pa), worried about what would emerge from the woodwork next to threaten the bank's existence – yet another government agency investigation, yet another customer lost, yet another press hammering as reporters discovered more about the wrongdoing? He sacrificed a lot of sleep in this period, and the common stock fell to not much over $20. He had to do something about the attitude employees had regarding the allocation of profits to shareholders. At a time when returns on capital were poor, the bankers still thought they could take away three-quarters of the profits in bonuses, leaving the scraps for shareholders. Apart from his day-to-day attempts to reset the culture, he delivered a public admonishment, combined with a statement of how a good compensation scheme works, by reproducing Salomon's third-quarter report in two-page advertisements in *The Financial Times, The New York Times*, the *Wall Street Journal* and *The Washington Post*. The key element was his letter – note his willingness to lose staff who didn't agree with his values (afterwards he did lose bankers by the dozen, as hundreds of thousands of dollars were lopped from their bonuses and competitors came calling):

> "Most of you have read articles about the high levels of compensation at Salomon Brothers. Some of you have also read discussions of incentive compensation that I have written in the Berkshire Hathaway annual report. In those, I have said that I believe a rational incentive compensation plan to be an excellent way to reward managers, and I have also embraced the concept of truly extraordinary pay for extraordinary managerial performance. I continue to subscribe to those views.
>
> But the problem at Salomon Brothers has been a compensation plan that was irrational in certain crucial respects. One irrationality has been compensation levels that overall have been too high in relation to overall results. For example, last year the securities unit earned about 10% on equity capital… yet 106 individuals who worked for the unit earned $1 million or more. Many of these people performed exceedingly well and clearly deserved their pay. But the overall result made no sense: though 1990 operating profits, before compensation, were flat versus 1989, pay jumped by more than $120 million. And that, of course, meant earnings for shareholders fell by the same amount… In effect, the fine performance of some people subsidized truly out-sized rewards for others.
>
> … Salomon is a publicly-owned company depending on vast amounts of shareholders' capital. In such an operation, it is

appropriate that the excess earnings of the exceptional performers – that is, what they generate beyond what they are justly paid – go to the stockholders... employees producing mediocre returns for owners should expect their pay to reflect this shortfall. In the past that has neither been the expectation at Salomon nor the practice. Salomon Inc's directors have decided that total compensation at Salomon Brothers in 1991 will be slightly below the level of 1990. Through 30 June 1991, however, compensation accruals had been made at a rate that considerably exceeded 1990's. Therefore, a $110m downward adjustment of the accrual was made in the third quarter.

In 1991 and in the future, the top-paid people at Salomon Brothers will get much of their compensation in the form of stock... [which] motivates managers to think like owners, since it obliges them to hold the stock they buy for at least five years and therefore exposes them to the risks of the business as well as the opportunities.

Contrast this arrangement with stock-option plans, in which managers commit money only if the game has already been won and then often move quickly to sell their shares.

We wish to see the unit's managers become wealthy through ownership, not by simply free-riding on the ownership of others, I think in fact that ownership can in time bring our best managers substantial wealth, perhaps in amounts well beyond what they now think possible... Within a relatively few years Salomon Inc's key employees could own 25% or more of the business, purchased with their own compensation.

The better job each employee does for the company, the more stock he or she will own. Our pay-for-performance philosophy will undoubtedly cause some managers to leave.

But very importantly, this same philosophy may induce the top performers to stay, since these people may identify themselves as .350 hitters about to be paid appropriately instead of seeing their just rewards partially assigned to lesser performers.

Were an abnormal number of people to leave the firm, the results would not necessarily be bad. Other men and women who share our thinking and values would then be given added responsibilities and opportunities. In the end we must have people to match our principles, not the reverse."

A few weeks later, once his key managers were in place (most notably Robert Denham, from Charlie Munger's law firm, as chairman) and stability and market confidence established, his New York time was reduced, allowing him to be absent from his beloved Omaha only one or two days per week.

In spring 1992, Salomon was permitted to resume buying notes and bonds in Treasury auctions for customers. Shortly afterwards, Buffett went home to Omaha. A couple of years later, he wryly noted, "Mozer's paying $30,000 and is sentenced to prison for four months. Salomon's shareholders – including me – paid $290m, and I got sentenced to ten months as CEO."[178]

Warren Buffett's best speech

In opening remarks, delivered to a Congress subcommittee investigating Salomon's violations, 4 September 1991, Buffett spoke bluntly of the foul-up at Salomon and, more significantly, the business ethos he holds dear; one which he was trying to instil in the bank. Each May, a video clip of this two minute speech (www.c-span.org/video/?21029-1/securities-trading-investigation) is played at Berkshire Hathaway's AGM, reminding Berkshire managers and shareholders alike the standard of integrity and common decency expected of everyone who works for the firm, or its subsidiaries and associates. If all high-flying executives in all companies followed these precepts, the world would be a much better place.

> "I would like to start by apologising for the acts that have brought us here. The nation has a right to expect its rules and laws to be obeyed, and at Salomon certain of these were broken.
>
> Almost all of Salomon's 8,000 employees regret this as deeply as I do, and I apologise on their behalf as well as mine.

My job is to deal with both the past and the future. The past actions of Salomon are presently causing our 8,000 employees and their families to bear a stain. Virtually all of these employees are hard-working, able and honest.

I want to find out exactly what happened in the past so that this stain is borne by the guilty few and removed from the innocent.

To help do this I promise you Mr Chairman and to the American people Salomon's whole-hearted co-operation with all authorities. These authorities have the power of subpoena, the ability to immunise witnesses and the power to prosecute for perjury.

Our internal investigation has not had these tools – we welcome their use.

As to the future, the submission to this subcommittee details actions that I believe will make Salomon the leader within the financial services industry in controls and compliance procedures.

But in the end, the spirit about compliance is as important, or more so, than words about compliance. I want the right words and I want the full range of internal controls.

But I've also asked every Salomon employee to be his or her own compliance officer. After they first obey all rules, I then want all employees to ask themselves whether they are willing to have any contemplated act appear the next day on the front page of their local paper, to be read by their spouses, children and friends, with the reporting done by an informed and critical reporter.

If they follow this test, they need not fear my other message to them: lose money for the firm and I will be understanding; lose a shred of reputation for the firm and I will be ruthless."

Every year in Omaha, at the end of the video of this speech, there is loud applause from 40,000 Berkshire shareholders, keen to show their agreement on how business should be conducted.

An even greater commitment to Salomon, and a sale

As Salomon grew in strength in the mid-1990s, Berkshire spent $324m on its common stock. That 6.6m shareholding, together with the rights attached to its preferred stock, gave Buffett effective control of 20% of the voting rights. This was reduced to 18% by the redemption of one-fifth of the preferred in 1995 (Berkshire receiving a cheque for $140m). In October 1996, one-fifth of the preferred stock was converted into 3.7m common stock.

Travelers Group, an insurance and brokerage firm, was looking to grow through acquisition and, in 1997, offered to buy Salomon – creating one of only a handful of giant financial companies in the USA, Europe and Japan. Berkshire received Travelers Group common and preferred stock to the value of approximately $1.8bn.

Thus, over a ten-year period, Berkshire put $700m into Salomon's preferred stock, and $324m into common stock, and received back $592m in preferred dividends, a $140m redemption payment, and $1.8bn in Travellers shares plus a few million in common stock dividends. A total of $1,024m went in and slightly over $2,532m came back, which works out at an annual return of 14.5% (allowing for timing of cash in and out) – not far short of Buffett's original target.

> "Looking back, I think of my Salomon experience as having been both fascinating and instructional, though for a time in 1991–1992 I felt like the drama critic who wrote: 'I would have enjoyed the play except that I had an unfortunate seat. It faced the stage'."[179]

I'll round off this morality tale of lost and re-discovered ethics, with Buffett's reminder to all his managers of the attitude he expects them to adopt, as set out in his letter to his All-Stars, 26 July 2010:

> "This is my biennial letter to reemphasize Berkshire's top priority and to get your help on succession planning (yours, not mine!). The priority is that all of us continue to zealously guard Berkshire's reputation. We can't be perfect but we can try to be. As I've said in these memos for more than 25 years: we can afford

to lose money – even a lot of money. But we can't afford to lose reputation – even a shred of reputation."

He asked managers to consider not just the legality of every act but the morality. Would they be comfortable seeing it splashed over the front page of a national newspaper? The rationale 'everybody else is doing it' was unacceptable and certainly wouldn't hold much water with a judge or reporter.

He told them that if any decision gave them pause to think, they should contact him, but the very act of hesitating was probably a good reason to abandon the idea.

"As a corollary, let me know promptly if there's any significant bad news. I can handle bad news but I don't like to deal with it after it has festered for a while. A reluctance to face up immediately to bad news is what turned a problem at Salomon from one that could have easily been disposed of into one that almost caused the demise of a firm with 8,000 employees."

In a business employing over 250,000 people, he continued, someone is likely to be doing something they and he would be unhappy about; that was unavoidable, However, by acting promptly and decisively, they could minimise such activity.

"Your attitude on such matters, expressed by behavior as well as words, will be the most important factor in how the culture of your business develops. Culture, more than rule books, determines how an organization behaves."[180]

Learning points

1. **There is no such thing as a guaranteed money-making investment when it comes to holding corporate common stock, preferred stock or bonds.** Make sure you are diversified.

2. **Look for three qualities in managers: integrity, intelligence and energy.** "If you don't have the first, the other two will kill you."[181]

3. **A rational compensation system aligns the interests of executives with those of shareholders.**

4. **Reputation can save a business.** It was Warren Buffett's reputation for probity and business competence that rescued Salomon – the regulators and the markets could trust him. "Reputation and integrity are your most valuable assets and can be lost in a heart beat." (Charlie Munger)

Investment 8

COCA-COLA

Summary of the deal

Deal	Coca-Cola
Time	1988–present
Price paid	$1,299m (1988–1994)
Quantity	7.8% of the share capital (grew to 9.4% due to share buy-backs)
Sale price	Part of Berkshire Hathaway today
Profit	20-fold so far
Berkshire Hathaway in 1988	Share price: $3,025–$4,900
	Book value: $3,412m
	Per share book value: $2,975

Warren Buffett had admired the Coca-Cola Company ever since he was a six-year-old, buying packs of six Coca-Cola bottles for 25 cents and then selling individual bottles for five cents (around his Omaha neighbourhood and on holiday at Lake Okoboji, Iowa). "I duly observed the extraordinary consumer attractiveness and commercial possibilities of the product."[182]

But for the following 52 years, he chose not to buy a single share in the company, despite being fully aware of the power of its brand, and its growth decade by decade. Both excellent economic characteristics, and the potential for growing owner earnings, are potent reasons for being drawn to a company, but they are insufficient for making a decision to buy its shares – you must always remember to ask the price. If the price does not allow for a significant margin of safety, then the code of the disciplined value investor dictates that it must be left alone. Admire from a distance, keep following the story but, if the price keeps going beyond the safe level, opt for masterly inactivity.

Something changed in the 1980s to make Buffett and Munger think that, at last, intrinsic value was jumping by leaps and bounds while the share price responded at a slow enough rate to allow the margin of safety to grow.

The big change was the two key people running Coca-Cola, Don Keough and Roberto Goizueta. They were demonstrating, in the reported numbers and the strategic positioning of the company, that they had cultivated a very strong economic franchise and were deepening and widening the moat protecting that franchise. In fact, the franchise was so strong that Buffett categorised Coca-Cola as that very rare thing, an "Inevitable".

Inevitables

Inevitables are the best type of companies to own. These are firms which will dominate their fields for an investment lifetime due to their enormous competitive strengths. They are found in sectors not likely to experience major change – a fast-changing industry precludes the possibility of dominance over a span as long as three decades.

To get in the right frame of mind to recognise an Inevitable, imagine that you are about to embark on a ten-year mission to Mars, and you are unable to change the constituents in your portfolio while you are gone. If you can make only one investment now what would you look for? Answer: certainty. Your chosen company would need to operate in a simple-to-understand industry, on a stable growth path, and it would be the dominant company; and the leader(s) likely to be loyal to the company for at least a decade.

Buffett believed Coca-Cola and Gillette could be considered Inevitables. Forecasters might differ in their predictions of how each business would be doing in ten years' time but no sensible observer could question that Coke and Gillette would dominate their fields worldwide for an investment lifetime. Both companies had significantly expanded their already huge shares of market during the past ten years, and all signs pointed to their repeating that performance in the next decade.

"Obviously many companies in high-tech businesses or embryonic industries will grow much faster in percentage terms than will the Inevitables. But I would rather be certain of a good result than hopeful of a great one… Considering what it takes to be an Inevitable, Charlie and I recognize that we will never be able to come up with a Nifty Fifty or even a Twinkling Twenty. To the Inevitables in our portfolio, therefore, we add a few Highly Probables."[183]

Market leadership does not equate to inevitable status. Polaroid, General Electric and Kodak enjoyed periods when they appeared unstoppable, but new technology introduced by more agile competitors outside their industry (e.g. digital), or simply the lack of true customer captivity ('share of mind') in an industry in which buyers can choose between a range of alternatives, means pricing power can be transitory. Thus, for every Inevitable, there are dozens of impostors: companies now riding high but vulnerable to competitive attacks.

"You can, of course, pay too much for even the best of businesses. The overpayment risk surfaces periodically and, in our opinion, may now be quite high for the purchasers of virtually all stocks, The Inevitables included. Investors making purchases in an overheated market need to recognize that it may often take an extended period for the value of even an outstanding company to catch up with the price they paid."[184]

We'll look at the characteristics of Coca-Cola which pointed to it being an Inevitable, in more detail, later in the chapter.

Coca-Cola – suitable for a value investor?

To simplistic value investors, the notion of paying an above-market average multiple of 15 times the previous year's earnings (what Berkshire Hathaway paid for Coke in 1988) didn't make sense – value investors don't pay high PE ratios, do they?

But Coca-Cola is an example of an excellent value investment which, although it seems expensive at the time, is easily justified if you think about not last year's reported earnings but the discounted value of the *future* owner earnings.

Buffett and Munger saw that Coca-Cola's consumer pricing power was so strong that owner earnings would grow dramatically as it expanded its international presence, while its hold over the distribution system in the US and elsewhere would be preserved. And it would at least maintain its 20–30% returns on capital employed as volume doubled, trebled, quadrupled.

The evidence that they were correct in their optimism is demonstrated in Table 8.1 and Figure 8.1. While the table does not show owner earnings directly, over a span of years the dividends on this permanent holding are the manifestation of those owner earnings.

Berkshire Hathaway accumulated $1.3bn shares in Coca-Cola by the time it had finished buying in 1994. Once the millions of shares were assembled, after receiving $88m in 1995, a long period of uninterrupted and growing dividends flowed to Berkshire. The average annual growth rate from 1995 to 2018 was 8.9%. By 2018, the pay-out had reached $624m.

The discounted value of a set of cash flows starting at $88m and growing in all future years at 8.9% is $2.8bn.[185] Paying $1.3bn for a holding with an expected present value of $2.8bn is a value investment with a sufficient margin of safety.

Of course, Buffett and Munger did not have a crystal ball to predict the future with such extreme accuracy, but they could work out estimates of possible outcomes and, given the strength of the management and the quality of the franchise, they could easily envisage something like the outcome that occurred.

Table 8.1: Berkshire's investments in Coca-Cola and income received

	Number of shares held in December	Cost of accumulated shares ($m)	Berkshire's approximate ownership of Coca-Cola	Dividends received that year ($m)
1988	14,172,500	592.5	4.2%	9 (est.)
1989	23,350,000 (9,177,500 shares bought in 1989)	1,023.9	7.0%	26 (est.)
1990	46,700,000 (a 2 for 1 stock split in 1990)	1,023.9	7.0%	37
1991	46,700,000	1,023.9	7.0%	45
1992	93,400,000 (a 2 for 1 stock split in 1992)	1,023.9	7.1%	52
1993	93,400,000	1,023.9	7.2%	64
1994	100,000,000 (6,600,000 shares bought in 1994)	1,299	7.8%	75 (est.)
1995	100,000,000	1,299	7.8%	88
1996	200,000,000 (a 2 for 1 stock split in 1996)	1,299	8.1%	100
1997	200,000,000	1,299	8.1%	112
1998	200,000,000	1,299	8.1%	120
1999	200,000,000	1,299	8.1%	128
2000	200,000,000	1,299	8.1%	136
2001	200,000,000	1,299	8.1%	144
2002	200,000,000	1,299	8.1%	160
2003	200,000,000	1,299	8.1%	176

	Number of shares held in December	Cost of accumulated shares ($m)	Berkshire's approximate ownership of Coca-Cola	Dividends received that year ($m)
2004	200,000,000	1,299	8.1%	200
2005	200,000,000	1,299	8.1%	224
2006	200,000,000	1,299	8.8%	248
2007	200,000,000	1,299	8.8%	272
2008	200,000,000	1,299	8.8%	304
2009	200,000,000	1,299	8.8%	328
2010	200,000,000	1,299	8.8%	352
2011	200,000,000	1,299	8.8%	376
2012	400,000,000 (a 2 for 1 stock split in 2012)	1,299	8.9%	408
2013	400,000,000	1,299	9.1%	448
2014	400,000,000	1,299	9.2%	488
2015	400,000,000	1,299	9.3%	528
2016	400,000,000	1,299	9.3%	560
2017	400,000,000	1,299	9.4%	592
2018	400,000,000	1,299	9.4%	624

Sources: W. Buffett, letters to shareholders of BH (1997–2018).

Figure 8.1 shows a renewal of investor interest in Coca-Cola shares after the initial period of Buffett's purchases (he bought in the second half of 1988 and first half of 1989). Between mid-1988 and the end of 1989 Coca-Cola's stock price nearly doubled.

This is a remarkable 18-month run, but it was to get even better. When it dawned on thousands of investors that Coca-Cola was likely to have a good rate of earnings growth, they piled in. So, even though Buffett bought shares in 1989 at a more generous price of $47.01, compared with an average of $41.81 paid in 1988 (not allowing for subsequent splits), it was worth it because the company was still undervalued. This was confirmed by the ten-fold rise in the next ten years.

Perhaps things got a little out of hand, as it did with most of the market, in the late 1990s, when Coca-Cola's shares sat on a price earnings ratio of 60. The puncturing of this bubble, and a few troubles in the early part of the 21st century (discussed later), resulted in a decade of share price falls. All through the downturn, Berkshire had the satisfaction of the flow of dividends, and by 2019 the shares bounced to 15 times what Berkshire paid.

Figure 8.1: Market value of Berkshire's Coca-Cola shareholdings (1988–2018)

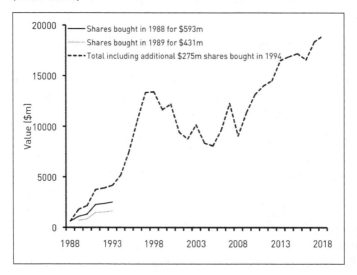

Sources: Berkshire Hathaway annual reports.

The Coke connection

The six-year-old Buffett's first entrepreneurial venture might have been with Coca-Cola but, by the time he was ten, he figured that the best seller was Pepsi because a customer could have 12 ounces for the same price as a six-ounce Coke. For the next 45 years, Buffett was a Pepsi drinker – I know, shocking isn't it!

So, how come Buffett changed the habit of almost half a century? This story goes back to the time when he and his wife Susie had recently settled into the five-bedroomed house he bought for $31,000, in 1958, in a quiet neighbourhood in Omaha (he still lives there – on YouTube videos you can see how modest it is, for a billionaire).

Across the street lived Don Keough, then a Butter-Nut coffee salesman with four kids. Keough ruefully recalls the time he turned down the offer of a lifetime from his friend living only a few yards away (in a TV interview hosted by former Disney CEO Michael Eisner): "I lived across the street from a guy who had no celebrity at the time. He didn't go to work. He did some funny thing on the telephone. His name was Warren Buffett. He came over to see me in 1960, and he said, 'Don, I was just thinking about you… You know you've got to think about college [for your children].'"

The 30-something Keough, taken aback, responded, "Warren I'm working on grade school right now, I'll get around to college a little later." Not to be shaken off that easily, Buffett launched into, "I'm forming a little partnership. A few of us have put $10,000 into it. I might be able to turn that into something."

Keough couldn't really understand why someone who didn't hold down a conventional job and bring in a salary could ask for investment money. "Remember, he didn't go to work. I worked. When I came home after working all day one of my kids would say 'we had a wonderful time with Mr Buffett today. He took us to the park', or 'he had a train set up on the third floor of his house'. And he said, 'If you give me $10,000 I might be able to do something about it.' Well, I didn't have it, but I could've borrowed it from my father. But can you imagine giving $10,000 to a guy who doesn't get up and go to work in the morning?"[186]

You can understand where the 1960 Keough was coming from – $10,000 was a third of the price of a house in a nice Omaha suburb in 1960. However, compounded at 25% for ten years – the average for the Buffett Partnership after Buffett's fee – followed by 20% per annum – the average return on Berkshire Hathaway, 1970–2018 – would have amounted to $93m. Enough for whole blocks of houses.

Having known Buffett as an ordinary, if slightly eccentric, neighbour and friend for a very long time, this comment from Keough on Buffett's character holds particular resonance:

> "He was exactly the same then as he is now... What you see is what you get. He had the same values. His story is not money. It's values. People should know about his values."[187]

An incensed Keough

Don Keough was a brilliant manager and when his company was taken over by the Swanson family of Omaha, and then by the Duncan Foods Company, he rose through the ranks. Coca-Cola bought Duncan in 1964 and, in 1981, Keough rose to the top, becoming president and chief operating officer, complementing Roberto Goizueta, Coca-Cola's chairman and CEO.

In 1985, Keough read a shocking article in the *New York* magazine which had the temerity to mention that Buffett was a guzzler of Pepsi-Cola Cherry Coke.

Keough couldn't let that rest, so he wrote to Buffett offering to send him in-development samples of Coca-Cola's 'nectar of the Gods', the soon to be launched Cherry Coke. It worked. In February 1986, Buffett wrote to Berkshire shareholders saying there had been a revolution:

> "I hope you come to this year's meeting, which will be held on May 20 in Omaha. There will be only one change: after 48 years of allegiance to another soft drink, your Chairman, in an unprecedented display of behavioral flexibility, has converted to the new Cherry Coke. Henceforth, it will be the Official Drink of the Berkshire Hathaway Annual Meeting."[188]

His habit now is to consume at least five bottles/cans of Cherry Coke per day. His offices are stuffed with the drink and attendees of the Berkshire AGM witness can after can being consumed as Buffett and Munger hold forth for six hours – obviously good fuel for the brain, if balanced with See's candy of course.

But, despite this remarkable 1985 beverage conversion, Buffett had still not persuaded himself that he should buy Coca-Cola's shares. That was still over two years away.

Coca-Cola's economic franchise[189]

The first Coca-Cola was drunk in 1886. A pharmacist, John Pemberton, mixed up a caramel-coloured liquid, then walked along his Atlanta street to Jacob's Pharmacy, where it was combined with carbonated water and sampled by customers. With positive feedback from the pharmacy's patrons, the drink was launched at five cents a glass. In the first year, an average of nine glasses were sold per day. John Pemberton's partner and bookkeeper, Frank Robinson, named it Coca-Cola and wrote it out in his script – the logo you see today.

What the company did over the next century was to create an economic franchise by first producing a product that people found pleasing, but second by being acutely aware of the power of psychology in encouraging repeated consumption.

There was also a determination to control a distribution system which ensured competing products were set at a disadvantage. And there was the exploitation of economies of scale, first in the United States and then in over 200 countries.

In many countries Coca-Cola operates on such a scale that it accounts for 50% or more of the carbonated soft drinks sold; and yet competition regulators rarely intervene in the market which indicates some cleverness in avoiding riling or waking-up the anti-trust watchdogs – another extraordinary resource possessed by the firm. Some market shares statistics: USA 43%, Mexico 48%, India 69%, Germany 79% (all carbonated brands included, e.g., Thums Up in India).

The psychology of drink choices

The creation and maintenance of conditioned reflexes is a key part of Coca-Cola's success. A considerable amount has been invested over the years in ensuring that the trade name and the trade dress act as stimuli inducing people to buy and consume Coke. The conditioned reflex is assisted by two types of habituation.

Operant conditioning

This means engendering human learning through frequent rewards for what is 'good', or punishment for what is 'bad'. Coca-Cola goes for positive reinforcement following regular behaviour, i.e. drinking Coke brings the rewards of hydration, calories, pleasant taste, cooling, caffeine and sugar stimulation (leading to a strengthening in the desired response, i.e. buying another can).

For Coca-Cola to make good use of operant conditioning it needs to:

(a) Maximise rewards from drinking – flavour, calories, etc.

(b) Minimise the risk of a diminishing reflex to drink Coke. This threat comes from the actions of competitors attracting customers and then introducing new operant conditioning, i.e. customers sample and like a competing drink, leading to them going back for more of that reward.

This means making sure that Coca-Cola will be available at all times everywhere (as far as reasonably practicable), so that competitors find it difficult to persuade consumers to give their drink a try. In this way, a habit in conflict with the habit of drinking Coke is rarely established.

An important economy of scale is created because people are more aware of your product than competing products, because they have tested/ tasted it in the past and it has always been around. This produces an informational advantage economy of scale. Munger puts it like this when writing about Wrigley's but we could substitute Coke for chewing gum:

> "If I go to some remote place, I may see Wrigley's chewing gum alongside Glotz's chewing gum. Well, I know that Wrigley is a satisfactory product whereas I don't know anything about Glotz's. So if one is forty cents and the other is thirty cents, am I going to take something I don't know and put it in my mouth – which is a pretty personal place, after all – for a lousy dime."[190]

Thus Coca-Cola creates in people a willingness to pay a premium to drink 'the real thing' despite less well-known similar beverages being offered at considerably lower cost.

Operant behaviour is voluntary, unlike the other type – Pavlovian conditioning.

Pavlovian conditioning

This is often called *classical conditioning*, and is caused by mere association. It draws on Ivan Pavlov's experiments with dogs. After repeated action, dogs salivate in response to stimuli, such as a bell being rung, with no food being present or detectable. This is involuntary.

While humans do not respond well to bells, they do subconsciously associate certain foods or drinks with objects or events, e.g., the Coca-Cola logo has a strong association with taste and thirst quenching. Or an event – like the start of a baseball game –might have a long association with the drink in the sub-consciousness of the individual; likewise a family gathering might stimulate the need for Coca-Cola to be there. Coca-Cola often advertises with a message that work breaks are for drinking its product – people then associate the pleasant event of a break with a drink like Diet Coke (particularly if semi-naked men straight from the gym are used in the advertisements, it seems).

The logo and promotion must continuously create, in consumer minds, an association with things they like or admire, e.g. attractive people, sports, good health, celebrations. The amount of advertising required to create this condition is very expensive but worth it. With $31.9bn revenue in 2018, the "aggregate amount provided by our Company to bottlers, resellers or other customers of our Company's products, principally for participation in promotional and marketing programs, was $4.3bn."[191]

If Coca-Cola is the biggest soft drink advertiser in many markets, it can, to a large extent, shut out competition because competitors advertising dollars are spread between too few ounces of drink.

Social proof gives a boost

Social proof is the psychological phenomenon of being influenced by what we see others doing and of what they approve. This may be conscious or unconscious. Thus, if everybody else is buying a product such as Coke, we tend to think it a superior drink. Human beings have a natural tendency to want to be in-step with others.

We often approach the difficulty of choice on a conscious level, e.g. "I don't know much about the different products in this field. It looks as though others know what they are doing. It makes sense to follow them."

Coca-Cola's ubiquity delivers social proof benefits in spades – potential consumers see people obviously enjoying drinking Coke in cafes, walking down the street, at a ballgame, on billboards and in TV advertisements.

How can a smaller or newer rival compete against this force, even with billions at its disposal for advertising? It's extraordinarily difficult to dislodge an incumbent benefitting from oodles of information advantages and social proof advantages.

Signalling

In some countries, *signalling* is an important motivator for buying the Coke brand; American cultural associations mean that young people, particularly, will pay a premium.

Other economies of scale

If a business sticks to its knitting, and establishes itself as the one with the greatest scale, then it can benefit from greater *specialisation of task*. Coca-Cola can assign a huge range of specialised manpower to say the establishment of new markets – such as in Soviet Bloc countries post-cold war – or it can continuously improve marketing in the US, by having specialists in, say, Facebook advertising. Also, greater volume gives economies in distribution, finance, manufacturing and sourcing.

The Coca-Cola Company is able to grow owner earnings and return on capital employed by sub-contracting most of the bottling and distribution to other companies. These other firms are required to spend a considerable amount on buildings, plant and machinery, leaving Coca-Cola with the lower capital commitment task of producing concentrate to ship to the bottlers, hence the high returns on equity capital (usually over 25%).

Coca-Cola ensures its bottlers are not treated as customers – that would be to give too much power away to them. They are required to comply with Coca-Cola's wishes in how they serve the retailers, be that in shops, kiosks, restaurants or sports stadia. This means retailers can be offered Coca-Cola's own package, including promotional materials, signage and fridge with its logo – this helps to reinforce Pavlovian conditioning by plastering the logo everywhere. It disadvantages competing soft drink makers by discouraging retailers from sourcing elsewhere – a 'free' fridge offer might come with the strings of giving prominent or exclusive space to Coca-Cola, and/or the fridge has to be in a prominent position, and/or permission to advertise Coke on the side of the building.

Lollapalooza at Coca-Cola

The *lollapalooza effect*, a term Charlie Munger employs, arises when many elements blend together to generate amplified results. It's not simply an addition of benefits; it is an enormous multiplication of value once factors are present in sufficient volume.

It's rather like in physics, when a combination of factors creates mundane effects until the point of critical mass is reached – and you get a nuclear explosion. Or in medicine, when the cure of cancer comes from using a combination of immunotherapy treatments, more traditional drugs, and radiotherapy.

Coca-Cola has this autocatalytic quality because it (a) has a taste people like and experience often, plus sugar, caffeine and a cooling benefit, i.e. operant conditioning, (b) Pavlovian conditioning, and (c) strong social-proof effects.

Porter's Five Forces

We can use Michael Porter's Five Forces[192] to consider the competitive position of Coca-Cola's industry:

1. **Supplier power?** Coca-Cola and other soft drink producers buy commodity products (e.g. sugar) sold in highly competitive markets with many alternative suppliers. Therefore, suppliers do not have much hold over the prices they can charge.

2. **Customer power?** Coca-Cola is the leading producer, but there are many others offering to supply retailers. However, demand from the ultimate consumer for Coca-Cola drinks – created by the psychological factors listed above – means that retailers have only limited power, even giant retailers such as the major fast-food restaurants and supermarkets.

3. **Substitutes?** There are many substitutes for carbonated sugar-based drinks and these are having an impact. Coca-Cola has responded by buying up many firms offering these alternatives, to increase its range – from coffee and juice, to water and energy drinks. Economies of scope – distributing different products through the same routes – help Coca-Cola stay ahead of the competition. Even with these alternative drinks available, many people on many occasions must just have a Coke, or Fanta, or Sprite, etc.

4. **Rivalry within the industry?** There are many suppliers, but Coca-Cola is usually the dominant firm in a market and is, to some extent, protected from rivals by its psychological advantages.

5. **Potential entrants?** Warren Buffett commented on the inadvisability of entering Coca-Cola's territory: "If you gave me $100bn and said take away the soft drink leadership of Coca-Cola in the world, I'd give it back to you and say it can't be done."[193]

This industry structure (power relationships) is likely to be stable in the future. Technological change may assist Coca-Cola's manufacturing processes, and those of its competitors, but won't change in any significant way the consumption of drink or the competitive dynamics within the industry.

What might change is social acceptability of sugar and caffeine. But then Coca-Cola has positioned itself to benefit from growth in other types of drink as well as more healthy variants of Coke (e.g. sugar-free).

A price war with Pepsi is a possibility. But this has been tried before to the detriment of both firms, so it may not have a high likelihood.

It's possible that governments/regulators may clamp down on Coca-Cola given its dominance of markets.

An impressive fortress with a deep and dangerous moat

In recognising all these advantages, Buffett and Munger thought there was considerable untapped pricing power at Coca-Cola – prices could be raised significantly without losing much custom.

> "There are actually people out there who don't price everything as high as the market will easily stand. And once you figure that out, it's like finding money on the street – if you have the courage of your convictions."[194]

Worldwide, Coke sold about 44% of all soft drinks, and Gillette had more than a 60% share (in value) of the blade market. Moreover, both Coke and Gillette had actually increased their worldwide shares of market in recent years. In his 1993 letter to Berkshire shareholders, Buffett commented on how he viewed Coca-Cola's and its fellow inevitable, Gillette's, strategic strengths:

> "Leaving aside chewing gum, in which Wrigley is dominant, I know of no other significant businesses in which the leading company has long enjoyed such global power... The might of their brand names, the attributes of their products, and the strength of their distribution systems give them an enormous competitive advantage, setting up a protective moat around their economic castles."

In contrast, he said, the average company did battle daily without any such means of protection.

> "As Peter Lynch says, stocks of companies selling commodity-like products should come with a warning label: Competition may prove hazardous to human wealth."

Why 1988?

Buffett and Munger had known about Coca-Cola's virtues for many years, and yet chose not to buy. This section provides a brief history, leading to the changes taking place in the 1980s.

The creation of the powerhouse

The inventor of Coca-Cola only saw two years of (very small) sales of his now world-famous drink before he died. Prior to his death, he sold stakes to various people with the majority interest being bought by Asa G. Candler – the most valuable items being the formula for the syrup and the copyright on the 'Coca-Cola Syrup and Extract' label registered at the US patent office. Candler gained complete ownership in 1891, paying out $2,300. He grew the soda fountain business beyond Atlanta, but it wasn't until a customer installed his own bottling machinery, in 1894, that we had the portable version of the drink. About the same time, the Coca-Cola script trademark was registered with the US patent office, but the company was still small, with an advertising budget of only $11,000 per year.

Warren Buffett, in his 1996 letter, reflected on the soundness of the strategy established in the 19th century – a quality drink distinguished by a strong brand:

> "I was recently studying the 1896 report of Coke (and you think that *you* are behind in your reading!). At that time Coke… had been around for only a decade. But its blueprint for the next 100 years was already drawn… Asa Candler, the company's president, said: 'We have not lagged in our efforts to go into all the world teaching that Coca-Cola is the article, par excellence, for the health and good feeling of all people.' Though 'health' may have been a reach, I love the fact that Coke still relies on Candler's basic theme today – a century later."

Candler went on to say, just as Roberto could now, "No article of like character has ever so firmly entrenched itself in public favor."

The number of bottlers grew to over 1,000 over the next 20 years, as the beverage went to every state in the union, as well as Canada, Cuba, Panama and the Philippines. Irritatingly, due to the lack of consistency in bottle design, competitors were able to pass-off their imitations easily, using a slightly different name but similar script. So, in 1916, the bottlers agreed to the distinctive contoured bottle, which, being so recognisable, helped reinforce the power of the brand.

Growing as a public company

In 1919, The Coca-Cola Company was purchased by Ernest Woodruff and his investor group for $25m, and later that year it was floated on the New York Stock Exchange at $40 a share (500,000 shares sold).

A few tumultuous years followed, in which the company was locked into high sugar prices and wasted time on lawsuits over trademark protection and bottling agreements. The shares fell to $19.50 by the end of 1920.

In 1923, Ernest persuaded his son, Robert, to leave his successful career as a motor company executive and lead the Coca-Cola company, taking a $50,000 pay cut. Thus began his six decades as president or chairman or senior director (semi-retired) of Coca-Cola.

Robert Woodruff was adamant that the drink must be consistently excellent and within an "arms reach of desire". He employed a team of highly-trained staff to encourage and help fountain retailers serve Coca-Cola to perfection, and to aggressively sell the drink. He also raised the quality consistency of the bottled version, and pumped money into advertising it. By 1929, bottles sales exceeded fountain sales.

Woodruff internationalised the company. Starting in only five countries in 1923, it had pushed into 30 by 1930. He carefully crafted the brand image; spending money on association with great events such as the Olympic Games (first in 1928).

In 1938, *Fortune*, while acknowledging the quality of the business, nevertheless worried that investors were taking an insufficiently-rewarded risk by investing in its shares at, what it judged to be, too high a price. In 1993, Buffett was also criticised for paying an excessive price so, in his 1993 letter to Berkshire shareholders, he reflected on what had happened to the share over the previous 74 years.

Coca-Cola had gone public in 1919 at $40 per share. By the end of 1920, negative market sentiment had seen the stock plummet by more than 50%, to $19.50. At year end 1993, however, one of those shares, with dividends reinvested, was worth more than $2.1m. Buffett quoted Ben Graham: "In the short-run, the market is a voting machine – reflecting a voter-registration test that requires only money, not intelligence or emotional stability – but in the long-run, the market is a weighing machine."

In 1938, *Fortune* reported that serious investors viewed the company with huge respect but could only conclude that they had missed the boat. Saturation or competition would surely limit further progress.

> "Yes, competition there was in 1938 and in 1993 as well. But it's worth noting that in 1938, The Coca-Cola Co. sold 207m cases of soft drinks... and in 1993 it sold about 10.7bn cases, a 50-fold increase in physical volume from a company that, in 1938, was already dominant in its very major industry. Nor was the party over in 1938 for an investor: though the $40 invested in 1919 in one share had (with dividends reinvested) turned into $3,277 by the end of 1938, a fresh $40 then invested in Coca-Cola stock would have grown to $25,000 by yearend 1993."

Since 1993, the share has risen five-fold. A single $40 share held from 1919 would be worth over $10m today. The increase since that 1938 article was published is over 3,000-fold.

A big break for internationalising the drink came in 1943, when the US government requested Coca-Cola be available to troops all over the world. The company responded by setting a low price of just a nickel for the military regardless of where they were or how much it cost the company to make and get it to them. Of course, the presence of Coca-Cola in every country where the US soldiers, airmen and sailors went helped create new markets, e.g. post-war Germany and Japan, as locals became attracted to the product and its image. By 1959, Coke was drunk in over 100 countries.

The turbulent 1970s

The 1970s were a decade in which the total return to shareholders averaged less than 1% per year. "Its empire was strung together as a loosely-knit chain of very eccentric fiefdoms, affording Atlanta virtually no control over how its bottlers chose to grow, or not grow, their Coca-Cola business."[195] Unknown to the company, the chairman was suffering from Alzheimer's and Parkinson's. It also had to cope with numerous disputes with bottlers. "The company had no sense of direction whatsoever… Unprofessional would be an understatement. We were there to carry the bottlers' suitcases."[196]

Governments in a number of countries made trouble for Coca-Cola, tinged by anti-Americanism, and consumer tastes were shifting to waters, juices, teas, etc. Coca-Cola also made some product gaffes and it had diversified into completely unrelated fields. Then it suffered the onslaught of the Pepsi Challenge – blind-tasting very small amounts of cola (Pepsi is sweeter and so often preferred in *small* quantities) – which caused some market share loss.

Figure 8.2: Coca-Cola's share price adjusting for splits (1971–1980)

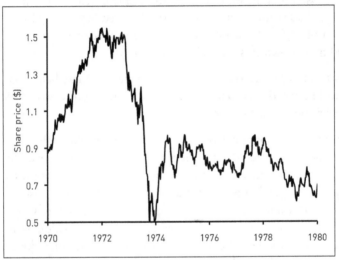

Source: www.advfn.com

Time for a change

In 1981, the man in charge of the 1970s errors departed, but the nonagenarian Robert Woodruff was in no mood to accept the chosen successor. Instead, he asked Roberto Goizueta to become chairman and CEO. A Yale graduate, Goizueta worked for Coca-Cola in his native Cuba, but in 1960 had been forced to flee. He held tightly to his

Coca-Cola shares and his job in the firm, and spent the next 20 years working his way up the ranks.

The moment he was asked to lead the company, Goizueta asked if he could have Don Keough at his side, a man many assumed to be the front-runner to be chairman. Keough was named president and chief operating officer and a given a great deal of freedom. The two worked together more like partners than boss and junior. Put crudely, Goizueta was the Atlanta strategist taking tough decisions on closures, etc., while Keough was the charismatic and energetic globetrotting team-builder and chief enthusiasm-inducer.

Keough describes Goizueta's attitude "We weren't here to be a nice company; we were here to be a growth company. We were going to get our balance sheet in order. And we were going to reward the hell out of performance, but we were no longer going to pay for perfect attendance."[197]

Employees were motivated to generate high returns for shareholders through bonus incentives, stock options and large stock grants when they retired. This made dozens, if not hundreds, of managers millionaires but, importantly, they only became rich if shareholders were doing well. Buffett commented in his 1993 letter:

"Don is one of the most extraordinary human beings I've ever known – a man of enormous business talent but, even more important, a man who brings out the absolute best in everyone lucky enough to associate with him. Coca-Cola wants its product to be present at the happy times of a person's life. Don Keough, as an individual, invariably increases the happiness of those around him. It's impossible to think about Don without feeling good."

He recalled the strong impression that Keough had made on him when, as "a coffee salesman with a big family and a small income", he had lived across the road in Omaha.

"The impressions I formed in those days about Don were a factor in my decision to have Berkshire make a record $1bn investment in Coca-Cola in 1988–1989. Roberto Goizueta had become CEO of Coke in 1981, with Don alongside as his partner. The two of them took hold of a company that had stagnated during the previous decade and moved it from $4.4bn of market value to $58bn in less than 13 years. What a difference a pair of managers like this makes, even when their product has been around for 100 years."

Some of Goizueta and Keough's triumphs

These achievements were apparent to the market and, of course, to Buffett by the summer of 1988, when he started buying.

Taking control of the bottling, distribution and marketing processes

They did this while still using bottlers, etc., but now more as sub-contractors than as customers – often with Coca-Cola holding influential equity stakes in them. Goizueta said in 1993, "The difference today? We used to be either cheerleaders or critics of bottlers. Now we are players."[198]

Diet Coke

A very successful drink, launched in 1982, and Cherry Coke in 1985.

Entered many new markets with gusto

The fall of the Berlin Wall was one opportunity taken. Coca-Cola invested $1bn in Eastern Europe. "The more distant a country's culture is from America's, it seems, the more potent Coke is as an icon of American culture and – especially in the former communist world – as a symbol of the market economy."[199]

And there was plenty of untapped potential in its older markets, where per capita consumption was significantly less than the 274 eight-ounce servings in the USA (1987 figure). Australia was at 177, Germany at 155 and Japan at 89, but Britain was only at 63 and Thailand just 26. "Coke executives become almost giddy thinking about what it would be like if Thais drank as much soda as Texans. Mr. Keough lights up when he talks of Indonesia, where a population of 180m in a hot, humid climate drinks only 3.2 servings of Coke products a year."[200] Japan set the target to aim for; by 1988, Coca-Cola was earning more there than in the US.

Dropping the strange accretions

Coca-Cola had acquired some very ill-fitting businesses, from aquaculture to industrial water treatment plants and a winery.

"It's simple," says Goizueta. "You make a chart. Across the top you put your businesses: concentrate, bottling, wine, foods, whatever. Then you put the financial characteristics on the other axis: margins, returns, cash flow reliability, capital requirements. Some, like the concentrate business, will emerge as superior businesses. Others, like wine, look lousy." He quickly sold off the lousy businesses. Everybody else around the company learned just as quickly how to make financial charts, which, among other things, calculated their cost of capital."[201]

Buffett was amazed at the menagerie of businesses that Coca-Cola (and Gillette) had collected in the 1970s. Coke had tried growing shrimp while Gillette had got involved with oil exploration.

> "Loss of focus is what most worries Charlie and me when we contemplate investing in businesses that in general look outstanding. All too often, we've seen value stagnate in the presence of hubris or of boredom that caused the attention of managers to wander. That's not going to happen again at Coke and Gillette, however – not given their current and prospective managements."[202]

Changed the company culture placing an emphasis on economic profit

Coca-Cola started to judge all company operations based on economic profit: after-tax operating profit in excess of a charge for capital.

> "Says Goizueta: 'When you get right down to it, what I really do is allocate resources – capital, manpower. And I learned that when you start charging people for their capital, all sorts of things happen. All of a sudden inventories get under control. You don't have three months' concentrate sitting around for an emergency. Or you figure out that you can save a lot of money

by replacing stainless-steel syrup containers with cardboard and plastic.'"[203]

Some of the more doubtful moves (but which seemed to work out)

Columbia Pictures was bought in 1982 for $750m

It never really belonged in a drinks business. But at least it was sold at a $500m profit (in 1989) and there was a lot of Coca-Cola product placement during those seven years – watch out for it in *Ghostbusters* and *Karate Kid*.

The Coca-Cola formula was changed in 1985

This sparked widespread 'Deprival Super-reaction Syndrome' – the tendency to be more influenced by minor decrements down than movements in the opposite direction, i.e. people overreact if you take away something that they are used to, even if it is a small thing.

The 'New Coke' resulted in nationwide protest and after 79 days 'Coca-Cola Classic' was returned to the market. The error was turned to the company's advantage, as people realised their affection for the original Coca-Cola, and vast amounts of media time was focused on the excited calls to bring it back. As a result, market share jumped higher than in 1984.

The deal

Coca-Cola's share price responded well to the changes Goizueta and Keough introduced after 1981, rising four-fold in the six years to September 1987. Then the stock market crash of October 1987 brought it down by a quarter (see Figure 8.3). And yet the annual report for 1987 showed good things happening to the underlying business. Revenue was up 9.8% at $7.7bn; after-tax income was over $900m in both 1986 and 1987, almost double that of 1981; return on equity was 27%; soft drink volume up 6%, and now available in more than 155 countries, accounting for more than 44% of all soft drinks sold in the world,[204] equivalent to 524m servings per day.

Figure 8.3: Coca-Cola's share price adjusted for splits (1980–1990)

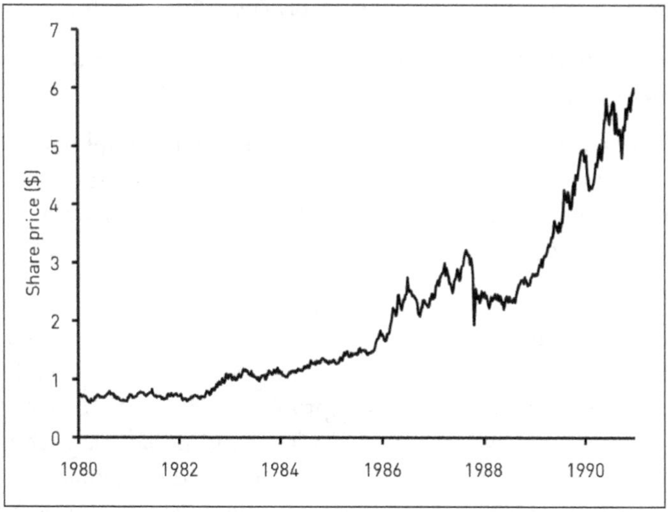

Source: www.advfn.com

The company exuded confidence in future growth, stating in the report:

> "Coca-Cola, it sometimes seems, is everywhere. And yet, given our recent growth and our worldwide opportunities, it is apparent that the size and scope of our system, the pervasiveness of our products and trademarks, can only increase."[205]

Buffett agreed, and started accumulating shares in noticeable amounts in the fall of 1988. Over in Atlanta, senior managers were naturally curious (perhaps concerned) about all this activity on the stock register. Upon investigation, they noticed that most of the purchases were made by a midwestern brokerage. It didn't take long for Keough to think of his old friend as the likely buyer. He gave him a call. "Warren, the trading in Coke stock suggests that someone is buying a lot of it. Could that possibly be you?" Buffett's response delighted Keough: "Well, keep it quiet between you and Roberto. But yep, it's me."[206]

And Buffett carried on buying. So, it wasn't a deal as such, just Buffett buying a large stake in 1988 (4.2% of Coca-Cola's stock) then adding more, in the first half of 1989, to take Berkshire's holding to 7%. Shortly afterwards, he was invited to join Coca-Cola's board of directors.

Buffett poked fun at himself for not recognising the value of Coca-Cola shares much earlier, in his 1989 letter to shareholders:

> "This Coca-Cola investment provides yet another example of the incredible speed with which your Chairman responds to investment opportunities... I've learned my lesson: my response time to the next glaringly attractive idea will be slashed to well under 50 years."[207]

There was a pause in the buying, 1990–1993, while the shares rose three-fold (see Figure 8.4). When the company came through with excellent numbers in the early 1990s (profits nearly doubled 1990–1994), Buffett and Munger still thought it a bargain and so, after a few months of observing the share going nowhere during 1993 and early-1994, Berkshire bought some more, taking the stake to one-twelfth of all Coke's shares, the largest shareholder.

Figure 8.4: Coca-Cola share price adjusted for splits (1987–1994)

Source: www.advfn.com

The 1994 purchases, even at a multiple of what was paid in 1988–1989 were well worth it. Figure 8.5 shows Coca-Cola's share trebling again over the rest of the 1990s.

Figure 8.5: Coca-Cola share price adjusted for splits (1994–1999)

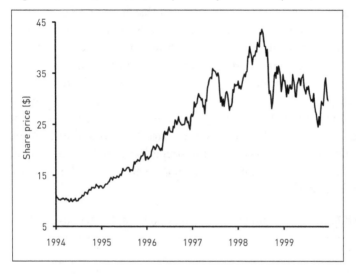

Source: www.advfn.com

But it would seem that the shares got ahead of the underlying performance of the business (in 1998, the price to earnings ratio rose to 60), as so many did in the late 1990s. They fell, and it wasn't until 2014 that they again reached the level of 1998 (Figure 8.6). It wasn't just the excessive price of the late 1990s that caused the stock market to be hesitant, there were some real problems. Not least was that Coca-Cola had lost Goizueta, who died after a short illness in 1997, followed by a series of CEOs who could not fill his shoes. Keough had retired in 1993, and wasn't enticed back, as an advisor to the board, until 2000. In 2004, aged 77 and disliking retirement, he returned as a director for another 13 year stint. "My idea of hell would be to go down to some watering hole, buy two pairs of pink pants, and wait for the cocktail hour."[208]

Why didn't Buffett sell at the top of the market?

Well, he says he is not able to play the game of in-and-out investing to exploit short-term or medium-term market moves. Second, he had made the commitment to Coca-Cola that it was one of the few permanent holdings of Berkshire; if his word is to mean something to the hundreds of executives calling him boss (and to executives yet to come aboard) then he must stick to it. Third, Coca-Cola was pumping out an increasing amount of money, in the form of dividends, for Buffett to invest elsewhere – dividends to Berkshire were $120m in 1998, but quadrupled to $488m in 2014 – thus the underlying business was performing even if Mr Market held the shares down. And fourth, there were good reasons to expect that the strengths of the business would be recognised again – in 2018 it made $6.45bn after tax, with $624m in dividends for Berkshire.

Figure 8.6: Coca-Cola share price adjusted for splits (2000–2019)

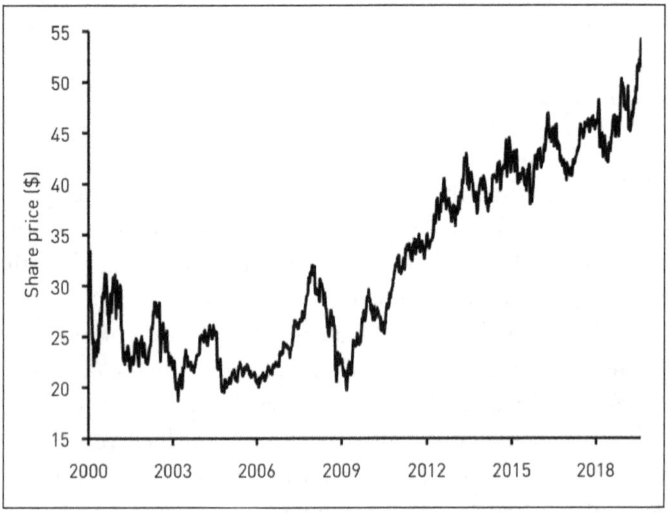

Source: www.advfn.com

Today, Buffett loves to observe people drinking Coke, or any of the other 500 brands sold by Coca-Cola, because he can bask in the warm glow of contemplating the other 1.9bn servings being consumed that day. Given Berkshire's 9.4% share, it benefits from 179m drinks being bought each day. And there is still much international growth to go for because the average person in most countries does not consume anything like as much as Americans. Berkshire Hathaway shareholders can look forward to dividends from Coca-Cola continuing to march upward – it won't be long before they surpass $1bn a year, closing in on the total paid for Berkshire's shares.

Learning points

1. **Look for a franchise strong enough to withstand years of poor management.** Despite many missteps, consumers continued to like the product and so it was able to bounce back from neglect and wrong turns.

2. **Inevitables are great companies to invest in, but only at a price giving a good margin of safety.** Buffett and Munger waited half a century until the conditions were right to buy.

3. **Analysis is easier, and assurance of success greater, when examining a company doing much the same as it has done for decades, and is likely to be doing it for many decades to come.** Many industries are just too complex and in flux to judge value within companies.

4. **Psychology is usually a much more important discipline than mathematics when trying to understand economic franchises.** People decide to buy Coke for a number of psychological as well as physiological reasons, ranging from a Pavlovian response to signalling and operant conditioning. Understanding psychological ideas is very useful for investors.

5. **The competence and integrity of the managers is vitally important.**

Investment 9

BORSHEIMS

Summary of the deal

Deal	Borsheims
Time	1989–present
Price paid	Not released
Quantity	Initially 80% of the shares. Bought more later.
Sale price	Part of Berkshire Hathaway today
Profit	Not released
Berkshire Hathaway in 1989	Share price: $4,800–$8,810 Book value: $4,927m Per share book value: $4,296

One of the great joys of being a Berkshire Hathaway shareholder is revelling in the whole weekend of events centred around the annual general meeting in early May. A fixture in the diaries of over 20,000 shareholders is a visit to the Borsheims store for the cocktail reception on Friday evening – it really does get crowded. People from all over the world mingle, express their wonder at the Berkshire phenomenon, and look at the jewellery and watches on display. Hundreds of thousands, if not millions, of dollars are taken by Borsheims on that evening alone – the anticipation and the party atmosphere seem to loosen the purse strings. But, so what? Spending at Borsheims is all part of the feeling of being a member of the Berkshire family, just as much as thinking through the rationale for the latest acquisition, or eating See's candy and drinking Coca-Cola during Buffett and Munger's six-hour Q&A.

The Berkshire connection has been a boon for Borsheims for over three decades. Even though it operates only one store, it sells to people – shareholders or not – from every corner of the globe. Buffett and Munger are great salesmen, rarely missing a chance to tell anyone who'll listen about the terrific range, the low prices and the trustworthiness of the people.

When four-fifths of the shares in a company with a mere 20,000 sq ft of sales floor were acquired by Berkshire in the spring of 1989, it was already an Omaha landmark, with both a dominant market share and enviable reputation. Immediately after buying, the Buffett marketing machine got to work. He helped organise buses for shareholders, for the evening after the AGM, to journey the mile or so to spend time looking around Borsheims. This Saturday evening tradition continues but, because demand grew, in 1990 they added a special opening for shareholders on the Sunday. Even this wasn't enough, so these two were joined, in 2000, by the Friday evening gathering, which helped to spread the burden of catering for the 40,000 shareholders in Omaha for the weekend.

So keen are Buffett and Munger to join fellow shareholders in chat (and sell to them), that they have themselves turned up on the Sunday afternoons, along with many of the Berkshire managers. Munger took to signing Borsheim receipts – helping to make it the biggest sales day of the year. "'Charlie will be available for autographs.' He smiles, 'However, only if the paper he signs is a Borsheim's sales ticket.'"[209] Buffett has taken to being a shopfloor sales assistant: "So come take advantage of me. Ask me for my 'Crazy Warren' price."[210]

Then there is the fun of shareholders taking on champion table tennis player, Ariel Hsing. For a number of years Buffett got Bill Gates to "try to soften her up" before other shareholders even made the attempt. There is more fun with the champion chess and scrabble experts, and – Buffett's favourite – bridge champions taking on all-comers including

Munger, Ajit Jain (Berkshire's insurance supremo) and Buffett himself. "Don't play them for money,"[211] he warns.

So important is Borsheims to the Berkshire Hathaway weekend, that the 2004 AGM was shifted to a weekend in April 2005: "we have scheduled the meeting for the last Saturday in April (the 30th), rather than the usual first Saturday in May. This year Mother's Day falls on May 8, and it would be unfair to ask the employees of Borsheim's and Gorat's [Buffett's favourite steakhouse] to take care of us at that special time – so we've moved everything up a week. Next year we'll return to our regular timing, holding the meeting on May 6, 2006."[212]

There is little doubt that Borsheims has been a great purchase for Berkshire, but we cannot quantify the level of success because the selling Friedman family asked for the price not to be made public. The subsequent profits flowing to Berkshire are too small, in the context of the giant corporation that Berkshire now is, to be separately discussed. However, we do know that costs have been held down by excellent management and by following the strategy of: operating only from the one store, buying in great volume, and passing on much of the resulting efficiencies to customers.

Sales had doubled in the three years after the firm moved to its current site in 1986 to when Berkshire acquired it. In fact, after Tiffany's of New York, Borsheims generated the largest sales volume from a single-store jeweller in the entire US. Since then, there have been many years of double-digit percentage growth as the store has grown from around 20,000 to over 60,000 sq ft on the same site. It has moved into selling through the internet, and selling by sending thousands of dollars-worth of jewellery for customers to look at in their homes all over the world, on a send-back-what-you-don't-want-no-obligation basis. Amazingly, it has suffered very few frauds – they really know their core customers.

There is no end of valuable endorsements and notable connections that come with being part of Berkshire. For example, Bill Gates, a friend of Buffett and Munger's, and director of Berkshire Hathaway, travelled to Omaha to select his engagement ring to offer to Melinda French in April 1993. Buffett met the couple at Omaha airport to escort them to the store. His sales pitch was that, when he bought an engagement ring in 1951, he spent 6% of his net wealth on it, and Bill Gates, the richest man in the world, worth tens of billions, should do the same. It didn't work, "We didn't have quite as big a day that Sunday as I had hoped,"[213] Buffett quipped.

Berkshire in 1989

Before discussing more detail about the Borsheims case it might be useful to know where Berkshire had got to in spring 1989. The money kept rolling in during the period 1987–1989, with the insurance businesses generating over $200m in both 1988 and 1989, and the controlled businesses producing well over $100m in each year for Buffett and Munger to invest elsewhere. All in all, those 24 months gave over $800m to be allocated to new exciting prospects, one of which was Borsheims.

Table 9.1: Net earnings after taxes attributable to Berkshire Hathaway from operating businesses

	1987 ($m)	1988 ($m)	1989 ($m)
Insurance underwriting	−20.7	−1.0	−12.3
Insurance investment income (dividends and interest)	136.7	197.8	213.6
Realised security gains	19.8	85.8	147.6
The Buffalo News	21.3	25.5	27.8
Fechheimer	6.6	7.7	6.8
Kirby	12.9	17.8	16.8
Nebraska Furniture Mart	7.6	9.1	8.4
Scott Fetzer Manufacturing Group	17.6	17.6	20.0
See's Candies	17.4	19.7	20.6
Wesco – other than Insurance	5.0	10.7	9.8
World Book	15.1	18.0	16.4
Other	4.3	17.0	2.8
Interest on debt	−5.9	−23.2	−27.1

	1987 ($m)	1988 ($m)	1989 ($m)
Charity donations by BH shareholders	−3.0	−3.2	−3.8
TOTAL EARNINGS	234.6	399.3	447.5

Source: W. Buffett, letters to shareholders of BH (1988–1989).

With monthly income averaging $37m, it's no surprise that Berkshire's shares rose on the stock market during 1989, from under $5,000 per share to over $8,500 (see Figure 9.1).

Figure 9.1: Berkshire Hathaway share price (1989)

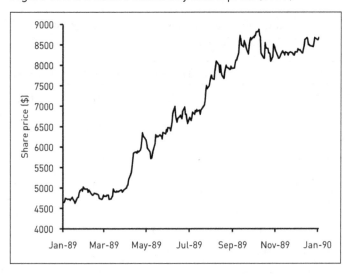

Source: www.finance.yahoo.com

Buffett commented on the progress made: "our performance to date has benefited from a double-dip: (1) the exceptional gains in intrinsic value that our portfolio companies have achieved; (2) the additional bonus we realized as the market appropriately 'corrected' the prices of these companies, raising their valuations in relation to those of the average business. We will continue to benefit from good gains in business value that we feel confident our portfolio companies will make. But our 'catch-up' rewards have been realized, which means we'll have to settle for a single-dip in the future."[214]

Warren Buffett worries about the popular notion of stock market efficiency

For some time, Buffett had been disturbed by the growing belief in the academic community, and by their Wall Street followers, that the equity market, through the buying and selling actions of thousands of 'informed' investors, 'correctly' priced shares. This meant that investors were unable to systematically select undervalued shares and thereby out-perform the stock market. They might manage, through luck, to occasionally achieve exceptional returns, but would eventually fall back to the averages (after allowing for risk).

This idea, that systematic out-performance was impossible, was directly opposed to the teaching of Benjamin Graham: that the market frequently made mountains out of molehills, that Mr Market can be irrationally pessimistic as well as irrationally optimistic, and that people base buying decisions on emotion and in herds, at least for some periods.

Graham would say to his classes at Columbia, including Buffett's, that "in the short run, the market is a voting machine but in the long run, it is a weighing machine." The market eventually catches up with the value, but there might be long periods offering opportunities to pay a price significantly less than intrinsic value.

The academics called their idea the efficient markets hypothesis (EMH) or efficient markets theory (EMT). This way of thinking was in direct conflict with Buffett's five decades of investment experience, as well as failing to explain the performance of the successful value investors that had gone before him. He decided to go on the offensive in his 1988 letter to shareholders – it was important that readers understood the teaching he received from Graham, and the knowledge he had gained from putting his money on the line.

Buffett criticised adherents of EMT. Observing correctly that the market was *frequently* efficient, they had incorrectly concluded that it was *always* efficient. The difference between these propositions was night and day.

> "In my opinion, the continuous 63-year arbitrage experience of Graham-Newman Corp., Buffett Partnership, and Berkshire illustrates just how foolish EMT is. (There's plenty of other evidence, also.) While at Graham-Newman, I made a study of its earnings from arbitrage during the entire 1926–1956 lifespan of the company. Unleveraged returns averaged 20% per year. Starting in 1956, I applied Ben Graham's arbitrage principles, first at Buffett Partnership and then Berkshire. Though I've not made an exact calculation, I have done enough work to know that the 1956–1988 returns averaged well over 20%. (Of course, I operated in an environment far more favorable than Ben's; he had 1929–1932 to contend with.)"

Over the same 63-year period, the general market delivered just under a 10% annual return, including dividends. That meant $1,000 would have grown to $405,000, if all income had been reinvested. A 20% rate of return, however, would have produced $97m. "That strikes us as a statistically-significant differential that might, conceivably, arouse one's curiosity." He went on:

> "Naturally the disservice done to students and gullible investment professionals who have swallowed EMT, has been an extraordinary service to us and other followers of Graham. In any sort of a contest – financial, mental, or physical – it's an enormous advantage to have opponents who have been taught that it's useless to even try. From a selfish point of view, Grahamites should probably endow chairs to ensure the perpetual teaching of EMT."

Buffett gave a speech at Columbia University, on the 50th anniversary of the publishing of Benjamin Graham and David Dodd's book *Security Analysis*. In 'The Superinvestors of Graham-and-Doddsville' he elegantly refuted the notion of the stock market always being efficient, and therefore unbeatable in the long run, by describing a place – an intellectual home – called 'Graham-and-Doddsville'. Those who resided there outperformed orangutans throwing dice. You can easily find the text of this speech, and a subsequent article of the same name, with a Google search.

Buffett on the advantage of avoiding churn

In the late 1980s Buffett was in full educational mode: trying to help fellow investors avoid common errors; recounting cautionary tales at Berkshire's AGMs; talking to MBA students; TV appearances; and through his annual letters to shareholders. One of the issues preying on his mind in 1989 was the mistake of rapidly changing the constituents of a portfolio – many so-called professional fund managers could have an annual churn rate (proportion changed) of over 100%.

By starting out with the intention of holding shares in your portfolio for many years, you can achieve much higher returns. This comes not only from a much better mindset, which is focused on the long-run prospects of the underlying business rather than the market's short-term obsessions, but also from savings on transaction costs and taxes on capital gains made. And then there are the human relationship issues of building up long-term friendships and understanding with business managers.

To illustrate, in his 1989 letter, Buffett asked us to consider the extremis position of starting with $1 and buying shares with it, then holding for one year during which a 100% return is made.

If the after-tax proceeds of the sale were used to repeat this process for the next 19 years – each time achieving a 100% return – the 34% capital gains tax would have delivered $13,000 to the government, leaving about $25,250 for the investor. Not bad.

If, however, a single investment was made which doubled 20 times over the 20 years, our dollar would have grown to $1,048,576. Cashing out would leave a profit of about $692,000 after a deduction of roughly $356,500 for tax.

The only reason for this staggering difference in results would be the timing of tax payments. The government, too, gains significantly from the second scenario although I it would have to wait for its money.

Buffett was clear, however, that these mathematics were not the reason they had adopted their strategy of long-term investment. It was possible, he said, that they could have earned even greater after-tax returns by moving rather frequently from one investment to another. Many years ago, that's exactly what he and Munger had done.

"Now we would rather stay put, even if that means slightly lower returns. Our reason is simple: we have found splendid business relationships to be so rare and so enjoyable that we want to retain all we develop. This decision is particularly easy for us because we feel that these relationships will produce good – though perhaps not optimal – financial results."

Giving up these relationships with "people we know to be interesting and admirable, for time with others we do not know and who are likely to have human qualities far closer to average" didn't seem to make much sense to Buffett. It would be akin to "marrying for money – a mistake under most circumstances, insanity if one is already rich."

A short history of Borsheims

The first store was established in Omaha by Louis Borsheim in 1870, the frontier days of this Union Pacific railway town. It was held by his family until 1947 when the small jewellery shop was bought by Louis and Rebecca Friedman, and their son Ike.

Rebecca has a link to another story in this book. She is one of the younger sisters of Mrs Rose Blumkin of Nebraska Furniture Mart fame (Investment 3 – bought by Berkshire in 1983). Mrs B spent years working hard and saving enough money to help one sibling at a time escape oppressive soviet Belarus. Rebecca and Louis used the money sent from Omaha to make their way to America via Latvia in 1922, a journey fraught with danger. They arrived in the USA with no assets to speak of but, through sheer hard work, intelligence and decency, accumulated enough capital over a quarter of a century to buy Borsheims.

Friedman's store was run with the same philosophy as Nebraska Furniture Mart: a single-location offering customers a wide range; sell cheap and tell the truth; the low prices obtained from suppliers (due to large volume), and the benefits of a low expense ratio, were passed on to customers leading to rapid turnover; and a family dedicated to getting every detail right.

Warren Buffett said that he had been remiss in not spotting the business as a potential acquisition soon after buying NFM in 1983. "Your chairman blundered… neglecting to ask Mrs B a question any schoolboy would have thought of: 'Are there any more at home like you?'"[215]

In 1986, Borsheims moved from the 7,000 sq ft (35 staff) downtown store to its current location at 120 Regency Pkwy, off Omaha's Dodge Street, eight miles from the heart of the town. This offered much more (and cheaper) space for growth and plenty of parking; in moving, it more than trebled its floorspace (it's doubled again since).

By then, Rebecca and Louis were in their eighties and taking more of a back seat, but still helping out most days. Ike was ably assisted by another generation. His son Alan, who started as a floor sweeper when five, and then served customers at ten, was, by 1986 (aged 31), a fully qualified and enthusiastic gemologist, with a special fondness for coloured stones. Sons-in-law Donald Yale (married to Janis Friedman), and Marvin Kohn (married to Susie Friedman), were working full time for the business – these daughters of Ike and Roz Friedman lent a hand at busy times.

Ike was greatly admired by staff and customers alike as a kindly, knowledgeable leader, and as the consummate retailer. One commented that "Ike Friedman was a remarkable character. A computer mind, [He] knew people by their jewelry, knew people by their previous purchases… Incredible negotiator, an incredible buyer, an incredible salesman."[216]

The deal

Legend has it that Donald Yale prompted Buffett to think about buying Borsheims. Buffett had shopped there for years, and as Christmas 1988 approached he was looking for a ring. Well known to the staff, a little banter was normal. While he was looking, Yale yelled out "Don't sell Warren the ring, sell him the store!"[217] After the holidays, Buffett called to ask if a sale was possible. A short meeting was arranged in February with Ike Friedman and Donald Yale at Friedman's house.

The deal was agreed in only ten minutes, during which Buffett asked five questions[218] (he already knew the business didn't have debt, and he knew about the excellent reputation it enjoyed):

1. What are sales?

2. What are gross profits?

3. What are expenses?

4. What is inventory?

5. Are you willing to stay on?

The first four – answered without referring to notes – confirmed that the business was in excellent shape. The fifth was answered in the affirmative, providing Buffett with the key people – Ike in particular – to take the business forward.

A cash payment was made for 80% of the shares, with a legal document that ran to only a page or so and cost $1,100 in lawyer's fees. They all agreed not to disclose the price – rumour has it that it was in the region of $60m, but I have no evidence to back that up. Ike thus became very cash-rich, and the remaining 20% of shares were split between Alan Friedman, Donald Yale and wife Janis, and Marvin Kohn and wife Susie.

Buffett wrote in spring 1989:

> "This purchase... delivers exactly what we look for: an outstanding business run by people we like, admire, and trust. It's a great way to start the year... Most people, no matter how sophisticated they are in other matters, feel like babes in the woods when purchasing jewelry. They can judge neither quality nor price. For them only one rule makes sense: If you don't know jewelry, know the jeweler... Borsheim's had no audited financial statements; nevertheless, we didn't take inventory, verify receivables or audit the operation in any way. Ike simply told us what was so – and on that basis we drew up a one-page contract and wrote a large check."[219]

Borsheims blossoms

Immediately after the deal, Buffett gave instruction to "forget that it happened, and just keep doing what you were doing."[220] That's it, there was no further instruction according to Donald Yale. No discussion on crucial matters such as growth plans, management hierarchy, decision-making or how they might boost profits. Just carry on doing what you are doing, using your initiative, and Berkshire will be in it for the long-haul, supporting you all the way.

> "All members of the Friedman family will continue to operate just as they have before; Charlie and I will stay on the sidelines where we belong. And when we say 'all members', the words have real meaning. Mr and Mrs Friedman, at 88 and 87 respectively, are in the store daily. The wives of Ike, Alan, Marvin and Donald all pitch in at busy times, and a fourth generation is beginning to learn the ropes."[221]

The support of Berkshire has been a great blessing. As well as the extra publicity, Borsheims has benefitted from the cash backing and creditworthiness of Berkshire (one of only a handful of AAA-rated companies), giving it enormous buying power. It can prepay for bulk purchases thereby obtain the lowest prices (it's very rare for jewellers to pay upfront).

Buffett ranked Borsheim's along with the Sainted Seven – those Berkshire-controlled businesses with economic characteristics ranging from good to superb, and managers ranging from superb to superb:

> "In the past, we have labeled our major manufacturing, publishing and retail operations 'The Sainted Seven.' With our acquisition of Borsheim's, early in 1989, the challenge was to find a new title both alliterative and appropriate. We failed: let's call the group 'The Sainted Seven Plus One'… most of these managers have no need to work for a living; they show up at the ballpark because they like to hit home runs. And that's exactly what they do."[222]

Shortly after the purchase, Ike was invited to a very special gathering of Buffett's investing friends – those who run value-orientated funds based on Benjamin Graham's principles:

> "Ike decided to dazzle the group, so he brought from Omaha about $20m of particularly fancy merchandise. I was somewhat apprehensive – Bishop's Lodge is no Fort Knox – and I mentioned my concern to Ike at our opening party, the evening before his presentation. Ike took me aside. 'See that safe?' he

said. 'This afternoon we changed the combination and now even the hotel management doesn't know what it is.' I breathed easier. Ike went on: 'See those two big fellows with guns on their hips? They'll be guarding the safe all night.' I now was ready to rejoin the party. But Ike leaned closer: 'And besides, Warren,' he confided, 'the jewels aren't in the safe.' How can we miss with a fellow like that."[223]

As Borsheims grew, it managed to keep its operating costs at about 18% of sales, less than half that of a typical competitor.

Sadly, in 1991, only two years after Berkshire had bought, Ike died suddenly from lung cancer. There was no succession plan in place. Alan Friedman had left to set up his own jewellery stores in Beverly Hills, selling his shares to Berkshire Hathaway. Yale became president and CEO and Marvin Cohn was named executive vice president. For three years all went smoothly but, in 1994, Janis Yale was struggling with cancer. Donald tried for a while to cope with both his executive and family responsibilities but held that his family was the priority, and so resigned as an executive, retaining a non-executive position on the board.

After a short interview with Buffett, Susan Jacques, aged 34, was appointed president and CEO. She had arrived in America, 14 years before, from Zimbabwe (then Rhodesia). In 1983, she met Alan Friedman while on a gemological course in Florida. She was offered a job at Borsheims as a lowly shop assistant, on $4 per hour. She jokes that she had three strikes against her becoming a leader in a trade dominated by middle-aged Jewish men: she was young, a woman, and was a *goy* (a non-Jew). But what Buffett was looking for was competence, energy and integrity, and she fitted the bill very well.

> "Though she lacked a managerial background, I did not hesitate to make her CEO in 1994. She's smart, she loves the business, and she loves her associates. That beats having an MBA degree any time. (An aside: Charlie and I are not big fans of resumes. Instead, we focus on brains, passion and integrity.)"[224]

In 2014, Susan Jacques left Borsheims to follow her passion by becoming president and CEO of the Gemological Institute of America, the place where she started out as a student in 1980. Buffett said, "I couldn't be happier or more proud of Susan. While it is with great sadness that I accept her resignation after her long and stellar career with Borsheims, I know she is accepting a role at GIA that she is passionate about and allows her to give back to the jewelry industry. I am confident that she will bring the same style of professionalism and collaboration to her new and exciting role in the gem and jewelry industry that she has honed throughout her years of service at Borsheims."[225]

The three hundred and fifty employee, 62,000 sq ft store, is now in the capable hands of Karen Goracke, CEO, with Marvin Cohn as executive vice president, and continues to go from strength to strength.

Learning points

1. **The benefits of combination.** Borsheims has been boosted by the extra attention it receives by being part of the Berkshire family, not least the loyalty of the shareholders. Also, Borsheims' buying power is enhanced by Berkshire's credit standing and deep pockets.

2. **Deep pervasive culture is valuable.** If a culture has been so developed as to have deep roots throughout the organisation, then the loss of a founder/key person will not be too detrimental to the business. When Buffett lost Ike Friedman, the cohesive collegial culture at Borsheims quickly found a knowledgeable and experienced replacement in Donald Yale. Similarly, when he had to leave, Susan Jacques moved up the ranks to continue the strategy, polices and attitude of the organisation; later she was ably followed by Karen Goracke.

3. **Do not over-exploit a virtuous circle.** Borsheims' low prices and costs, buying power, and large range attract customers from far and wide. This enables high volume which, in turn, leads to low prices and costs, greater buying power and range. The benefits of this virtuous circle must, for the greater part, be passed onto customers. If Borsheims becomes greedy on operating margin then competitors will grab customers.

4. **The stock market is not a perfect weighing machine.** It is efficient in pricing shares for most of the people most of the time. But that

still leaves many opportunities to exploit inefficiencies, and thereby outperform. This is especially so if you concentrate on understanding the business, assessing the quality of the people running it, build in a margin of safety on the price paid for shares, do not aim for unrealistic share returns, and exploit Mr Market's emotions.

5. **Don't churn.** Holding shares for short periods leads to the wrong mindset, higher taxes and transaction costs, and therefore lower returns.

Investment 10

GILLETTE-PROCTER & GAMBLE-DURACELL

Summary of the deal

Deal	Gillette-Procter & Gamble-Duracell
Time	1989–present
Price paid	$600m (plus $430m for P&G shares 2006–2008)
Quantity	$600m preferred shares, later exchanged for common stock in Gillette (11% of its equity), which were exchanged for P&G shares (3%), which were exchanged for 100% of Duracell.
Sale price	Duracell is part of Berkshire today
Profit	Nine-fold, at least
Berkshire Hathaway in 1989	Share price: $4,800–$8,810
	Book value: $4,927m
	Per share book value: $4,296

This case study demonstrates the value of recognising economic franchises which have formed over time by making a deep impression on the minds of consumers. People form attachments to products they have long been familiar with and have come to trust. Once a brand has this 'share of mind', it is difficult for potential rivals to challenge the incumbent. This kind of deep and wide moat around a franchise castle permits exceptional rates of return on equity capital, because of the improved pricing power a strong brand brings.

But even strong consumer product companies can become vulnerable. In the late 1980s, Gillette was going through such a phase, not on the product attractiveness side but on the financial structure side. It had been attacked by Wall Street raiders, and chose to mollify aggressive shareholders by borrowing a great deal and buying back its own shares. Things went too far; it started to run out of money and remained a subject of interest to activists and private equity players. It needed a large cash injection quickly, and it needed a friendly large shareholder who would not sell out to raiders, or sack the managers, doing untold damage to the long-term health of the businesses. Berkshire Hathaway, Warren Buffett and Charlie Munger fitted the bill. They could come up with $600m almost at the drop of a hat. They would allow the directors to manage in the long-term interests of the firm and they would scare off the big beasts of Wall Street.

At first, Berkshire bought preferred shares to receive a very generous dividend. But it wasn't long before the preferreds were converted to common stock, and then the shares moved to a multiple of the $600m put in.

A few years later, the opportunity arose to combine Gillette, with its extraordinarily strong brands, with Procter & Gamble – the company holding the world's broadest set of strong brands. Buffett and Munger jumped at the chance of Berkshire being the largest shareholder in the combined company. They could see the quality of the franchises, and they could see potential for synergy in linking operations, not least the improved bargaining power vis-à-vis supermarkets.

Later, when the share price of Procter and Gamble was high, and the directors were willing to part with one of their businesses, Duracell, at what Buffett and Munger thought a bargain price, Berkshire swapped its holding in P&G for 100% of Duracell. This gem came with a cash dowry of $1.8bn. That deal was in 2015 and Duracell is now seen as part of a bigger plan readying Berkshire for the shift from a carbon-powered world to electric power. Duracell sits nicely with Berkshire Hathaway Energy and BYD electric cars and batteries. Even without the potential from collaboration with BHE and BYD, Duracell has one-quarter of the world's battery market and a very strong brand.

The creation of Gillette's economic franchise

A middle-aged travelling salesman, King Gillette, who also filed patents from time to time, thought he could do better than the safety razors on the market in the 1890s. These were of a similar shape to today's razors but had only one sharp side. Annoyingly, it was necessary to sharpen it on a leather *strop* or to employ a professional to hone it properly. It wasn't long before the blade could be sharpened no more. These complications were a nuisance to this salesman, especially as he was often forced to shave on a moving train.

Gillette worked on some ideas and, in 1895, came up with a thin rectangular sheet of metal, sharpened on both sides, cheap enough to be thrown away and easily replaced. But it took six years, working with MIT graduate engineer, William Emery Nickerson, to figure out how to produce in high volume. Sharpening thin cheap steel was not easy; Nickerson had to create his own machinery.

Gillette and Nickerson established their company in 1901, but it wasn't until 1903 that shavers and blades rolled off the production line. By the end of the following year, over 91,000 razors had been sold. It was quite a novelty for customers to buy a razor followed by a series of blade packs. In 1904, a patent was granted for a razor with a blade, with sharp edges on both sides, which could be thrown away when blunt. The retail price, at $5 for the safety razor plus a pack of 20 blades, seems hefty at about half a week's wage, but clearly the convenience was worth it. A pack of 20 blades was $1.

The Gillette Company might have been slow to find a way to mass produce but, once they found it, they were very fast in ramping up production and in expanding abroad. By the end of 1908, manufacturing plants were in Britain, Canada, France and Germany as well as the United States.

Competitors could see the advantage Gillette had in the market place so it wasn't long before they too offered doubled-edged blades. Patent battles were inevitable, often followed by Gillette buying the opponent.

John Joyce, a major investor and director, battled King Gillette for control of the company. In the end (1910), Gillette sold a substantial proportion of his controlling stake to Joyce. He then semi-retired but was titled company president and would frequently visit foreign branches (his face was famous from the image on the packaging). Gillette concentrated more on travelling, property and buying shares in the stock market, while Joyce managed the business day-to-day. When Joyce died in 1916, his friend Edward Aldred, an investment banker, bought the Gillette shares in Joyce's estate.

A breakthrough came when the company was awarded a contract to supply razors to US armed forces in the first world war as part of the soldiers' field kits – 3.5m razors and 32m blades. Naturally, the returning soldiers held onto their razors and, more importantly to the company, the habit of using Gillette's blades.

Gillette has been credited with inventing the business strategy of selling a product cheap, often at a loss, to increase the installed base, followed by the sale of a complementary product at high prices. Business schools call it the 'razors-and-blades strategy', but it has been applied to many industries from games consoles to music streaming (freemium model).

But it's not true that King Gillette hit on this idea. In fact, until 1921, while the product was still under patent, Gillette asked for high prices for the handle. Gillette had chosen to market itself as at the quality end of the market, and was charging up to five times other brands for the initial set. But once the patent expired it no longer had the exclusive right to offer its particular shape of handle, so it lowered the price of its old model to match or undercut competitors, while introducing a new patented handle selling at a premium price. This had the effect of pressuring/excluding competitors at the low end of the market – thus following a razors-and-blades strategy – but it also offered a special upgraded version.

In theory, it should have come under competitive pressure to lower blade prices after their patent expired in 1921 and they could be copied. But, by then, millions of men around the world were in the habit of buying Gillette's quality blades, and the powerful marketing reinforced the message that it was worth paying extra for 'the best a man can get'. Brand investing really paid off, inducing a strong psychological loyalty effect. In fact, it was so good that, in the 1950s, Gillette's US market share was 70–75%, with high shares in many other countries.

Diversifying

In the 1950s and 1960s, cash was accumulating in the company and the directors saw opportunities for investing in adjacent and not-so-adjacent market areas. First, foamy shaving cream was introduced in 1953. Two years later, the company went for something completely outside the field of male grooming by acquiring Paper Mate, a manufacturer of ballpoint pens. Returning to the main theme in 1960, Right Guard antiperspirant was launched and, in 1967, the German company Braun, most famous for electric shavers, but also offering a range of other electric products, was purchased. Then they felt the pull of pens again and bought the Parker and Waterman companies. These are just the highlights – the whole list is too long to present here. Suffice to say, the company became highly diversified.

While this accumulation of brands was going on, the Gillette razor (and other products) were rapidly expanding sales into over 200 countries. It wasn't long before over 60% of sales were outside of the USA.

Colman Mockler, a Gillette lifer having joined in 1957, was appointed CEO in 1975. He thought the company had diversified too far, lost focus, and was operating some businesses offering only small rates of return on capital (his career had developed through the finance side of the business). The newly installed CEO inherited a business selling items ranging from lighters to deodorants, and making a respectable $78m in earnings on worldwide sales of $1.5bn. His approach to bump up shareholder returns was to concentrate particularly on those markets where consumers were in the habit of frequent purchases, where high volumes could be achieved. He sold off leather goods, plant food, and some other divisions, and he pumped the money into those areas where the company possessed a clear competitive advantage. He also increased the advertising budget to reinforce the brand image-based economic franchises.

A serious competitive threat

The French company BIC shook a number of markets with a series of disposable products. They first entered America in the 1958 with disposable pens, which greatly affected Gillette's Paper Mate. 1973 saw the BIC disposable lighter, which lowered sales of Gillette's 'Cricket' lighters.

Both the pen and the lighter markets were important to Gillette, but not crucial. The big attack on its core was yet to come. Gillette's razor blades contributed over 70% of its profits, so when BIC introduced the one-piece disposable razor in 1975, the company felt under real threat. Its response was to both lower prices and to emphasise its better quality. This was implemented well, and Gillette's profits rose. The first twin-bladed disposable razor was launched by Gillette in 1976, followed by the first pivot-headed razor in 1977. Some of the surplus cash was used to buy Oral-B toothbrushes in 1984.

Under attack from Wall Street raiders

The profit build-up of the early and mid-1980s made the company attractive to a number of Wall Street players with easy access to vast amounts of debt capital (this the era of the junk bond craze). Ronald O. Perelman, who had taken control of Revlon for $1.8bn the year before, launched a $4.1bn takeover bid for Gillette in 1986. Revlon had already acquired 13.9% of Gillette's shares. Both companies operated in personal care products and, it was argued, there were sales and distribution synergies to be had.

Mockler fought hard, but the outcome was that Gillette agreed that it buy back those of its shares held by Revlon for $558m ($59.50 per share). This was higher than the market price of $56.625. Analysts on Wall Street saw the transaction as 'greenmail',[226] with Revlon walking away with a profit of $43m plus getting Gillette to pay $9m of its legal expenses. Meanwhile, remaining shareholders saw the share fall to $45.875.

To add more harassment, Revlon came back the following year with two more unwelcome offers. Feeling under pressure to improve performance, Gillette restructured senior management, sold underperforming units, modernised factories, moved production to low-cost locations, and reduced employee numbers.

Despite all this, it found itself a target again in 1988. This time Coniston Partners, a New York investor group, holding 6% of its shares, pushed to replace four members of Gillette's 12-strong board with its own nominees. They wanted Gillette to be sold or to be split up. There was a tense fight, but in the end Gillette shareholders voted against Coniston's ideas. But it was very close, with 48% of shareholders voting with Coniston. Under pressure from the largest shareholder, i.e. Coniston, and fearful of more unsolicited bids, the Gillette board came up with a plan to repurchase one in seven of its shares – this time open to all shareholders. In all, 16m were purchased, costing $720m.

Most of the money for this was borrowed, significantly increasing the interest burden (up to a 10% annual rate was paid). This worried investors, resulting in the share price falling 5% on the August 1988 buy-back announcement. The company tried to reassure shareholders by forecasting that total debt would fall to 'only' $1bn by 1992, assisted by high cash inflow. But investors could see the balance sheet showed negative net assets ($85m of negative equity at one point in 1988), and Gillette had an expensive capital expenditure programme and brand enhancement spend. At least profits were still flowing: in 1988 earnings were $269m rising to $385m in 1989, on turnovers of $3.6bn and $3.8bn respectively.

Gillette directors were forced to recognise two things:

- First, they had struggled to remain independent – perhaps it was only a matter of time before one of the big Wall Street beasts took them over.

- Second, they were carrying too much debt, making the company vulnerable to financial distress.

They needed to shore up defences. They needed a white squire able to put in significant non-debt capital and block aggressive outsiders. But where could you find one of those with a few hundred million dollars to hand?

The deal

Warren Buffett was able to sit in Omaha, reading his six daily newspapers, and observe from a relaxed distance the tribulations at Gillette; the way it had been bounced into weakening its balance sheet, ever fearful of another disruptive bid battle. One spring evening, when reading Gillette's

1988 annual report he had an idea, "It was my thought that they might be interested in a big investment in their shares because they had used up all their capital in repurchasing shares… I'll propose myself."[227]

Over at Gillette HQ, Director Joseph J. Sisco – a famed State Department diplomat and Buffett's fellow director on GEICO's board – was having similar ideas. Buffett called Sisco to ask if he would approach Colman Mockler, to see if Gillette might be amenable to discussing an investment from Berkshire. "I told Joe, look, if they have an interest, fine. If they don't, that's fine too."[228]

Sisco had no hesitation in supporting the idea, and he was sure that the two Midwesterners would hit it off. Sure enough, when Mockler and Buffett met a few days later, in Omaha, they got on very well, both enjoying the simple foods at the Omaha Press Club (hamburgers and Coca-Cola). Buffett said, "I liked him, the chemistry was good. It was like meeting a girl, it didn't take five minutes. And I could tell he was very able."[229]

Buffett suggested a preferred stock purchase at any amount between $300m and $750m – Mockler could pick the number. After lunch, Buffett drove his guest back to the airport in his ageing car, not having discussed any of the deal terms.

Gillette's directors had recently committed over $120m, from their already depleted cash pile, for production of their revolutionary Sensor shaver (to be launched soon), and were spending yet more money on international expansion. Thus, at the 15 June 1989 board meeting, they expressed keenness for taking Berkshire's money but – of course – on the right terms. Mockler reported that he admired Buffett and that the investment "would support the belief that Gillette can carry out its strategic plans without undue concern for the disruptions and distractions of the past few years."[230] They were attracted by Buffett's avowed intent not to engage in hostile takeovers, and his record of sticking to that rule. One of his other rules when buying large influential share stakes was also attractive to the Gillette team, "Management in place (we can't supply it)."[231]

The first proposal from Buffett was for Berkshire to buy $600m of newly-issued preferred stock carrying a right to be converted into common stock. The preferreds were to pay a 9% per annum dividend and be convertible at a common stock price of $45. There was an alternative offer from Buffett: a dividend, of an even more generous 9.5%, and a conversion price of $50. The common stock was then selling in the market at around $40–$43.

Mockler and the board thought these arrangements too onerous for Gillette's common stockholders and rejected them. But they agreed to discuss alternative terms with Charlie Munger during a series of meetings in July. The two parties finally settled on an annual dividend of 8.75% and a $50 conversion price. On 20 July 1989, Berkshire bought $600m preferred and Buffett and Munger looked forward to receiving a quarterly dividend amounting to $13.125m, which they could then deploy to other investments.

Buffett joined Gillette's board of directors and agreed that Berkshire's stake would not be sold, except in the case of a change of control, or if its insurance regulators (much of the money came from insurance float) forced a sale in the event of Gillette falling into financial distress. If Berkshire's preferred shares were to be sold, Gillette itself would have first right of refusal. And, with Buffett on board, Gillette quickly changed the vending machines and cafeterias so they stocked Coca-Cola rather than Pepsi.

An element of the deal: if Gillette's common stock stood above $62.50 for at least 20 consecutive days then Gillette could insist on conversion of the preferred into common stock. Doing this would make Berkshire a holder of 11% of the common stock.

Gillette used the $600m to pay back high-interest loans, strengthen the balance sheet, and preserve cash flow – allowing the large capital spend to continue.

The financial press thought the company had been far too generous to Berkshire given that preferred shares issued by other companies, of a similar calibre, offered several percentage points less. One of the directors, Rita Ricardo-Campbell, later wrote a book on hostile mergers in which she defended the deal. "There were, as I recall, no alternative deals sought by Gillette or offered to it. A lump-sum investment of $600m is not easily found… Gillette's advisors said that the investor's return would probably be about 25%. From Buffett's point of view, there is a risk in any investment, including convertible preferreds, as his USAir and Salomon holdings illustrate."[232]

Buffett commented on Gillette in his 1989 letter to Berkshire shareholders: "Gillette's business is very much the kind we like. Charlie and I think we understand the company's economics and therefore believe we can make a reasonably intelligent guess about its future. (If you haven't tried Gillette's new Sensor razor, go right out and get one.)" Commenting on his key person, he said: "We only want to link up with people whom we like, admire, and trust... Colman Mockler, Jr at Gillette... meet[s] this test in spades."

At a time when he couldn't find attractive common stock investments, Buffett went for the safer option of preferred shares, saying that he thought they would at least return the amount invested plus dividends, in almost all conditions bar, say, another Great Depression or large fraud. But he did add that he would be disappointed if that is all Berkshire gets, because "we will have given up flexibility and consequently will have missed some significant opportunities that are bound to present themselves... The only way Berkshire can achieve satisfactory results from its four preferred issues is to have the common stocks of the investee companies do well."[233]

The fact that Gillette had a major, stable, and interested shareholder, was seen by Buffett as likely to increase profits for other Gillette shareholders. "Charlie and I will be supportive, analytical, and objective... Experienced CEOs... at certain moments, appreciate the chance to test their thinking on someone without ties to their industry or to decisions of the past... Charlie and I feel that our preferred stock investments should produce returns moderately above those achieved by most fixed-income portfolios and that we can play a minor but enjoyable and constructive role in the investee companies."[234]

Gillette's golden years

The Sensor

In October 1989, the Sensor razor was unveiled. This offered thinner twin blades, individually mounted on springs, allowing a closer shave due to continuous adjustment to the contours of the face. It was an instant hit. So successful was it that the company suspended advertising, for a while, so that the production team could catch up.

So, despite costing almost $200m to develop over 13 years, followed by $100m for advertising, it made a mint for Gillette. Factories produced around the clock, seven days a week. Within two years the one-billionth blade cartridge was sold.

Gillette's profits after tax went from $285m in 1989, to $368m in 1990, to $427m in 1991; and were headed for a whopping $513m in 1992.

Common stock

The common stock rocketed, and the board insisted that Berkshire's preferreds be converted into 12m common shares on 1 April 1991. Given that these shares had a market value of over $1.3bn, and being a participant in the profits of a company on a fast-growth trajectory, Buffett and Munger were quite content to switch to the common stock.

Sadly, in January 1991, Colman Mockler died of a heart attack aged 61. In his 1990 letter to shareholders, Buffett paid this tribute:

> "No description better fitted Colman than 'gentleman' – a word signifying integrity, courage and modesty. Couple these qualities with the humor and exceptional business ability that Colman possessed and you can understand why I thought it an undiluted pleasure to work with him and why I, and all others who knew him, will miss Colman so much."

He also referenced a *Forbes* cover story about Gillette, published a few days before Colman died. The article lauded the company's devotion to quality; a mindset that has caused it to consistently focus its energies on coming up with something better, even though its existing products already ranked as the class of the field. In so depicting Gillette, Buffett said, *Forbes* had painted a portrait of Colman.

Why did Buffett hold on to Gillette's common stock?

After conversion of the preferred shares into 12m common stock in 1991, Berkshire could have sold for over $1.3bn, more than double the original investment less than two years previously. So why didn't Buffett cash in his chips at that point?

Presumably, he thought through the likely owner earnings over the next decade and beyond. After that, he estimated, probably in his head, the present value of the future annual owner earnings to arrive at a rough estimate of intrinsic value. The factors informing this estimate are qualitative and far from precise. They are based on judgements about matters such as the sustainability of the strength of brands in the minds of people in various countries; in the competence of the managerial team, and in the likelihood of the directors acting in shareholders best interest.

We do not know what numbers Buffett came up with in 1991. What we can do, however, is look at the dividends actually paid to Berkshire over the following ten years. And we can look at Berkshire's share of Gilllette's undistributed earnings (see Table 10.1). Perhaps Buffett had in mind numbers similar to these? If so, his 1991-self would have judged that it wouldn't be many years until Berkshire's dividends, plus its share of retained earnings in Gillette, amounted to more than $100m for a typical year. (We can't automatically use the numbers in the table as perfect representations of owner earnings, because some of the retained earnings might be swallowed up by large capital expenditures, or extra investment in working capital to maintain the company's economic franchises, but the numbers still give some idea of the ballpark figures for owner earnings.)

He might also have thought, given a strong managerial team constantly leveraging market positions with new products and new marketing triumphs, that the dividends plus retained earnings amount would grow year-on-year. If that turned out to be the case, then the intrinsic value of those 12m shares would exceed the market price of $1.3bn by a significant margin.

Table 10.1: Berkshire's share of Gillette dividends and undistributed earnings (1991–2000)

Year	Dividends ($m)	Berkshire's share of undistributed operating earnings* ($m)	No. of Gillette shares held by Berkshire** (m)
1991 (9 mos)	11	20	12 (until 1 May) then 24
1992	17	33	24
1993	19	38	24
1994	23	44	24
1995	25	n/a	24 (until 1 June) then 48
1996	33	63	48
1997	40	70	48
1998	41	n/a	48 (until 15 May) then 96
1999	55	45	96
2000	61	43	96

* Less a hypothetical tax if it was paid over to Berkshire.

** Berkshire did not buy any more shares but there were 2 for 1 share splits.

Sources: W. Buffett, letters to shareholders of BH (1991–2000); Media Corporate IR Net, stock split history (1950–1998), media.corporate-ir.net.

In terms of franchise strength, Buffett put Gillette in the same category as Coca-Cola:

"Coca-Cola and Gillette are two of the best companies in the world and we expect their earnings to grow at hefty rates in the years ahead. Over time, also, the value of our holdings in these stocks should grow in rough proportion."[235]

It didn't seem difficult, to him, to conclude that Coca-Cola and Gillette possessed far less business risk over the long term than, say, any computer company or retailer. Coke sold about 44% of all soft drinks worldwide, and Gillette had more than a 60% share (in value) of the blade market. Apart from Wrigley, Buffett couldn't think of any other significant businesses which had enjoyed such global dominance in their sector.

> "Moreover, both Coke and Gillette have actually increased their worldwide shares of market in recent years. The might of their brand names, the attributes of their products, and the strength of their distribution systems give them an enormous competitive advantage, setting up a protective moat around their economic castles."[236]

New, new, new...

Large amounts of cash flowed in and the managers were hungry for more world-beating products. In 1992, the Oral-B Indicator toothbrush was introduced, and the Gillette Series line of men's toiletries – including antiperspirant, shaving cream and aftershave – were developed and launched.

Parker Pen was bought for $484m in 1993, allowing Gillette to claim top position worldwide for writing instruments, with its Parker, Paper Mate and Waterman brands. In the same year, Gillette launched its 'shaving system', SensorExcel, promising 'five soft, flexible microfins'. Also in 1993: Braun's FlavorSelect coffeemaker; Oral-B Advantage toothbrush; and Custom Plus men's and women's disposable razors with pivoting heads.

There followed a few bolt-on acquisitions, but the really big one was the $7.8bn purchase of Duracell in 1996, world leader in alkaline batteries. The idea was to combine with Gillette's marketing channels to reach customers in 200 countries. Duracell became the firm's second-highest-ranking division in terms of sales.

Another highlight that year was the SensorExcel for Women, which helped to propel companywide sales to nearly $10bn, and profits to $949bn. The success in female shaving products was consolidated, in 2000, with the introduction of a series of products under the Venus brand.

There was something of a hiccup to sales and earnings growth in the period 1998–2000. Stationery and small appliances lost money, and the battery business was subject to aggressive competitive attack by Energizer and Rayovac, both of which offered cheaper products for similar performance. Another competitor with an eye on Gillette's high margins was Schick-Wilkinson; it introduced the Quattro (with four blades), gaining an extra three percentage points of market share.

As sales fell, directors responded by cutting staff but could not prevent a decline in Gillette's shares. Despite the drop, the market value of Berkshire's holding in Gillette had risen from $600m a decade before to over $3bn (Figure 10.1).

"It's pleasant to go to bed every night knowing there are 2.5bn males in the world who have to shave in the morning."[237]

Figure 10.1: Market value of Berkshire's holding in Gillette (1989–2005)

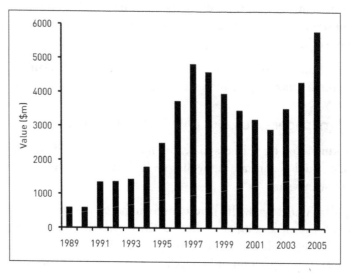

The Kilts era

In February 2001, after 14 consecutive quarters of missed earnings targets, and five years of flat sales, Jim Kilts was hired, from Kraft, to revive Gillette.

Kilts was Gillette's first outside CEO for 70 years. Characteristically, Buffett made up his mind to hire Kilts after just one meeting:

> "It was a natural move… He made as much sense in terms of talking about business in general as anybody I've ever talked to. If you listen to Jim analyze a business situation, you get absolutely no baloney. And frankly, finding someone like that is a rarity."[238]

Kilts improved hundreds of operating details to ensure top performances from the brands.

> "It's not rocket science, as Kilts himself readily admits. But it is a meticulous and exacting process nonetheless. Instead of dreaming up grand visions for Gillette's future, Kilts stays up at night worrying about whether he should sell batteries in packages of six or eight. Rather than rally the troops with big speeches on how Gillette can change the world, Kilts presents slides on how their SG&A (Selling, General & Administrative) expenses compare with those of competitors. It's not glamorous, it's not sexy; it's a buttoned-up, old-school approach to business. And it works."[239]

You can see from Figure 10.1 that Kilts' approach paid off – Berkshire's holding jumped above $4bn, and then $5bn.

Reward managers, yes, but only when warranted

Buffett's admiration for Kilts is apparent in his 2005 letter to Berkshire shareholders, and in contrast to the distaste Buffett has for unjustified rewards for managers.

Praising Kilts, Buffett said, "It's hard to overemphasize the importance of who is CEO of a company." Before Kilts' arrival, Gillette was struggling having made a number of costly errors in allocating capital. In particular, the acquisition of Duracell cost shareholders billions of dollars but this loss was never made visible by conventional accounting. Simply, the company gave up more in business value than it received. Buffett was amazed how often this yardstick was overlooked by managements and investment bankers when considering acquisitions.

"Upon taking office at Gillette, Jim quickly instilled fiscal discipline, tightened operations and energized marketing, moves that dramatically increased the intrinsic value of the company... Jim was paid very well – but he earned every penny. (This is no academic evaluation: as a 9.7% owner of Gillette, Berkshire in effect paid that proportion of his compensation.) Indeed, it's difficult to overpay the truly extraordinary CEO of a giant enterprise. But this species is rare."

Buffett felt that, too often, executive pay was disproportionate and unaligned with performance. Investors were often guaranteed a bum deal as the hand-picked teams and consultants of mediocre CEOs helped push through ill-designed compensation policies.

He used the example of ten-year fixed price options as an illustration of such misaligned reward. If "Fred Futile, CEO of Stagnant, Inc.", is given an option on 1% of the company, his self-interest is obvious – he will want to maximise the value of the share price. He can choose to skip dividend payments and instead use the company's earnings to buy back stock.

Imagine Stagnant lives up to its name and, for each of the ten years after the options grant, earns $1bn on $10bn of assets. Initially, this represents earnings of $10 per share (100m shares outstanding). If Fred eschews dividends to repurchase shares, and the shares constantly sell at ten times earnings, the share price will have appreciated by 158% by the end of the option period. This is because the number of shares will have reduced to 38.7m and earnings per share will have increased to $25.80. By withholding earnings from shareholders, Fred can get very rich – making $158m – without the business improving one jot.

Even worse, Fred could make more than $100m even if Stagnant's earnings fall by 20% over the period. Where, asked Buffett, is the alignment in interests of management and shareholders?

Even dividend policies (e.g. one-third of earnings) can provide generous rewards for managers who achieve little.

"It doesn't have to be this way: it's child's play for a board to design options that give effect to the automatic build-up in value that occurs when earnings are retained. But – surprise,

surprise – options of that kind are almost never issued. Indeed, the very thought of options with strike prices that are adjusted for retained earnings seems foreign to compensation 'experts', who are nevertheless encyclopedic about every management-friendly plan that exists. ('Whose bread I eat, his song I sing.')"

Buffett was equally scathing about severance pay. "Getting fired can produce a particularly bountiful payday for a CEO. Indeed, he can 'earn' more in that single day, while cleaning out his desk, than an American worker earns in a lifetime of cleaning toilets."

Procter & Gamble

In international markets, Gillette and Procter & Gamble face a mighty competitor in the Anglo-Dutch giant Unilever, with its terrific range of personal care and food products. Unilever was bigger than both the American companies in many countries, and enjoyed greater leverage with retailers.

Jim Kilts approached P&G with a plan to merge (after obtaining Buffett's approval). The two companies had little product overlap, which increased the chances that the anti-trust regulators would not block the deal. Gillette's razor business, in particular, neatly extended P&G's beauty and grooming business. A merger would strengthen bargaining clout with retailers. For example, Walmart was able to bargain hard with suppliers, and it accounted for 17% of P&G's sales and 13% of Gillette's. By bringing together 21 'must-have' brands, each with between $1bn and $10bn of annual sales, the P&G–Gillette combination would be able to withstand pressure from the professional buyers supermarkets employed. "Retailers can't afford not to stock their brands. The merger is an attempt to increase the balance of power with the big supermarket groups," said an analyst on the announcement. [240]

Kilts told the press he was optimistic about the merger because of the dominant scale it would bring: "strength plus strength equals success." As well as improving bargaining power, P&G anticipated both revenue and cost synergies. Also, the combined marketing budget (over $3bn) would add a great deal of muscle when negotiating with media companies and advertisers.

P&G offered 0.975 of its shares for each share of Gillette, in January 2005, amounting to about $57bn (29% of the combined entity). The new P&G would have a market capitalisation of around $200bn and sales of $61bn, making it the world's number one household goods supplier.

As Gillette's largest shareholder, Buffett was invited to make a comment in the official announcement. He called the acquisition "a dream deal" that would "create the greatest consumer products in the world."

On 1 October 2005, Berkshire Hathaway's 96m Gillette shares were swapped for 93.6m P&G shares. Before the end of 2005, Buffett had bought another 6.4m P&G common stock to take the holding to 100m, which was 3% of P&G, with a market value of $5.8bn. "We didn't intend to sell our Gillette shares before the merger; we don't intend to sell our P&G shares now," he wrote in his 2005 letter to Berkshire shareholders.

It wasn't long before P&G, as promised, was buying back its shares. So, even though Berkshire's holding of 100m shares remained the same, at year-end 2006, its percentage of P&G's equity was up by 0.2% to 3.2%. In 2007, Berkshire bought 1.472m more P&G shares. But during 2008, 9.53m were sold, followed by more in 2009 (Figure 10.2). Buffett said that he and Munger expected P&G to trade higher in the future, but, "We made some sales early in 2009 to raise cash for our Dow [Chemical] and Swiss Re purchases and late in the year made other sales in anticipation of our BNSF purchase."[241] The aftermath of the 2008 crash was a good time to pick up bargains, even more attractive than P&G. The Burlington Northern Santa Fe purchase of 2010 used $22bn of cash, some of which was raised by selling P&G shares. In 2012, it was the turn of the H. J. Heinz deal to draw on Berkshire's cash ($12bn). Another reason for selling P&G was that Buffett saw many opportunities to improve the quality of the franchises of subsidiaries. In 2012, for example, 26 companies were bought as bolt-on acquisitions for subsidiaries, costing $2.3bn.

Figure 10.2: Procter & Gamble share price (October 2005–February 2016)

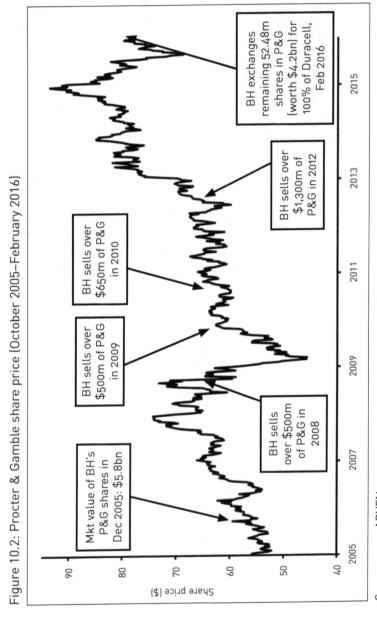

BH exchanges remaining 52.48m shares in P&G (worth $4.2bn) for 100% of Duracell, Feb 2016

BH sells over $1,300m of P&G in 2012

BH sells over $650m of P&G in 2010

BH sells over $500m of P&G in 2009

BH sells over $500m of P&G in 2008

Mkt value of BH's P&G shares in Dec 2005: $5.8bn

Share price ($)

90

80

70

60

50

40

2005   2007   2009   2011   2013   2015

Source: www.ADVFN.com

Duracell

When Duracell was bought by Gillette in 1996 for $7.8bn, it was the market leader in alkaline batteries; its brilliant marketing, with the Duracell Bunny, had created a global brand. Duracell accounted for one-quarter of Gillette's sales. But it didn't take long for competitors to offer cheaper versions. A price war ensued and two years of falling market share. Operations seemed to move into a lacklustre phase, with failed marketing campaigns. It even allowed the Bunny mascot trademark to lapse in the USA allowing Energizer to file its own bunny mascot. There was also a run-up of overhead costs.

Jim Kilts imposed financial discipline and invested in new marketing, but Duracell didn't really recover lost ground – annual revenue growth slowed to 1% and market share was lost. In 2014, P&G decided its optimum strategy was to concentrate on the 65 brands generating the most profit, such as Tide, Head & Shoulders and Pampers, and to sell off the slow-growing divisions.

Buffett saw an opportunity because he had "always been impressed by Duracell as a consumer and as a long-term investor."[242] After all, it still had 24% of the world market for batteries. He agreed to exchange the $4.2bn of P&G shares held by Berkshire for all the shares in Duracell, but only after P&G injected $1.8bn in cash into the battery company, thus the net price was $2.4bn, less than a third of what Gillette had paid for it 20 years earlier (the deal was completed in February 2016).

Why choose Duracell over P&G?

Both Duracell and P&G are consumer businesses with strong brands and predictable cash flow. Both are easy to understand and have strong competitive advantages; and both are run by competent and honest managers. So why did Buffett choose to put all his eggs into the Duracell basket and none in P&G?

I suspect the decision had a lot to do with price. In 2015, P&G was trading on a price to earnings ratio above 20, indicating Mr Market had faith that earnings would grow significantly. Duracell was seen by P&G as, at best, destined for slow growth, as it had been bypassed by rechargeables.

But Buffett noted its cash flow was strong and P&G was willing to sell it at seven times adjusted earnings before interest, tax, depreciation and amortisation. This EBITDA measure makes Buffett and all rational share valuers shudder because, not least, it leaves out the need to spend on capital items and to pay taxes. But even if we deduct reasonable estimates for these, Duracell was being sold on a low double-digit multiple of after-tax earnings.

Table 10.2: Fair values of assets and liabilities (and goodwill) of Duracell at acquisition by Berkshire Hathaway

	$m
ASSETS	
Cash and cash equivalents	1,807
Inventories	319
Property, plant and equipment	359
Goodwill and other intangible assets	2,416
Other assets	242
Assets acquired	5,143
LIABILITIES	
Accounts payable, accruals and other liabilities	410
Income taxes, principally deferred	494
NET ASSETS	4,239

Source: Berkshire Hathaway annual report (2016).

In Table 10.2, we can see that Duracell's use of net *tangible* assets was nothing like the net $4.2bn paid for the company. Taking net assets of $4.2bn, then deducting $2.4bn of goodwill and intangibles, we get $1.8bn. But, within that, we see that the balance sheet carried $1.8bn in cash. The vast majority of this was not needed for Duracell's operations, meaning that it could carry on producing batteries with very few net tangible assets. This allowed Buffett to invest the cash in other shares. It also meant that high rates of return on net tangible assets could be expected as the company grew.

Buffett was not too concerned about flat sales; he stated in his 2007 letter to shareholders that "Long-term competitive advantage in a stable industry is what we seek in a business. If that comes with rapid organic growth, great. But even without organic growth, such a business is rewarding. We will simply take the lush earnings of the business and use them to buy similar businesses elsewhere."

The attraction of Duracell also had something to do with Buffett preferring to own a business outright. Buffett told the *Financial Times*, "I love adding good operating businesses to Berkshire... We have been saying in our annual reports for 30 years now that we want to exchange marketable securities for operating businesses, so that is the direction we want to go... Duracell is a leading global brand with top quality products, and it will fit well within Berkshire Hathaway."[243]

The arrangement of swapping shares for shares neatly put off the evil day of having to pay capital gains tax, but the injection of $1.8bn gave Buffett another pot of money or further investment – it was freed from Berkshire's P&G holding without tax payable immediately. Berkshire's 1.9% stake in P&G cost $336m but was being sold for $4.2bn. If it had been sold for cash, a 38% capital gains tax would have been levied. By swapping the 52.5m shares for Duracell, capital gains tax was deferred and Buffett and Munger had a couple of billion more to invest.

Then there was the distinct possibility that Duracell may not always be as slow-growing as thought by P&G and Wall Street analysts. It was already in rechargeable batteries and was investing in renewable power. There is much potential in the consortium it helped to create to develop wireless charging technologies for cars – other members include German carmakers. The same technology could be used for battery charging for a wide range of devices. It has expanded into areas such as smartphone batteries, jump-starters and coin-sized batteries.

It turns out that the market for all types of battery is growing – from alkaline and lithium to zinc-carbon and nickel-cadmium – as the sales of consumer electronics and other electrical products in an ever-growing variety zoom. The different types fulfil different roles, effectively segmenting the market. For example, in areas where customers want to avoid frequent battery changing, such as electronic door locks, hearing aids or smoke detectors, the long-lasting alkaline is ideal – and Duracell still has the strongest brand. Also, alkaline batteries work well in freezing conditions, e.g. in cold stores, whereas other battery types do not. The global alkaline battery market is about $7bn and Duracell commands about $2bn of that. Billions of new middle-class consumers will be buying an expanding range of electronic goods, from TV remote controls to torches, and many will decide to buy market-leading and quality-renowned Duracell batteries.

Then, there are synergy potentials with Berkshire's other companies. Duracell is working with the Chinese company BYD, in which BH has a major stake, to sell a home energy storage system. Duracell is a sister company to Berkshire Hathaway Energy, formerly MidAmerica Energy, which generates vast amounts of electric power for homes and businesses in the US and UK. It invests billions every year in renewable forms of energy, and there is much potential for working with Duracell, e.g. power storage in batteries. Buffett and Munger have cleverly positioned BH to benefit from the shift from a carbon-based economy to one based on ecologically-friendly generated electricity.

A summary of the money in and money out

There were quite a few payments by Berkshire, and sales, over the three decades, so a summary table might help clarify.

Table 10.3: Berkshire investments in Gillette, Procter & Gamble, and Duracell

Date	Investment made	Returns to Berkshire
20 July 1989	Preferred stock $600m	
July 1989– April 1991		Gillette preferred dividends $89m ($45m after tax)
April 1991– September 2005		Gillette common stock dividends (over $600m before tax)
2005	Bought more shares in P&G, paying $340m	
2007	Bought more shares in P&G, paying $90m	
October 2005– February 2016		P&G dividends $1.4bn
2008–2012		From sale of P&G shares, over $2.95bn
February 2016		Received $4.2bn shares in Duracell
TOTAL	$1.03bn	$9.26bn (approx.) before tax deduction

Learning points

1. **An investor able to inject large sums into a company, and do it in a non-threatening way, can get a bargain from the managers.** Following the generous return gained from the Gillette purchase in 1989, Buffett and Munger assisted other companies restore balance sheet strength without imposing onerous conditions on the directors, e.g. Goldman Sachs and General Electric following the 2008 financial crisis. Smaller investors do not have this power, but we can try to be understanding and supportive of directors rather than aggressive and critical. That way, we might obtain not only more pleasant engagement, but more information, and greater likelihood of directors listening to our thoughts on the company.

2. **Occasionally, a scarcity of reasonably priced common stock can justify investing in preferred stock offering higher yields.** Ideally, the preferred would have a convertibility right so participation in exceptionally good company performance is possible.

3. **Relationships between individuals is crucial; like, trust, admire.** Warren Buffett and Charlie Munger enjoyed their relationship with Colman Mockler, Jim Kilts and later with Alan G. Lafley at P&G. Investors should take time to meet the directors of their companies.

4. **Corporate raiders can destroy or wound a business.** Financial players drawing on vast amounts of debt capital, whether they be private equity, hedge funds or other vehicles, can put a company into play often leading to a perfectly good business being endangered. Sometimes they take control and then over-borrow and under-invest in competitive advantage maintenance. Other times they induce damaging reactions, e.g. the incumbent managers irrationally buy back shares or fall for greenmail.

5. **Even good businesses can become flabby.** The managers can fall into complacency about franchise maintenance, or keep too much money in the business (earning poor rates of return), or allow overheads to rise wastefully. Buffett and Munger were forced to intervene at various points in their three-decade association with Gillette, P&G and Duracell to recommend changed leadership in order to get back on track.

6. **Managers should be rewarded in proportion to returns generated for shareholders.** Be wary of share options giving a managerial incentive to retain capital and boost earnings per share without adding much value to shareholders.

7. **An excellent business is not always an excellent investment.** In 2015, Buffett and Munger still saw the brands within P&G as constituting an excellent set of businesses. But the price of owning those businesses was too high. Another excellent business, but with slow sales growth, was Duracell with its high rates of return on net tangible assets. It was an excellent investment because it was being offered at a lower price relative to its likely future owner earnings.

A Distance Travelled

In 1976 you could pick up a share in Berkshire Hathaway for $40. The entire company had a book value of about $58m and market capitalisation under $40m. Warren Buffett owned over two-fifths of those shares.

Just 14 years later, you would have to pay $8,600 for one share – a rise of 21,400%. If you'd invested $10,000 in 1975, by January 1990 your Berkshire shares would be worth $2,150,000. Warren Buffett still held over 40% of these shares and so was a billionaire.

The transformation of Berkshire Hathaway in just 14 years is breathtaking. At the beginning it had an ailing textile operation which "was a significant disappointment" and did not "offer the expectation of high returns on investment."[244] It also owned a small insurance underwriting business possessing a float amounting to $87.6m, mostly invested in equities such as 9.7% of The Washington Post. It could also look forward to a good flow of income from its ownership of Illinois National Bank. Then there was its holding of a minority of the shares in Blue Chip Stamps, which in turned owned See's Candies and 64% of Wesco.

In 1989, Berkshire Hathaway had an insurance float of $1.54bn which produced a net income from interest and dividends of over $200m. It owned all or most of the shares in high-returns-on-capital businesses such as The Buffalo News, Fechheimer, Kirby, Nebraska Furniture Mart, Scott Fetzer Manufacturing Group, See's Candies, Borsheims and World Book. These wonderful companies, year after year, fed profits back to the centre for Buffett and Munger to invest in other opportunities.

It also owned 18% of Capital Cities/ABC's shares (worth $1.7bn), as well as 7% of Coca-Cola (worth $1.8bn) and over 14% of The Washington Post (worth $0.5bn).

On top of that collection, it held 51% of GEICO, which the market valued at over $1bn, and shares in Federal Home Loan Mortgage Corporation worth a nice round billion. Then there was an assortment of preferred stock, including Salomon and Gillette, totalling nearly $2bn.

But that's not all

Warren Buffett and Charlie Munger's personal reputations had grown. Back in 1976 only a handful of shareholders turned up to the AGM. The press were not interested, with Berkshire Hathaway being thought of as a pretty small mixed-bag conglomerate run out of Omaha, of all places, by a couple of unconventional, even eccentric, Midwesterners. Why would you pay attention to Berkshire Hathaway when there are far more exciting things happening on Wall Street?

But, by 1989, the name of the company, and of Warren and Charlie, were known throughout the land. Thousands came to Omaha to listen to their wisdom expressed in a clear down-to-earth way, and thousands more read Buffett's chairman's letters. The press regular reported their deals and clamoured for interviews. Buffett and Munger rubbed shoulders with the great and the good of American society, helped not least by Kay Graham and by the publicity around the saving of Salomon.

Prospective sellers of businesses often thought of Berkshire Hathaway as a safe haven for their creation, somewhere it would be nurtured and grown without loss of integrity.

Berkshire Hathaway was also becoming the go-to sanctuary for the largest companies in the land, if they needed money quickly, and needed a finance provider who would not interfere in their business, and would refuse to sell to one of those brutal Wall Street raiders. Sure, Berkshire charged a high dividend on preferred shares issued, but at least you knew you were safe from financial distress and from constant attacks.

In short, Berkshire was in a powerful position in 1989. It was one of the largest corporations in the United States, and had plenty of money to invest in more wonderful businesses as it enjoyed the flow of income from its collection of companies.

Just as Warren Buffett was coming up to his 60th year and Charlie Munger his 66th, we find these two still tap-dancing to work. They were so excited about going into the office every day, thinking about all that cash flowing to them and thinking what else they might buy. In the next few years, they discovered some great businesses in which to place their money, from Wells Fargo and American Express to Dairy Queen, NetJets, General Re and Moody's. Buffett and Munger were having the time of their lives. But these stories (and others) will have to wait for another volume in the series.

Notes

1. W. Buffett, letter to shareholders of BH (2005).
2. H. L. Butler, 'An Hour with Benjamin Graham', *Financial Analysts Journal* (November/December 1973). Reprinted in J. Lowe, *The Rediscovered Benjamin Graham* (John Wiley & Sons, 1999).
3. Insurance Hall of Fame Biography: www.insurancehalloffame.org/laureateprofile.php?laureate=141
4. R. P. Miles, *The Warren Buffett CEO*, p.29 (John Wiley & Sons, 2002).
5. Ibid.
6. W. Buffett, letter to shareholders of BH (1983).
7. W. Buffett, letter to shareholders of BH (1986).
8. Ibid.
9. W. Buffett, letter to shareholders of BH (1984).
10. W. Buffett, letter to shareholders of BH (1995).
11. W. Buffett, letter to shareholders of BH (1986).
12. W. Buffett, letter to shareholders of BH (2001).
13. W. Buffett, letter to shareholders of BH (2004).
14. W. Buffett, letter to shareholders of BH (1995).
15. W. Buffett, letter to shareholders of BH (2010).
16. L. Simpson, Q&A, Kellogg School of Management (2017).
17. Ibid.
18. L. Simpson, *The Washington Post* (11 May 1987).
19. Miles, *The Warren Buffett CEO*, p.58.
20. Simpson in Miles, *The Warren Buffett CEO*, p.61.
21. Simpson, Q&A.
22. Simpson, *The Washington Post* (11 May 1987).
23. Simpson, Q&A.
24. Simpson, *The Washington Post* (11 May 1987).
25. W. Buffett, letter to shareholders of BH (1995).
26. T. Nicely in A. B. Crenshaw, 'Premium Partners', *The Washington Post* (18 September 1995).
27. W. Buffett, letter to shareholders of BH (2006).
28. W. Buffett, letter to shareholders of BH (2015).

29. W. Buffett, letter to shareholders of BH (2016).
30. T. Nicely in Miles, *The Warren Buffett CEO*, p.37.
31. Ibid, p.38.
32. Miles, *The Warren Buffett CEO*, p.40.
33. Ibid, p.39.
34. W. Buffett, letter to shareholders of BH (1996).
35. W. Buffett, letter to shareholders of BH (2009).
36. Ibid.
37. J. R. Laing, 'The Collector: Investor who piled up $100m in the 1960s piles up firms today', *The Wall Street Journal* (31 March 1977).
38. W. Buffett, letter to shareholders of BH (2006).
39. K. Graham, *Personal History*, p.581 (Vintage Books/Random House, 1997).
40. Ibid.
41. M. B. Light, *From Butler to Buffett: The Story Behind the Buffalo News* (Prometheus Books, 2004).
42. Ibid.
43. BCS annual report (1981).
44. Light, *From Butler to Buffett*.
45. Ibid.
46. S. Lipsey, 'New Addition to Blue Chip Ranks', *The Buffalo News* centennial publication (12 October 1980).
47. Light, *From Butler to Buffett*.
48. S. Lipsey, quoted in Miles, *The Warren Buffett CEO*, p.237.
49. C. J Loomis, 'The Inside Story of Warren Buffett', *Fortune* (11 April 1988).
50. S. Lipsey, quoted in Miles, *The Warren Buffett CEO*, p.247.
51. Ibid.
52. W. Buffett, letter to shareholders of BH (2012).
53. W. Buffett, letter to shareholders of BH (2006).
54. Ibid.
55. Video, 'Rose Blumkin: Omaha's Nebraska Furniture Mart', YouTube.
56. D. Burrow, 'From Mrs B to Mr K: Do not underestimate the best country in the world', *Omaha World Herald* (28 October 1962).
57. W. Buffett, letter to shareholders of BH (2003).
58. www.berkshirehathaway.com/2013ar/linksannual13.html
59. Documentary, 'The History of NFM: 75th Anniversary', YouTube.
60. G. Collins, 'Rose Blumkin, "Exemplar of the American Dream", remembers the tough road from Minsk to Omaha', UPI (9 June 1984).
61. Ibid.
62. A. Smith, *Supermoney*, p.190 (John Wiley & Sons, 1972, reprinted 2006).

63. Collins, 'Rose Blumkin, "Exemplar of the American Dream".
64. Buffett, speaking at BH shareholders meeting (2014).
65. BH annual report (2013).
66. K. Linder, *The Women of Berkshire Hathaway*, (John Wiley & Sons, 2012).
67. Buffett, speaking at BH shareholders meeting (2014).
68. Ibid.
69. Ibid.
70. W. Buffett, letter to shareholders of BH (1983).
71. C. Munger, 'Academic Economics: Strengths and Faults after Considering Interdisciplinary Needs', from the Herb Kay Undergraduate Lecture, University of California, Santa Barbara Economics Department (3 October 2003). Reproduced in P. D. Kaufman (editor), *Poor Charlie's Almanack: The Wit and Wisdom of Charles T. Munger* (The Donning Company Publishers, Virginia, 2005).
72. W. Buffett, letter to shareholders of BH (1990).
73. W. Buffett, letter to shareholders of BH (1983).
74. Ibid.
75. W. Buffett, letter to shareholders of BH (1984).
76. W. Buffett, letter to shareholders of BH (1987).
77. I. Blumkin, quoted in 'The Blumkin Legacy: One Influential Family, Three New Inductees into the Omaha Business Hall of Fame', YouTube.
78. R. Blumkin, quoted in Joyce Wadler, 'Blumkin: Sofa, So Good', *The Washington Post* (24 May 1984).
79. W. Buffett, quoted in S. P. Sherman and D. Kirkpatrick, 'Capital Cities' Capital Coup', *Fortune* (15 April 1985).
80. T. S. Murphy, quoted in an interview with A. Blitz, Harvard Business School Director of Media Development for Entrepreneurial Management, ABC (December 2000).
81. Ibid.
82. Ibid.
83. W. Buffett, letter to shareholders of BH (1985).
84. W. Buffett, letter to shareholders of BH (2015).
85. Buffett, quoted in Sherman and Kirkpatrick, 'Capital Cities' Capital Coup'.
86. Murphy, interview with A. Blitz, Harvard Business School Director of Media Development for Entrepreneurial Management.
87. Ibid.
88. Ibid.
89. W. Buffett, letter to shareholders of BH (1985).
90. Ibid.

91. Ibid.
92. Ibid.
93. Murphy, interview with A. Blitz, Harvard Business School Director of Media Development for Entrepreneurial Management.
94. Ibid.
95. Ibid.
96. Ibid.
97. Ibid.
98. Sherman and Kirkpatrick, 'Capital Cities' Capital Coup.
99. Murphy, interview with A. Blitz, Harvard Business School Director of Media Development for Entrepreneurial Management.
100. W. Buffett, letter to shareholders of BH (1985).
101. Murphy, interview with A. Blitz, Harvard Business School Director of Media Development for Entrepreneurial Management.
102. Ibid.
103. W. Buffett, letter to shareholders of BH (1991).
104. W. Buffett, letter to shareholders of BH (1985).
105. W. Buffett, letter to shareholders of BH (1986).
106. W. Buffett, letter to shareholders of BH (1991).
107. Ibid.
108. W. Buffett, letter to shareholders of BH (1995).
109. C. J. Loomis, *Fortune* (1 April 1996).
110. A *white squire* is a friendly company which buys a stake in a takeover target or potential target. A squire does not require a controlling interest, as a *white knight* would.
111. The encyclopedias were also sold abroad. The author, when 18, sold World Book door-to-door in Western Australia in 1989 – or at least tried to.
112. R. J. Cole, 'Boesky Makes Bid For Scott & Fetzer', *The New York Times* (27 April 1984).
113. 'Bid Turned Down By Scott & Fetzer', *The New York Times* (9 May 1984).
114. R. Schey in Miles, *The Warren Buffett CEO*.
115. 'Scott & Fetzer, Kelso Deal Off', *The New York Times* (6 September 1985).
116. W. Tilson, 'Three lectures by Warren Buffett to Notre Dame Faculty' (edited), www.tilsonfunds.com/BuffettNotreDame.pdf (1991).
117. Loomis, 'The inside story of Warren Buffett'.
118. Ibid.
119. R. W. Stevenson, 'Berkshire to Buy Scott & Fetzer', *The New York Times* (30 October 1985).

120. W. Buffett, letter to shareholders of BH (1985).
121. Ibid.
122. Ibid.
123. Ibid.
124. W. Buffett, letter to shareholders of BH (1999).
125. W. Buffett, letter to shareholders of BH (1992).
126. W. Buffett, letter to shareholders of BH (1994).
127. Ibid.
128. Ibid.
129. Ibid.
130. Ibid.
131. Ibid.
132. W. Buffett, letter to shareholders of BH (Appendix) (1986).
133. Ibid.
134. W. Buffett, letter to shareholders of BH (1986).
135. W. Buffett, letter to shareholders of BH (Appendix) (1986).
136. Ibid.
137. W. Buffett, letter to shareholders of BH (1994).
138. Ibid.
139. Ibid.
140. W. Buffett, quoted in M. Urry, 'Weekend Money', p.1, *Financial Times* (11/12 May 1996).
141. Buffett, speaking at BH annual meeting (1996).
142. www.cleveland.com
143. R. Schey in Miles, *The Warren Buffett CEO*.
144. W. Buffett, letter to shareholders of BH (1986).
145. W. Buffett, letter to shareholders of BH (1982).
146. W. Buffett, letter to shareholders of BH (1986).
147. Ibid.
148. W. Buffett, letter to shareholders of BH (1987).
149. Ibid.
150. Ibid.
151. W. Buffett, letter to shareholders of BH (1990).
152. C. J. Loomis, 'The Value Machine Warren Buffett's Berkshire Hathaway is on a buying binge. You were expecting stocks?', *Fortune* (19 February 2001).
153. P. Byrne, quoted in A. Kilpatrick, *Of Permanent Value: The Story of Warren Buffett* (Literary Edition), p.607 (AKPE, 2006).
154. R. W. Chan, *Behind the Berkshire Hathaway Curtain: Warren Buffett's Top Business Leaders*, p.96 (John Wiley & Sons, 2010).
155. W. Buffett, letter to shareholders of BH (1986).

156. Ibid.

157. Ibid.

158. Ibid.

159. Ibid.

160. P. Lynch, *Beating the Street*, p.141 (Simon & Schuster, 1994).

161. W. Buffett, letter to shareholders of BH (1986).

162. Ibid.

163. Ibid.

164. A *thrift* bank is a type of small financial institution in the US primarily for savings deposits and home mortgages. They differ from larger commercial banks in offering higher savings account yields and limited lending to business.

165. A. Bianco, 'The King of Wall Street: An inside look at Salomon Brothers' stunning rise to pre-eminence – and how it wields its power', *BusinessWeek* (5 December 1985).

166. Preferred shares give the buyer the option to either hold onto the shares collecting the dividends annually until a date in the future, or a series of dates, or to convert the preferreds into common stock. In the case of these preferreds, Salomon agreed to redeem one-fifth of them annually between 31 October 1995 and 31 October 2000. On redemption, dividends ceased and the nominal value returned to the holders.

167. W. Buffett, letter to shareholders of BH (1987).

168. W. Buffett, 'How to tame the casino society', *The Washington Post* (4 December 1986).

169. W. Buffett, letter to shareholders of BH (1987).

170. Ibid.

171. J. Sterngold, 'Too far, too fast; Salomon Brothers' John Gutfreund', *The New York Times* (10 January 1988).

172. W. Buffett, quoted in A. Schroeder, *The Snowball*, p.463 (Bloomsbury, 2009).

173. W. Buffett, quoted in C. J. Loomis, 'Warren Buffett's wild ride at Salomon', *Fortune* (27 October 1997).

174. W. Buffett, letter to shareholders of BH (1991).

175. Reported in *Omaha World-Herald*, 2 January 1994.

176. *Omaha World Herald* (2 January 1994).

177. K. Eichenwald, 'Salomon's 2 Top Officers to Resign Amid Scandal', *The New York Times* (17 August 1991).

178. W. Buffett, quoted in 'Now Hear This', *Fortune* (10 January 1994).

179. W. Buffett, letter to shareholders of BH (1997).

180. W. Buffett, letter to shareholders of BH (2010).

181. W. Buffett, in J. Rasmussen, 'Buffett talks strategy with students', *Omaha World Herald* (2 January 1994).
182. W. Buffett, letter to shareholders of BH (1989).
183. W. Buffett, letter to shareholders of BH (1996).
184. Ibid.
185. This is my 1994 intrinsic value estimate, based on the rate of return being the US government Treasury 10-year rate at 7% in 1994, and then adding the risk premium above the government bond of 5%, giving a required rate of return on a Coca-Cola share of 12% per year. This uses the dividend growth model: Intrinsic value = next year's dividend divided by required rate minus growth rate. Perfect hindsight makes the maths easy. See G. Arnold & D. Lewis, *Corporate Financial Management*, Ch.17 (Pearson, 2019) for equity valuation models.
186. D. Keough, 'Conversations with Michael Eisner', www.youtube.com/watch?v=6jABoeJk2E4, CNBC Prime (January 2009).
187. D. Keough, quoted in Kilpatrick, *Of Permanent Value*, p.463.
188. W. Buffett, letter to shareholders of BH (1986).
189. Much of this section draws on the ideas presented by Charlie Munger in a series of public talks now compiled in Kaufman (editor), *Poor Charlie's Almanack*. Particularly, 'Practical Thought About Practical Thought?' (20 July 1996).
190. Kaufman (editor), *Poor Charlie's Almanack*, p.177.
191. Coca-Cola annual report (2018).
192. M. E. Porter, *Competitive Strategy* (The Free Press, 1980; Simon & Schuster, 2004).
193. W. Buffett, in J. Huey, 'The World's Best Brand', *Fortune* (31 May 1993).
194. Kaufman (editor), *Poor Charlie's Almanack*, p.210.
195. Huey, 'The World's Best Brand'.
196. R. Goizeuta, life-long manager and future CEO, quoted in Huey, 'The World's Best Brand'.
197. Huey, 'The World's Best Brand'.
198. Ibid.
199. Ibid.
200. R. W. Stevenson, 'Coke's Intensified Attack Abroad', *The New York Times* (14 March 1988).
201. Huey, 'The World's Best Brand'.
202. W. Buffett, letter to shareholders of BH (1996).
203. Huey, 'The World's Best Brand'.
204. Excluding the Soviet Union and China.
205. Coca-Cola annual report (1987).

206. W. Buffett, quoted in C. J. Loomis, *Tap Dancing to Work*, p.113 (Penguin Books, 2013).

207. W. Buffett, letter to shareholders of BH (1989).

208. D. Keough, speaking to *Atlanta Journal-Constitution* (22 February 2004).

209. W. Buffett, letter to shareholders of BH (1997).

210. W. Buffett, letter to shareholders of BH (2011).

211. W. Buffett, letter to shareholders of BH (2013).

212. W. Buffett, letter to shareholders of BH (2004).

213. Kilpatrick, *Of Permanent Value*, p.617.

214. W. Buffett, letter to shareholders of BH (1989).

215. W. Buffett, letter to shareholders of BH (1988).

216. S. Jacques, who started as a sales assistant and later became CEO, in Miles, *The Warren Buffett CEO*, p.285.

217. Kilpatrick, *Of Permanent Value*, p.613.

218. Ibid, p.614.

219. W. Buffett, letter to shareholders of BH (1988).

220. Kilpatrick, *Of Permanent Value*, p.614.

221. W. Buffett, letter to shareholders of BH (1988).

222. W. Buffett, letter to shareholders of BH (1989).

223. Ibid.

224. W. Buffett, letter to shareholders of BH (2007).

225. GIA, www.gia.edu (2014).

226. In *greenmail* (green being the colour of a US dollar), a takeover target removes the threat by offering to buy-back shares from a hostile company at above the market price. Significantly, it does not offer the same price to other shareholders. It is illegal in many countries.

227. W. Buffett, quoted in G. McKibben, *Cutting Edge: Gillette's Journey to Global Leadership*, p.225 (Harvard Business Review Press, 1997).

228. Buffett in McKibben, *Cutting Edge*, p.226.

229. Ibid.

230. Ibid, p.227.

231. Buffett and Munger's business acquisition criteria are stated in most of Buffett's annual letters to shareholders.

232. R. Ricardo-Campbell, *Resisting hostile takeovers: the case of Gillette*, p.212 (Praeger, 1997).

233. W. Buffett, letter to shareholders of BH (1989).

234. Ibid.

235. W. Buffett, letter to shareholders of BH (1991).

236. W. Buffett, letter to shareholders of BH (1993).

237. W. Buffett, quoted in J. Eum, 'Warren Buffett's idea of heaven: I don't

have to work with people I don't like', *Forbes* (4 Feb 2014).

238. W. Buffett, quoted in K. Brooker, 'Jim Kilts is an old-school curmudgeon. Nothing could be better for Gillette', *Fortune* (30 December 2002).

239. Ibid.

240. S. Mesure and D. Usborne, 'P&G's $57bn Gillette deal sets fresh challenge for Unilever', *The Independent* (29 January 2005).

241. W. Buffett, letter to shareholders of BH (2009).

242. J. Stempel & D. Krishna Kumar, 'Buffett's Berkshire Hat', *Reuters* (13 November 2014).

243. C. Barrett, S. Foley & R. Blackden, 'Berkshire Hathaway to acquire battery business from Procter & Gamble', *Financial Times* (13 November 2014).

244. W. Buffett, letter to shareholders of BH (1976).

245. www8.gsb.columbia.edu/articles/columbia-business/superinvestors

Index

Index

Index

CPSIA information can be obtained
at www.ICGtesting.com
Printed in the USA
BVHW080510231019
561797BV00005B/10/P